APPLICATIONS OF
PSYCHOLOGY
IN THE
LAW PRACTICE

A Guide to Relevant Issues, Practices, and Theories

J. THOMAS DALBY, Ph.D.
EUNICE L. CLAVNER, Editor

General Practice, Solo & Small Firm Section
American Bar Association

Cover design by Frank Leone.

The materials contained herein represent the opinions of the authors and editors and should not be construed to be the action of either the American Bar Association or the General Practice, Solo and Small Firm Section unless adopted pursuant to the bylaws of the Association.

Nothing contained in this book is to be considered as the rendering of legal advice for specific cases, and readers are responsible for obtaining such advice from their own legal counsel. This book and any forms and agreements herein are intended for educational and informational purposes only.

© 1997 American Bar Association. All rights reserved.
Printed in the United States of America.

01 00 99 98 97   5 4 3 2 1

Dalby, J. Thomas (John Thomas)
   Applications of psychology in the law practice: a review of relevant issues, practices, and theories / J. Thomas Dalby.
        p. cm.
   Includes bibliographical references (p. 181).
   ISBN 1-57073-432-1 (pbk.)
    1. Psychology. 2. Psychology, Forensic 3. Lawyers--U.S.--
Handbooks, manuals, etc.   I. Title.
BF1121.D24   1997
150'.24'344--dc21   97-1220
                                                            CIP

Discounts are available for books ordered in bulk. Special consideration is given to state bars, CLE programs, and other bar-related organizations. Inquire at ABA Publishing, Book Publishing, American Bar Association, 750 North Lake Shore Drive, Chicago, Illinois 60611.

Contents

Acknowledgments   v

About the Author   vii

Introduction   ix

1. **Psychology and Law: Strange Bedfellows**   1
2. **Models of Behavior**   11
3. **Psychological Research and Assessment Methods**   23
4. **Personality Tests**   35
5. **Cognitive and Neuropsychological Assessment**   51
6. **Other Tests**   65
7. **Diagnosis: Understanding the Diagnostic and Statistical Manual of Mental Disorders (DSM–IV)**   77
8. **Treatment**   105
9. **Psychological Testimony**   119
10. **Psychological Consultation on Legal Issues**   127
11. **Negotiation and Mediation**   137

Appendix A: Finding Expertise in Psychology   147

Appendix B: Ethical Principles of Psychologists and Code of Conduct   155

Appendix C: Guidelines for Child Custody Evaluations in Divorce Proceedings   171

Appendix D: Glossary   177

Bibliography   181

Acknowledgments

I WISH TO THANK THE PEOPLE who assisted with the completion of this book. Eunice (Mickie) Clavner of Cleveland combined her skills as an educator with those of a practicing attorney to steer the book in the right direction and to adjust the "voice" of the text. Her assistance was invaluable.

Dr. Michael C. King provided assistance with the presentation of the material on neuropsychology. I also thank Professor Chris Levy for suggesting the addition of a chapter on mediation and negotiation.

About the Author

J. THOMAS DALBY, PH.D., is a forensic psychologist and trial consultant who has been in practice for nineteen years. He has conducted more than seven thousand forensic examinations in criminal, civil, and administrative law matters and has given expert evidence in more than five hundred trials. Dr. Dalby also has consulted internationally on the preparation and presentation of information at trial and on creative approaches in legal argument. He consults with police forces on criminal investigations and with private businesses in the area of workplace conflict. He is currently manager of the Department of Psychology at the Calgary General Hospital and is adjunct associate professor of psychology, psychiatry, and clinical psychology at the University of Calgary. He is a principal in Spectrum Psychology Group, an association of specialty practitioners that serves the legal, healthcare, and corporate communities. Dr. Dalby is the author of more than ninety professional publications and also has published short fiction.

Introduction

THE PAST TWO DECADES HAVE SEEN a remarkable expansion of the role psychology plays in the legal process. In the area of criminal law, the application of psychology, once confined to opinion evidence on a defendant's competency to stand trial and to occasional insanity pleas, now has expanded to include nearly every aspect of the criminal justice system. Today's criminal justice system could not function effectively without the participation of psychologists and other mental health experts.

Applications of psychology have flourished as well in other areas of law. For example, in civil litigation involving personal injury and workers' compensation cases, where allegations of psychological harm are increasing. Almost as a matter of course, family law now employs psychologists to provide evidence relevant to child custody and to issues of abuse.

With the expanded applications of clinical psychology came the realization that more experimentally oriented psychologists also could offer information that would be useful in the legal process. Psychological research has been applied to dozens of issues in such legal arenas as sentencing, eyewitness testimony, lie detection, jury behavior, trademark recognition, product liability, and recovered memory.

The purpose of this book is to provide busy lawyers with a single reference that can help them to understand the various applications of psychology so that when they are presented with a psychological report, they can comprehend the principles used and the strengths and weaknesses of the arguments made. Should lawyers need to employ their own experts in psychology, finding the experts will be facilitated by the book's comprehensive listing of local and national resources. The book also will help lawyers to discover areas of law for which they had not previously considered psychology as a resource. Lawyers may find that the book even assists their courtroom tactics and procedures by citing psychological studies that evaluate courtroom methods. Many lawyers tell me that they have an interest in psychology—how could they not, because the true subject of law, as of psychology, is human behavior.

CHAPTER ONE

Psychology and Law: Strange Bedfellows

In 1908 Hugo Münsterberg, a professor of psychology at Harvard University, proclaimed in his best-selling *On the Witness Stand* that although the lawyer and the judge and the jury member do not think that they need psychology, public opinion will persuade them otherwise. Münsterberg addressed his appeals to the public, often through popular magazines, trying to convince them that psychology had an application in almost every aspect of their lives. The legal profession soundly rejected his territorial intrusions. His vision for the application of psychology to the law was far-ranging but his critical tone toward those already participating in the legal system was such that his exclusion was assured. Münsterberg's pleas for acceptance are no longer necessary. Today there is scarcely an area of law that does not turn regularly to psychology for information, opinion, or guidance. The union of the two disciplines has not always been a smooth one, but it now seems a symbiotic relationship. It flourishes vigorously and extends well beyond its initial application to mental health issues arising in criminal matters.

The growth of psychology in the past fifty years has been exponential, and psychology touches almost every aspect of your life. An engineering psychologist may have helped design the car that you drive; the LSAT test you may recall taking was crafted using psychometrics; the movies, plays, and novels you enjoy frequently address psychological themes. The number of psychologists in North America has increased more than tenfold in the past fifty years, whereas the general population has yet to double. The increasing demand for psychological information is not unique to law; it is a society-wide phenomenon.

Psychologists' Involvement in the Law

Gary Melton, of the law/psychology program at the University of Nebraska–Lincoln, has pointed out the mushrooming involvement of psychologists in legal decision making. Psychologists are being appointed to faculties of law; the American Psychological Association has become a prolific amicus curiae in the Supreme Court; and the ranks of psychologists belonging to psychology-law societies have risen dramatically from virtual nonexistence in the early 1970s. Melton proposes that the influence of psychology on the legal system, although growing, remains less than it should be. To help lawyers make the most of psychology in their practice, this book reviews relevant issues, practices, and theory. It is intended as a guide to help lawyers understand and use psychological information. It is not intended as a substitute for a psychological expert. Indeed, the book's primary goal is to promote the appropriate use of psychologists in legal cases and to assist lawyers in interacting with them. The book contains a bibliography that directs readers to comprehensive reviews of the information surveyed. Citations to case law related to psychological issues would be a book in themselves. Rather than provide scattered legal sources, I have avoided them altogether. A well-trained forensic psychologist will provide these citations for a specific state and application. Meyer (1995) provides a good thumbnail summary of many of the relevant case references.

Psychology is the scientific study of behavior. The often-stated goals of this discipline include description, explanation, prediction, and control of behavior. The naive critic of the discipline may argue that understanding human behavior is just "common sense." As the English historian Mandell Creighton has suggested, however, all true knowledge contradicts common sense. Rigorous scientific studies have shown time and again that our customary beliefs of why or how humans respond in certain situations are frequently at odds with the facts. Common sense relies on our personal experience and intuition—both of which are subject to strong forces of misleading bias.

To those outside the discipline of psychology, there is an assumption of unity of interpretation or commonality of vision in this discipline. Although psychologists share a core training in scientific methodology, the contents of their study are widely diverse. Some have more accurately described psychology as a loose confederation of scientific professionals spanning topics across the biological and social sciences. The American Psychological Association (APA), for example, has forty-six divisions that represent distinct areas of research. Even within these areas, there is much diversity. It is quite possible for two psychologists to know little more about each other's area of interest than does the layperson.

Today, all psychologists have some form and degree of specialization, making it very difficult to be a general psychologist. Some of the major specialties that you may deal with are as follows:

Clinical psychologists. The largest group of psychologists (approximately 45 percent) focus on the assessment, diagnosis, and treatment of mental disorders. In addition to academic training, clinical psychologists must receive practical training and serve internships to obtain a license to practice.

Counseling psychologists. Although related to clinical psychology, counseling psychologists typically work with less impaired clients or with individuals experiencing common life problems for which they seek assistance. Counseling psychologists constitute the second largest group (approximately 12 percent).

Developmental psychologists. Developmental psychologists investigate the psychological and biological changes that occur throughout life, with many focused particularly on childhood development. They are usually members of a university faculty, although they may conduct some of their research in applied settings. Their work may be relevant to cases of child custody when the developmental needs of children at particular ages are in dispute or in criminal matters when children's testamentary capacity or abilities are called into question.

Educational and school psychologists. Educational psychologists are involved in the development of instructional material for a wide range of educational institutions as well as of procedures for industrial and business training. School psychologists provide assessment and consultation services within school systems to assist children with school performance or school adjustment difficulties. Legal action to ensure that special-needs children receive the services they require will need the opinion of an educational or school psychologist.

Engineering psychologists. Engineering psychologists are interested in the capabilities and limitations of humans in their interactions with machines and other environmental systems. The environment or machine can be ergonomically designed to provide optimal levels of safety, efficiency, and comfort. Engineering psychologists appear in trials with issues of product liability or inappropriate design of manufactured items that cause harm to their users.

Experimental psychologists. Experimental psychologists investigate fundamental psychological processes (learning, memory, perception, motivation), and they are nearly always affiliated with a college or university. They conduct their work primarily in laboratories. Many trials have highlighted the importance of witnesses' memories. Some experimental psychologists have studied the situations under which memory frequently fails and when it is most robust. Experimental psychologists who specialize in the study of perception also have been pivotal in many legal cases involving accident reconstruction.

Forensic psychologists. Although many types of psychologists can contribute to legal issues, forensic psychologists do so on a regular basis and have specific training in legal issues. They may specialize in one area of law (criminal) or have a more eclectic practice.

Health psychologists. In recent years it has become accepted, even in traditional medical circles, that psychological factors exert a tremendous effect on physical disease, and that these factors sometimes are the key to treating the condition. The discipline of health psychology also encompasses efforts to prevent disease and promote the maintenance of health. In personal injury litigation, health psychologists often address the interaction of psychological and physical variables in quantifying elements such as pain.

Industrial and organizational psychologists. The goals of industrial and organizational psychologists are to understand and improve workplace behavior, including productivity, motivation, job satisfaction, and commitment. Within the work environment, they may focus sometimes on the individual worker and at other times on the organization as an entity. They may also comment upon issues of employment litigation, workplace testing/promotion, and conflict.

Neuropsychologists. Clinical neuropsychologists assess the behavioral results of brain injuries and participate in consultations regarding rehabilitation of this population. Their most common appearance in courtrooms relates to personal injuries. With the growing number of aging citizens, however, they are increasingly addressing issues of competence in this population.

Personality and social psychologists. Personality psychologists research individual variance in human traits and abilities and develop theories to explain these variations. Social psychologists investigate how people interact with one another. They make significant contributions to the understanding of aspects of the legal system (e.g., juries) and of society's attitude toward the administration of justice.

To become a psychologist, it is necessary to acquire four or five years of graduate training after receiving a bachelor's degree. The traditional doctoral degree awarded in all sciences, the doctor of philosophy (Ph.D.), is the most common degree. In the past twenty years, however, some universities have awarded a doctoral degree unique to psychology, the doctor of psychology (Psy.D.). Universities awarding this degree reason that because most psychologists apply psychology rather than conduct research, this emphasis should be reflected in the training of doctors of psychology. In some jurisdictions, individuals with a master's degree in psychology also may practice psychology. Before being licensed, however, all psychologists who practice clinical and related health-service work are required to take written and oral examinations after a period of internship.

The fields of clinical psychology and of psychiatry overlap to some degree, and members of these disciplines frequently collaborate. A psychiatrist must hold an M.D. degree and serve a residency in the assessment and treatment of mental disorders. Psychiatrists (being physicians) may prescribe drugs for patients and admit patients to hospitals. Many psychologists, however, have expertise in the effects of drugs on behavior and have been admitted as expert witnesses in this area. Psychologists have achieved limited hospital admission privileges in a small number of hospitals, and there are groups of psychologists lobbying for the right to prescribe drugs for mental conditions, although this goal is not universally endorsed by the profession as a whole.

Conflicting Values

As you have seen, psychologists can be researchers or practitioners or both. However, psychologists who do only basic research are shrinking in numbers. Increasingly, these psychologists are pressured to conduct more practical research that addresses society's needs. Finding funding for more basic research that has no specific application has become difficult. This is unfortunate because, just as engineering requires knowledge from physics and medicine needs information from biochemical investigations, the core knowledge in applied psychology is derived from more basic experimental psychology.

At times there are conflicting values between the roles of scientist and practitioner. All psychologists are trained as scientists. However, many practitioners conduct no formal research beyond their dissertation project. Although most retain the critical skills of the scientist in their work, a few drift into subjective and intuitive interpretations while retaining the impression that their conclusions are scientific. Without some continuing contact with the scientific lifeblood of the discipline, there is the danger for the practitioner to proffer pseudoscientific ideas and opinions. These "junk-science" psychologists are often solo private practitioners without university or health service affiliations. Of course, many capable psychologists are solo practitioners, but this setting has fewer checks and balances to prevent the professional from drifting into murky waters.

Use in the Courtroom

Given the breadth of the discipline, what are some of the tasks that psychologists may be asked to do in the courtroom? The longest standing use of psychology is in criminal courts, where the issue of competency or fitness to stand trial is common when the accused is suspected of having a mental disorder. The primary importance of an individual's ability to participate fairly in his or her defense cannot be underestimated. Competency deals primarily with the individual's comprehension of the legal circumstances and his or her ability to gauge the seriousness of this plight. Although some competency statutes (which vary from state to state) cite the ability of the individual to assist counsel as an issue, this is a secondary concern. Only a small percentage of individuals who are assessed for competence to stand trial are found to lack the requisites to participate in their defense. Having even a major psychotic disorder does not necessarily render a person unfit. Mental retardation may also interfere with competency to stand trial, but rarely is a person with mild or even moderate mental retardation found unfit.

Criminal Trials

The most visible appearance of mental-health professionals in a criminal trial (which often precipitates chastisement from the public) is in a case that involves an *insanity defense*. In such a case, psychologists often work in tandem with their psychiatric colleagues. The general public has the misperception that insanity defenses are common events. Studies have shown that individuals who are found not guilty by reason of insanity tend to serve longer terms of incarceration (albeit in mental hospitals) than they would have served if they had pled guilty. Some efforts have been made to reform laws that allow this to happen, but the variability of law from jurisdiction to jurisdiction makes reform uneven. In some cases, a sequential hospitalization/incarceration arrangement is a preferred arrangement.

Another common application of psychology in criminal cases is the preparation of a *presentence report*. Judges have indicated that at this stage of the process, they want the offender "individualized," so that they may exercise appropriately the wide latitude they often possess in sentencing. Relevant questions posed by judges can include the following: What is the offender's personal history (developmental, educational, work, relationships)? Does the offender have prior offenses? Does she or he have a mental condition? If so, is it amenable to treatment? What form of treatment? Is the offender considered dangerous? Although the correctional system operates independently of the courts, judges want to balance the need for deterrence with the chance of remediation in meting sentences.

Civil Trials

In the civil law arena, clinical reports by psychologists are most prevalent in personal injury litigation and child custody matters. In personal injury litigation, claims of psychological injury have risen dramatically. In many personal injury cases, the physical injury is minor or absent altogether. Assessing claims of psychological injury is far more complex than assessing claims of physical injury. The psychologist assessing a plaintiff must determine the degree of impairment, if present, and provide an opinion on the pathway between specific events, such as a motor vehicle accident, and the plaintiff's mental condition. The psychologist's comments about the prognosis and about the recommended treatment for the condition are also necessary elements in these assessments. As a matter of course, courts now accept this form of psychological evidence. Psychological assessments in personal injury suits often address posttraumatic stress, brain trauma, cervical or whiplash injury, psychological reaction to burns or disfigurement, amputation, pain, and sexual dysfunction. Of course, the psychologist must also appraise objectively the possibility of malingering in personal injury assessments. This is not just a dichotomous judgment of the plaintiff's overall conduct, for specific compensable injuries can be exaggerated as well.

Family Law

Domestic law governing the status of the family, the settling of family disputes, and the maintenance of an individual family member's welfare has long accepted evidence from psychologists on the clinical concerns raised. In this forum more than any other, judges have expressed reservations over the boundaries of comments by psychologists. Subjective dogma has often been offered instead of objective scientific comment. This has been unfortunate, for the wealth of scientific information accumulated from studies of child development and family functioning could offer great assistance to judges. The task of adjudicating domestic issues becomes more difficult as the population of single parents and blended families increases and abuse within families is identified more frequently. The roles that psychologists play in these matters are as advocates, impartial observers, and, more recently, mediators. The impartial custody evaluator gathers as much information as possible about parental ability and capacity and offers this information to the courts. When a bilateral assessment of parents is conducted, the evaluator may make specific recommendations about custody, but many feel that this intrudes too far into the realm of the judge. Unilateral objective assessment of a parent may address the competency of that individual to parent but not the relative status of the other parent.

The ethics in this field are complex, and I will discuss them in chapter 9. Courts in adoption or other child custody matters often ask professionals other than psychologists to conduct "home studies." The advantages of engaging psychologists for this task are their more specialized knowledge of mental pathology and normal development, as well as their ability to measure objectively human skills such as parenting. In addition, psychologists, of all professionals, likely have the most to offer in drawing information from scientific literature on germane issues in these situations.

Sexual abuse in the family is another issue that appears in domestic law settings. This issue has surfaced in a number of trials (e.g., the Menendez brothers, Susan Smith) as a mitigator of adult conduct. Adults have also launched suits for damages against their parents for alleged sexual abuse. Understanding mechanisms of memory becomes critical to adjudicating these conflicts.

Other Situations

Issues of mental competency arise in a host of other situations. Is a person competent to manage his or her necessary daily needs or finances? Does (or did) the person have testamentary capacity—often a question raised in a house divided, when the individual's rights collide with the family wishes. Is the person competent to enter a contract—or give informed consent to participate in medical research? Is he or she able to refuse medical care, even when this jeopardizes his or her life? Can a minor's wishes be accepted, overriding the direction of a parent? Contextual understanding of individual cases and careful application of clinical and scientific information can add to understanding in each of these situations.

Lawyers practicing administrative law are increasingly seeking psychological assessments of their clients who are appearing before disciplinary bodies and tribunals. Physicians, lawyers, teachers, police officers, nurses, accountants, and, yes, even psychologists appear in hearings about their competence and/or conduct. The key issue is often whether the professional has a mental disorder and the estimated potential for her or his therapeutic change. When the record of the professional under review reflects only minor transgressions, most boards are quite willing to have the individual undergo rehabilitation rather than permanently remove her or him from the field.

In cases of suspicious death, a psychologist may perform a psychological autopsy. Suicide exclusion clauses in life insurance policies mean that challenges to benefits may occur. In such a case a psychologist who specializes in the study of suicide gathers data and presents a retrospective profile of the deceased. Then, using suicidology research as a base, she or he suggests a probability level of suicide. Often this information is combined with evidence from an accident-reconstruction expert. The prediction of suicide, even given the best data, is imprecise and the weight given to the expert offering a psychological autopsy should be considered in this light.

Most lawyers consider some of the clinical applications I have cited when they think of psychology applied to the law. Yet some of the most powerful psychological arguments arise from the scientific, not the clinical, developments in the discipline. Questions begging empirical behavioral answers arise from many areas of law. In negligence and product-liability work, the use of an engineering psychologist can be vital. Is the product designed to be safe to humans, given the abilities and habits of this poor species? Was the product tested with an adequate sample of people over a suitable age range or simply designed on theory? Is a particular road sign designed so poorly as to contribute to motor vehicle accidents? Are warning labels on products comprehensible to the general population who will use the product? Often previous research may provide ready answers for these inquiries, but engineering psychologists can undertake tailor-made research investigations for presentation at trial.

Experimental psychologists may have much to offer in a suit alleging infringement of trademark. Using data from research on the perceptions of a product by consumers and their decision-making processes, experimental psychologists can test the question of buyer confusion. Identification of products is far more complex than simple visual stimuli (e.g., a red and white package), and the ability of consumers to distinguish subtleties is well known.

CHAPTER **TWO**

Models of Behavior

PSYCHOLOGY HAS FOUR MAIN GOALS: to describe, to explain or understand, to predict, and to change or alter behavior. In this chapter I explore the second, and perhaps the most difficult, of these goals—to explain why people behave the way they do. When examining an individual's behavior, and sometimes even our own, a ready explanation is not always at hand. Why did Jeffrey Dahmer sadistically slay seventeen young men? Why did people vote for Bill Clinton? Why did people riot in Los Angeles after a legal decision? We are often left saying "God only knows." Indeed, when asked why they behaved in particular ways, people often offer what they believe are "common sense" explanations—yet dozens of studies show clearly how little insight people have into the forces that shape their behavior. In psychology, the study of behavior has led to the development of theory to address the question "why." Just as any object can be viewed from different perspectives, human behavior can be observed from diverse vantages. This is not to say that the viewpoints are constantly in direct opposition. Sometimes they are, but more often the explanatory values of different models can be summed to approximate a complete understanding of human behavior. For example, an individual's intelligence can be viewed as an inherited trait or as a trait that is dependent on the quality of the learning and the experiences the individual has received. The complete answer is, of course, that both of these elements are powerful in explaining (thus predicting) behavior. The controversy, in this example, is simply how much each explanatory model contributes to intelligence.

The appearance of a psychologist as an expert witness in a trial will be more productive and the lawyer will be better prepared if the lawyer knows the school or model of behavior the psychologist advocates. In this chapter I discuss the five basic models that have been developed to understand human behavior. The discussion will review the strengths and weaknesses of each model in the legal arena. I will present the case of Albert DeSalvo, commonly remembered as the Boston Strangler, to illustrate possible explanations for his aberrant behavior from each of the models.

DeSalvo typically strangled women in their apartments (often using their own stockings). His sexual drive was very strong, and he sought satisfaction five or six times per day. DeSalvo was a construction worker by trade. He was not very intelligent. His childhood was economically deprived, and his alcoholic father frequently beat both him and his mother. DeSalvo's father even sold him and his sister as slaves to a farmer for several months. DeSalvo engaged in breaking and entering as a youth. While serving with the United States Army in Europe, he married a German woman and soon had several children. He began his criminal spree by posing as a scout for a modeling agency and convincing (sometimes forcing) hundreds of women to have sex with him. He began to kill in June 1962, and when he was through on January 4, 1964, he had murdered thirteen women. It was while he was detained in a mental hospital for a series of rapes that he claimed to be the Boston Strangler. He had little insight into his motivations.

Psychoanalytic Model

When they think of psychology, many lawyers imagine an aging and bearded gentleman with a Viennese accent who sits behind a Victorian lady as she reclines on a brocade couch, revealing her latest dream. The image of Sigmund Freud (1856–1939) is well entrenched in the public's mind. Although he had a profound impact on the beginning of psychological explanations and treatment of behavior, Freud's influence on modern psychology is not pervasive. This is particularly true in courtroom applications. However, elements or ideas drawn from psychoanalysis continue to form the basis of some psychological legal defenses.

Freud's views developed out of clinical work with troubled individuals. He became convinced that unconscious mental processes underlay most abnormal behavior. The aim of his therapy was to assist the patient to gain insight into these hidden influences. In classic analytic theory the symptoms presented by the patient are the end product of the following chain: conflict → anxiety → defense → symptoms. Conflicts arise between the universal biological needs and the restraints imposed on our seeking to satisfy those needs. Freud argued that the roots of these conflicts are established in early childhood.

Freud pictured the personality as being composed of three elements: the *id*, the *ego*, and the *superego*. The *id* (the *it*) appears earliest in the development of the child and is governed by biological instincts and drives to satisfy these instincts. Freud separated the instincts into life instincts and death instincts. The life instincts are dominated by sexual drives, and the death instincts show up in the form of aggressive and hostile behavior. The instincts were thought to be biologically entrenched, but society placed strong sanctions on the expression of these drives which, in turn, led to conflict. Early in life this conflict is not present, as the child is selfish and seeks immediate gratification and has few inhibitions on satisfying his or her needs. This lack of restraint cannot continue throughout life, so the *ego* and *superego* develop as balances to the id. The *ego* (Freud's German term was *das Ich* or the *I*) represents the rational and realistic part of the mind and controls all voluntary action. In contrast the *superego (over the I)* is concerned with moral judgments and is composed of *the conscience*, which triggers guilt feelings over transgressions, and the *ego ideal*, which rewards morally proper conduct with feelings of pride. The id and superego are in opposition and are managed or balanced by the ego. When this balance is not maintained in either direction, mental pathology is created. If not balanced in adults, the id leads to psychopathic persons, who only seek satisfaction of their own needs. If the superego is not balanced by the id, then the person becomes very limited, constricted, and rigid in his or her conduct.

Freud suggested that personality develops in five *psychosexual* stages: *oral, anal, phallic, latency,* and *genital*. Each stage provides the foundation for the following stages. If the developmental tasks to be completed at each stage are not finished, then development will be thwarted and the person will be *fixated*. Finally, during periods of great stress in adulthood, the person may *regress* to an earlier stage of development. For example, a person who increases his or her food intake during times of stress may be thought to have regressed to the oral stage, a more secure time of life. With these concepts in mind, I review Freud's five stages of development, the approximate ages at which these stages occur, and the critical aspects of each stage.

1. **Oral stage** (birth to six months). During the oral stage, the infant is preoccupied with sucking. Freud took the bold step of postulating that this behavior is not only adaptive from a nutritional motive, but

that the child derives sexual pleasure from it. The child is highly dependent on the mother to meet its needs during this time, and any disruption to this relationship leads to anxiety.

2. **Anal stage** (six months to end of second year). During the anal stage, the child discovers that sexual satisfaction can be gained from anal functions. This is a forerunner to later mature sexual development, but it is an advance from strictly oral satisfaction. In this phase of development, the child fuses sex and aggression and attempts to control his or her parents during toilet training. The child can please or displease the parents by toilet performances. The reactions of the parents to the child's toilet training may also shape the child's personality: A strict and demanding parent may cause the child to be obstinate, whereas a supportive and encouraging parent may help a child become generous and productive.

3. **Phallic stage** (three to six years). It is during the phallic stage that the development of girls and boys diverges. Both begin to have stirrings of sexual feelings (hence the label), with boys becoming attracted to their mothers (Oedipus complex) and girls to their fathers (Electra complex). Boys (unconsciously, of course) will abandon their incestuous wishes for their mothers because of fear that their fathers will castrate them. Instead boys seek to identify with their fathers and thereby obtain their mothers vicariously. Freud's explanation of female development is even more interesting. Girls notice that they lack external genitalia and feel castrated. They blame their mothers for this tragedy, withdraw from them, and seek affection from their fathers. Like boys, girls recognize unconsciously that their mothers may seek to harm them and abandon their quest, seeking an affiliation with their mothers once again.

4. **Latency stage** (six to twelve years). Freud thought that little happened during the latency stage other than a child's continued strengthening of identification with the same-sexed parent, including not only an imitation of the parent's overt behavior but an incorporation of the parent's values and ideals.

5. **Genital stage** (after twelve years). During the genital stage, the individual strives to achieve sexual and personal maturity. The success of the goals in this stage depends upon how appropriately previous stages were achieved. The genital stage provides the foundation for effective adult relationships that allow for affectionate and altruistic interactions.

Anxiety results, according to psychoanalytic theory, when unconscious conflict occurs. This symptom is a signal for the individual to engage a *defense mechanism*. These are psychological tactics to distort reality, thereby reducing conflict and the resulting anxiety. Of the many psychological defenses, the following are some of the more important ones that were developed more fully by Freud's daughter, Anna:

1. **Repression.** A method of resolving conflict by sweeping painful memories to the far inaccessible recesses of the mind. Some suggest that long-lost memories of sexual abuse as children are repressed only to be brought out by treatment. This idea has received strong challenges from scientists who are expert in memory processes.
2. **Suppression.** Unlike repression, this is a conscious way of avoiding thinking about unpleasant material, often by engaging the mind on another topic.
3. **Denial.** A primitive method that distorts reality by the refusal to perceive or acknowledge it.
4. **Projection.** Attributing one's own unacceptable motives or characteristics to others.
5. **Displacement.** The discharge of pent-up feelings or drives that cannot be directly expressed by choosing to vent them in safer environments or situations.
6. **Regression.** A return to an earlier stage of life in which demands were less onerous.
7. **Identification.** Assuming the personal characteristics of another individual to satisfy one's needs vicariously.

How might Freud explain Albert DeSalvo's crimes? He would first point out how important DeSalvo's early environment was in the development of his deviancies. DeSalvo developed no superego, as any moral boundaries were erased when his father systematically broke his mother's knuckles or indentured his children for his own gain. Instead, DeSalvo was all id, dominated by his sex drive and clearly fixated at the phallic stage of development with attraction to his mother. Unable to unleash his anger on his father, he displaced his sexual anger toward mother (and wife) substitutes. After strangling his victim, he often tied a bow under her chin, displaying the rigid obsessive-compulsive features of his personality. Denial of reality (or wish fulfillment) was also evident in some cases, as he claimed to have had sexual intercourse when he had not. Although this is a potential explanation based on the general psychoanalytic theory, there are others. One hypnoanalyst, who saw DeSalvo, thought that in attacking these women he was somehow attacking his crippled daughter (the explanations can get a little far-fetched).

The main criticism levied against the psychoanalytic viewpoint is that although the ideas proposed are interesting (and occasionally bizarre), there is little scientific evidence to support them. Many treatment-outcome studies of psychoanalysis show equivocal response even after years of treatment. Rather, the buttress for using this system of thought comes from practitioners who say it is useful for them in explaining behavior to their patients. The concepts presented in this model of behavior do not lend themselves to empirical tests. This does not mean that they are wrong necessarily, but when psychoanalytic explanations for a behavior conflict with a theory that has a proven scientific basis, the latter typically will be preferred. A psychoanalytic explanation in court may end up sounding mystical, but it will not be held in a favorable light against strong opposition from biological or cognitive explanations. The appeal of provable hypotheses is a very powerful element in the courtroom.

Behavioral Model

An American model of behavior—behaviorism—rapidly eclipsed the classical analytic approach that was dominant in the early part of this century. The fundamental tenet of behaviorism is the rejection of subjective experience as an appropriate subject of scientific study. Rather, only directly observable behavior is accepted as legitimate data, and the environmental conditions that control behavior must be explored.

The origins of the behavioral view came from the work of Ivan Pavlov (1849–1936), a Russian physiologist. Pavlov won a Nobel Prize in 1904 for his work on the digestive processes in dogs. In the course of his work, he discovered accidentally that dogs developed a conditioned reflex of salivating both to the reaction of food in their mouth and to the sight and smell of food—and even to the sound of the footsteps of the assistant bringing the food. Following this observation, Pavlov continued to study the process of *classical conditioning*, whereby neutral objects or events, through repeated pairings with natural causes of behavior, take on powerful eliciting properties that lead to strong positive or negative reactions. This discovery added a new way to explain behavior—that many of our behaviors are not innate but passively learned through exposure to particular environments. Many phobias and other abnormal behaviors that are seemingly irrational arise in this way, as well as everyday likes and dislikes. For example, people may develop a fear of hospitals if they have undergone painful procedures in a hospital. The person develops a conditioned avoidance of hospitals because of the pain and suffering associated with the hospital. However, he or she will experience less anxiety when seeing a hospital on television than when seeing a real one.

Operant conditioning is thought to require a more active role of the participant than classical conditioning, whereby emitted behaviors are reinforced or punished. Again, most of the basic theory underlying operant conditioning arose from studies of animals in laboratories, then broadened to encompass human examples. That human behavior can be shaped by rewards and punishments was not a discovery of modern psychology. What psychology offered was the development of a technology for changing behavior and a systematic understanding of how rewards and punishments worked. With this information it became easier to predict with a measure of precision how strongly behavior can be altered. Why did you become a lawyer? Was it because of severe toilet training or because you saw that some tangible (or less tangible) rewards would accompany this vocation, such as status, income, or social influence? Likewise, consequences shape our interests, both positively and negatively.

A third form of learning is *modeling*. Through observation and imitation, new behaviors are added to our repertoire. A child reared in a home in which he or she daily observes abusive conduct toward women has an increased risk of developing parallel behavior simply through this exposure. Many behaviors that we acquire primarily in this way are language, social rituals, and vocational skills. In addition to learning specific information (how to arrange a place setting on a table) by observing, we often take on the general ideas or attitudes of prominent or influential people in our environment. Observational learning is perhaps the most complicated form of learning because it nearly always involves cognitive processing. We are selective in what behavior and what models we imitate. We are more likely to imitate high-status models and ones who share similar features (age, socioeconomic background, education, values). Much has been written about the shaping power of television as an explanation of behaviors such as violence. Reasonably strong evidence exists to show that watching violence stimulates aggression in the viewer and whets the appetite for watching similar programs.

Had Albert DeSalvo *learned* to rape and kill women? A behaviorist might claim exactly that. His first model was his father, who gave ample demonstrations of physical violence. As a youth, DeSalvo prostituted himself to gay men because he "needed the dough." He began to rape and was reinforced for this behavior time and time again (by his estimate, sexually assaulting two thousand women). Although not bright, he was verbally persuasive—again reinforced for his repeated lies and evasion of punishment. He was trained in violence in the military.

Humanistic Model

The humanistic model stems from the writings of Carl Rogers (1902–1987) and Abraham Maslow (1908–1970). Their approach was somewhat reactionary to the dominant research-oriented forms of treatment offered in the early 1960s. At that time both behaviorism and psychoanalysis proposed that human behavior is shaped or determined by forces outside of the person's control. Humanism strongly opposed this deterministic philosophy, arguing the opposite—that we can control our own behavior.

Humanistic approaches to understanding human behavior are diverse. They do not share a common methodology, only an attitude—to study humans as individuals and to understand their activity from their subjective perspective. This opens up a challenge as to the "generalizability" or relevance of these findings to other persons. Humanists seek to enrich human lives by helping people to understand themselves and to develop to the fullest. An assumption that people are fundamentally good underlies humanism. This is not surprising given that most of the therapeutic extensions of this approach are not with people who suffer mental disorders but who are simply seeking an enriched life. Humanists argue that it is counterproductive to view or study people by their "functions" such as learning abilities. Instead they promote the idea to see people as wholes and not to diagnose "abnormalities" of behavior. Humanists often reject the basic tenets of science, suggesting instead that people do not always follow the behavioral rules of other models and that people are individual, unpredictable, and unique. Sources of information about a client can be very intuitive rather than objective.

Humanistic psychology is not a tidy collection of knowledge-based practitioners. It is often thought to include Eastern philosophies of Buddhism and Taoism, with methods of treatment directed toward "personal growth and human potential."

In the legal arena the nonscientific aspects of this approach are quickly exposed and easily ridiculed. Embedded within humanistic approaches, however, are legitimate ideas borne from the founders of the approach, which over time have seeped into the practice of most clinicians. These ideas include the value of positive regard for clients, the utility of warmth, respect, and sympathy—things we all look for in a therapist whose assistance we seek. However, the fuzziness of some of the concepts has led to the birth of "alternative," "fringe," or just plain bizarre conduct by individuals under the guise of professional respectability. Sifting wheat from chaff in this field requires some doing, but obvious nonscientific approaches, such as rebirthing, primal integration, or sand play, may alert the observer to the nature of the practice.

Because the humanistic model has little to say about abnormal behavior in general, humanists would struggle to present any tenable hypothesis about the Boston Strangler's behavior. They might say that DeSalvo chose his behavior, but the assumption that he was fundamentally "good" would be a stretch for any theorist.

Biological Model

It is unlikely that psychoanalytic or humanistic models of behavior are especially applicable to lions, tigers, and bears. Yet we, like they, are animals. The biological model suggests that many of our behaviors are the result of the same genetic and physiological forces that shape other animals' behaviors. Therefore, by studying the behavior of other animals and the biological forces that sculpt their behavior, we may gain insights into some of the behaviors that parallel our own. As well, by studying humans who are biologically injured or different, we may be able to uncover fundamental aspects of why we do what we do.

Our physiology has much to do with the way we think and behave, and that physiology is what we share with other animals. Many aspects of our behavior—our group interactions, our sexual behavior, and even our eating—may be explained by our genetic heritage from centuries or hundreds of centuries past. Our behavior has been slowly shaped by the demands of our species to survive. That genetic traits can strongly affect very specific behaviors, as well as general tendencies, has been repeatedly demonstrated in studies of identical twins who were separated at birth, as well as studies of adopted children and studies of traits within families.

The brain is the most vital aspect of our physiology when we consider behavior. This soggy organ, weighing in at three and a half pounds in the mature adult, has been responsible for every accomplishment of our civilization. It is a tangled network of 180 billion cells that keeps the heart beating, regulates body temperature and a myriad of other vital functions, and, at the same time, allows the opportunity of complex speech and thought.

The brain and central nervous system mediate all behavior. We receive information from the world around us, process it, and then formulate actions based on the results of processing. Of course, much of this operation occurs automatically without much comprehension on our part. As I shall show in chapter 5, the brain is specialized in the organization of tasks, much as a large law firm organizes special divisions or areas of practice. Damage to particular regions brings predictable alterations in behavior. Regional destruction of the cortex can occur through a variety of diseases or traumas and sometimes even through the application of treatments (e.g., electroconvulsive therapy, or ECT).

In the normal person many behaviors are the result of physiological responses. In times of stress the autonomic nervous system regulates a complicated series of physical reactions. Heart rate, blood pressure, and the chemical makeup of our body can alter quickly and radically. Hormones, such as adrenaline, are released into the bloodstream, and behavior can become highly aroused or agitated. Violent outbursts, panic attacks, or other highly emotional responses can result.

Albert DeSalvo's behavior may have a number of biological explanations. A sociobiologist might argue that rape is adaptive, biologically based behavior in that it propagates the genetic material of the rapist. Is *rape* common in other animal species? Yes. Perhaps a biological explanation might acknowledge the abnormality of DeSalvo's conduct and suggest some malformation of his brain. Needing to release his sexual drive many times a day may point to some physiological excess. DeSalvo himself wondered why he had this terrible, unceasing urge.

DeSalvo also inherited some potent genes—that of a violent, destructive, and cruel man. Psychopaths manifest certain personality features—glib, superficial, charming, and without remorse. DeSalvo also displayed many of the narcissistic features seen in psychopaths, considering himself special and superior. Did he have a mental disorder arising from his biological state? Several psychiatrists at his competence hearing called him a chronic schizophrenic (this severe psychosis is a highly unlikely conclusion based on current diagnostic criteria).

Cognitive Model

Psychology's formal origins in European laboratories in the late nineteenth century placed cognition high on the list of essential features of study. This interest lapsed, only to reemerge beginning in the late 1950s. Psychologists then began to see the limitations of behaviorism and again began to inquire into the operations of the black box of the human mind. There was not an outright rejection of behaviorism. Indeed many psychologists successfully integrated both cognitive and behavioral perspectives. Cognitive psychologists suggested that thinking was the relatively unique *human* aspect of the brain, and that thought processes such as language, memory, attention, and other mental functions mediated much of our more complex behavior. Our cognitive abilities—to think, remember, and anticipate—are both an advantage and a hindrance in our daily life. They may make our life efficient or counterproductive by developing false ideas or misunderstanding experiences. The cognitive perspective focuses on humans as thinking beings, not simply biologically programmed animals or beings driven by unconscious forces.

In the late 1950s social psychologists began to study a phenomenon they called *attribution*. According to this theory, everything has to have a reason. Whether the reason is accurate is irrelevant. Imagine that you are a member of a jury hearing evidence in a murder trial. You listen for evidence that can explain to you what happened. Did the behavior of the accused occur because he or she reacted to a unique situation? Would other people in the same situation respond similarly? Is this a pattern of behavior that the accused has exhibited in other situations? If the last is confirmed, most jurors assume that the behavior could be attributed to the character of the person (internal cause). However, the jurors might accept an external cause if the behavior was not typical. Guilty or not guilty will depend on the "common sense" causes that people intuitively generate.

Using this basic phenomenon to understand an individual's behavior began to gather strength in the clinical psychology community. In the early 1960s two clinicians, Albert Ellis and Aaron Beck, proposed that cognitive processes are at the center of most behaviors and emotions. To these men, and to other cognitive theorists, emotional and behavioral distress is linked to irrational and distorted cognitive processes. Cognitive therapists suggest that we hold a unique set of assumptions about ourselves to guide us through life and to assist in our reaction to situations. If, for example, we assume that we should be thoroughly competent, adequate, and achieving in all possible respects if we are to consider ourselves worthwhile, then it is probable that we will be miserable and disappointed with ourselves. We also often display habitual, self-generated thoughts that can contribute to our state of emotional distress: "my parents think I'm no good," "my future looks grim," and so forth. These thoughts cause cascading emotional reactions. In our assessment of the world, we continually display many illogical thought processes. We often see only the negative consequences of an event, exaggerate the importance of undesirable events, and draw broad negative conclusions on the basis of one insignificant event.

Cognitive theory has received a great deal of attention and support from research findings. Therapies based on this theory are very popular and again show empirical support for their effectiveness in changing abnormal behavior.

Albert DeSalvo's cognitions are the source of some interest in explaining his behavior. When the murders stopped (before his confession), he recalled that his wife was treating him better and that he was feeling better about himself because he had received several pay raises. He worshipped his wife, but she rejected him and often insulted him in public. She vilified his sexual drive, calling him dirty and an animal. Did he repeat these statements to himself and grow angry over their truth? He certainly showed many cognitive distortions—suggesting that the women he raped enjoyed it. Was he angry over his lowly station in life, as one theorist suggested, and thus convinced himself that his crimes were a way of putting something over on high-class people?

Each of the theories or models I have reviewed can add to our understanding of "why." The days are past when complex human behavior can be explained completely by one theory.

CHAPTER THREE

Psychological Research and Assessment Methods

TRADITIONAL COMPARISONS BETWEEN LAW and psychology have emphasized their contrasting histories and methodologies. Western legal method can be traced to the Greek forum before the birth of Christ. Debates emphasizing polar rational arguments with supporting (but debatable) facts were laid before a judge who would render a decision. The wisdom of the past guided the decision maker. Attempts to settle disputes often preceded this final decree.

Psychology's birth was much later. As a scientific discipline, psychology began in the laboratories of Germany in the late nineteenth century, with methods directly borrowed from other sciences spawned during the scientific revolution two centuries before. Science, of course, existed long before this, but during the seventeenth century it became organized and systematized, rather than an individual enterprise. The distinct organized emergence of scientific study of behavior developed after 1879, when Wilhelm Wundt founded his laboratory at the University of Leipzig.

What is science? Most answers to this question emphasize the objectivity and hard-nosed methodology, even technology, involved. This is a facade. Science is an attitude and a way of thinking. In a self-description, Sir Isaac Newton, the most celebrated natural philosopher and mathematician of the modern era, likened himself to a boy playing on the seashore, diverting himself now and then with finding a smoother pebble or a prettier shell while the great ocean of undiscovered truth lay before him. This humility is lost on many scientists. Newton, however, captures the true nature of science—childhood curiosity, the drive to know about things observed. Thus science is only a reflection of natural human tendencies. Whether the subject is the orbit of Mars or the migration of birds or the behavior of a jury, the product sought is a sensible explanation for observed regularities.

The *objective* search for the truth in science, as contrasted with the *subjective* approach of law, is another caricature. If science were conducted by robots, one could argue that it is objective. However, the human factor in science makes complete objectivity impossible. Debates between scientists can be as irrational, acrimonious, and partisan as any between lawyers. Scientists have many personal and professional motives beyond a cerebral search for the ultimate truth. This is not to say that their results are necessarily tainted or without merit, rather that human elements can never be discounted fully in their work.

Scientific Truth

I would like to talk a little about the idea of scientific *truth*. The great scientific philosopher Thomas Kuhn has rigorously presented a model of the evolution of scientific ideas. It is a cyclical process. In the early stages of the process continual competition exists among a number of distinct views or explanations. Then one theory gains ascendancy and becomes a paradigm or standard explanation. At this stage "normal science" goes on to articulate, extend, and test the limits of the theory. Eventually some problems crop up with the established order of the theory. This perception that something is not quite right with the theory leads to a crisis stage, but there is resistance to novel ideas. At the height of the crisis it becomes obvious that the established tradition is incomplete and a revolution occurs, in which there again is a body of competing ideas. The pathway to *truth* can be seen as an ascending helix with progress *toward* truth seen in every revolution. Historians of science have noted that this model describes events surprisingly well. The problem with this model is that we never know when we have reached the real truth. This is reality—all we can say is that *right here and now* we believe a theory or explanation to be the truth. To say that we know without a doubt that something is the final truth is naive. There are certainly other kinds of truths besides scientific truth. For example, there are religious truths and mathematical truths that are often independent of scientific quests.

On many occasions scientific results, including those from psychological research, are presented in the courtroom as a buttress to an argument. It is necessary to understand the basic elements of how these scientific theories were developed and tested and how good they really are. Just because a research study has been published does not establish it as the standard or even as the most accepted work in the field. Scientific ideas must be presented as a *body* of work that reflects a consensus in the field, if this is possible. As I discuss later, it is an ethical responsibility of psychologist expert witnesses to present a fair picture of the particular research problem, not to hide dissenting views.

Steps in Psychological Research

To help you to understand the steps involved in psychological research, I will summarize the process. At every step there are a diversity of methodologies and a variety of problems, because there is no study that is exempt from criticism. Most scientists, however, easily grade a research product on a continuum of quality. Research begins with a problem or question. This can arise from reading previous research or from clinical observations of patients or from social issues. When a question or problem arises, the first thing a scientist should do is review the existing literature to see how this question or problem has been addressed and if it has been resolved. There is little value in launching a study into an area that has well-accepted findings.

If the literature reveals incomplete or unsatisfactory answers to the research question, then the scientist must define his or her question in clear, specific terms. There follows a hypothesis (from the Greek meaning *suggestion*). The hypothesis is an idea about the relationship between events or an explanation for why things happen. The hypothesis is usually stated in a way that makes it testable. Objective data will be collected to test the hypothesis. We can never absolutely prove most hypotheses, but research can lend support to the ideas. Testable hypotheses become the basis for the research study. The quest for understanding of human behavior has a similar tradition. From the earliest civilizations, humans have attempted to examine and explain their conduct. These efforts are abundantly portrayed in the works of philosophers, theologians, and playwrights.

To address a research question a scientist can choose from a variety of methods. These methods are often placed into two groups: the naturalistic, correlational study and the experimental study.

Correlational Study

The correlational study is one step beyond casual observation of events in the environment. Suppose that you had a hunch that more experienced lawyers use shorter closing arguments. You might further surmise that over time they have determined that this is a more effective strategy or that, with their years of experience, they are able to submit their argument more tersely to the judge or jury. The hypothesis that you hold has come to you from casual observations. Your observations may not be accurate, however. You may have been too influenced by one trial in which you observed the most senior partner of a prestigious firm give a dynamic five-minute closing. This may have colored your overall perception of the two variables (length of argument and time at bar). To test your hypothesis, you observe sixty lawyers. You objectively and systematically record lengths of their arguments by gauging quantifiable data (time elapsed or number of words) and the years that each lawyer has practiced. Once you have collected your data, you subject them to a statistical analysis. How do we know if the statistical result is significant? In inferential statistics there is a convention that, in most cases, a *significant* probability would be one that would occur by chance in less than 5 percent of cases. In scientific papers the notation that you will see in the Results section will signify $p < .05$ or an even more stringent $p < .01$ (i.e., probability by chance less than 1 percent) when the statistical finding is significant. The result of the statistical analysis never proves beyond all doubt that A caused or is somehow related to B, it simply denotes how probable this is.

In our case the correlation between the two variables appears as illustrated in figure 3.1.

In a statistical correlation you are trying to determine if there is a real relationship between two variables. If there is no relationship the correlation coefficient (mathematical outcome) will be 0. If there is some relationship the value will range from -1 to 1. A minus value indicates a negative correlation, that is, when one variable gets larger, the other gets smaller. A positive correlation indicates that when one variable increases, so does the other. In figure 3.1 I have plotted years of experience on the vertical axis and time elapsed in the closing argument on the horizontal axis. This creates a scatter plot of the sixty lawyers who were observed. Is there a relationship? A correlation statistically draws a straight line through the data and determines the slope of that line (a vertical line or no slope would indicate no correlation).

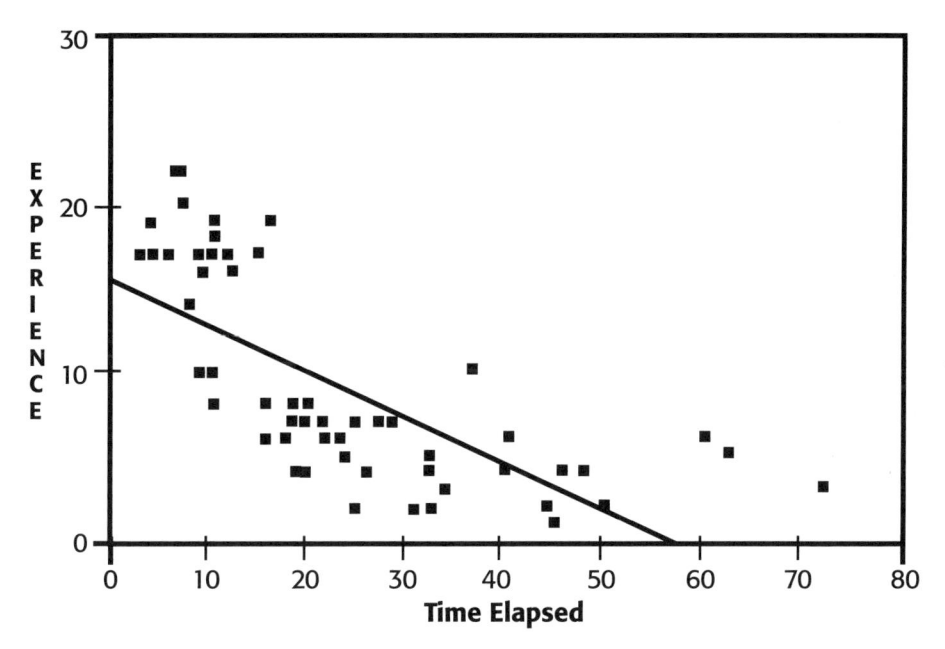

FIGURE 3.1. Correlational Scatter Plot

The correlation coefficient in this diagram is -.7, indicating a very strong relationship between the two variables. There is a statistically significant relationship between the number of years lawyers have practiced law and the amount of time they spend in their summations. The more experience, the shorter the argument. The correlation supports your hypothesis, but it does not explain why this occurs. That will be left for your next study.

One may challenge whether your sample was appropriate. It is necessary to calculate the minimum number of subjects required because if the sample is too small your theory may not hold up and be rejected simply because not enough lawyers were observed. Estimating sample size is done easily at the planning stage of the project. Others may argue that the sample is inappropriate because of other features (the lawyers observed all went to Ivy League schools, the study used only males, it used lawyers practicing only criminal law). The scientist must try to defend against these arguments or, in the design of the study, to balance or somehow account for the differences by incorporating these variables. It will be impossible to control for every possible variable that could have some influence on the outcome. That is why there is often a progression of research studies on the same topic, each attempting to look at just some of these variables and make a small advance over previous work.

Correlations can be used to make predictions. If you know how long a lawyer has been practicing, you can make predictions about how long she or he will take in making a closing argument. This prediction is not infallible, however, for it is based on group data and general relationships. Individuals can always deviate from the norm. Given the strength of the correlation in your study, however, you could predict with some confidence.

When we examine correlations it is important to realize that the relationship described is not necessarily causative. The length of time in practice does not *cause* a lawyer to give shorter arguments, this factor is simply related to the trend. It may be that age, not experience, is the critical factor (something you have not measured), and that people generally are more concise in their speech as they age.

In the study of mental disorders two kinds of correlational research are often used, *longitudinal studies* and *epidemiological investigations*. Longitudinal studies follow the same subjects over a long period of time. Are particular behaviors and characteristics of individuals stable over time or do they change at particular ages? Although the most accurate way to answer this question is the longitudinal study, such a study is very difficult to conduct because of the pragmatic considerations of following people over extended time periods. Epidemiological investigations determine the *incidence* and *prevalence* of conditions in a given population. *Incidence* refers to the number of *new* cases that appear in a given time period and *prevalence* is the *total* number of existing cases at a particular time. For example, the lifetime *prevalence* of schizophrenia, the most serious of the psychoses, is about 1 percent. Thus, during a lifetime, approximately 1 percent of the population will develop schizophrenia. This does not mean that we all share this risk, for people who have a close relative with schizophrenia have a much higher individual risk. That risk averaged over the population is about 1 percent. The *incidence* of schizophrenia (the new cases per year) is only about one per ten thousand, but due to the chronic nature of this disorder the cases accumulate over the years.

Experiment

Unlike a correlational study, an experiment is designed to answer questions regarding causation. One of the advantages it has over other investigation methods is that it allows the researcher to control conditions and attempt to eliminate influences on behavior other than the one being studied. Suppose that, building on our correlational study, we surmise that more senior lawyers give shorter arguments for a reason: They are more effective. Is this true? Do shorter arguments have a greater impact on judges and juries? This is a testable hypothesis, using an experimental research design. We enlist a mock jury and prepare the arguments for both sides of the case. However, we change the length of the arguments. For both pro and con in the argument we have two conditions, long (two-hour) and short (ten-minute) summaries. The arguments are given by the same lawyers (who are as similar in as many respects as possible). The reason for this last condition is that we do not want extraneous influences such as age, sex, style of dress, regional accent, and the like to have any influence on the decision of the jury—only the length of the argument. We then present a number of conditions (long and short arguments, both pro and con) to juries (balanced on all the factors we possibly can) and see if our *independent variable* (length of summary) causes changes in the *dependent variable* (positive or negative jury decision). Again, we gather our data and submit them to a statistical test that will tell us if the outcome is beyond mere chance and that, indeed, our intervention had an effect on outcome. If a significant statistic results, we will be able to proclaim that a brief closing argument produces a positive influence on jury decisions.

The way in which subjects are chosen to be in a research group is important. Often in an experiment a *control group* will be employed. If we were testing a new treatment experimentally, we would compare the results of the individuals who had received a treatment (drug, psychotherapy) with those who had not received it (controls). If the experimental group (receiving the treatment) had a better outcome statistically compared to the control group, we could conclude that the treatment is superior to no treatment. To counter the possibility of a placebo effect (improvement based solely on expectations from a treatment), the control group may receive an inert substance or condition designed to counter this biasing influence. *Bias* is possible from numerous sources and the experimenter attempts to control or counterbalance as many of these as possible. Two methods for reducing bias are *random assignment* and *blinding*. *Random assignment* of subjects to a group can prevent one group becoming systematically different from the other group(s) in a study. This is a statistical control designed to increase the probability that the groups will be the same. Even when the study has been extremely well designed, the investigator must still be alert to bias arising as the study unfolds in an unexpected way. We all know about best-laid plans.

When we have humans participate in behavioral experiments they do not sit passively—they have expectations. They know they may be subjected to some form of observation or examination, they may have some treatment given to them, and they may change because of this treatment. Most research subjects give freely of their time and are cooperative souls. This is a problem. They may try to figure out how they *should* behave and act accordingly to help the scientist trying to make a better world for us all. To overcome this bias, *blinding* is often used in an experiment. This means that the subjects will not be told if they have received an active treatment or a placebo. Sometimes it is also a good idea to keep those conducting the study in the dark. Those investigators who are watching the subjects for expected changes may inadvertently score differently the behavior of those receiving the experimental treatment. If a treatment is expected to improve depression, the investigator may look more intently for this change. If the investigator is unaware of which subject has received which treatment, he or she is unable to allow preconceptions to interfere with ratings. When both the subjects and investigators are unaware of the conditions received by the subjects, this is called a *double-blind* study.

One of the problems of some experiments is the issue of *generalizability*. In psychology many experiments are conducted at universities, and undergraduate students serve as subjects. Can the results of these studies be extended to the population as a whole? Maybe not. The average undergraduate student represents a narrow age range, has an I.Q. above that of the general population, and tends, as well, to have educated parents. If a study of attitudes or abilities is conducted with a sample of this group, the conclusions could safely be generalized only to other undergraduate students with similar parents. A related issue arises about the setting in which studies are conducted. If we are studying the process of memory in the laboratory, will the artificial tasks we give subjects parallel the process of memory in the real world? We hope so, but we always have to keep in mind that we must account for the gulf between the controlled laboratory and the uncontrolled natural environment.

The *case study* is another method of scientific investigation often used in the analysis of abnormal behavior. A case study is an intense examination of a single person or small group of individuals who typically present a notable or unusual feature. In a case study the subject's background, current symptoms, and test findings are presented with some interpretation about how this single case fits into what is known about the particular disorder and its treatment. For example, about ten years ago my colleagues and I reported a then unusual case of identical twin brothers. One of the young men had clear and prominent symptoms of a manic-depressive disorder whereas the other had equally conspicuous symptoms of schizophrenia. The importance of the case was that a prevailing theory at the time suggested that these two disorders were genetically independent. A single case such as this one challenged that idea because obviously the two men had identical genes and were expressing different mental disorders. Other clinicians reported similar cases and, incrementally, support for an alternate theory developed, which was then scrutinized using more large-scale techniques. Case studies can be used to illustrate new therapeutic techniques, or novel applications of existing treatments, and to generate new hypotheses to be tested in correlational or experimental studies. They are, of course, limited by their very nature in terms of generalizability and subjectivity of the report. This does not mean that all studies of a single person are subjective. True experiments can be conducted with a single person (called single-subject experimental designs). In these situations a single subject is observed and measured (called a *baseline period*) prior to any manipulations. This establishes the pretreatment condition of the subject. Then a reversal design is implemented in which a treatment is given, then taken away, then given again. This is often referred to as an A-B-A-B design. When the condition is reversed and the behavior changes or reverts to its original form, the researcher has demonstrated experimentally a link between the treatment and the behavior.

Other Research Techniques

I should briefly mention a number of other research techniques. *Historical research* has the purpose of systematically reconstructing the past by collecting, evaluating, and validating facts to reach definable conclusions. The investigation of the Shroud of Turin is an example of historical research. *Surveys* are another form of research. Surveys are often used by epidemiologists to collect data from a large sample (or even the whole population) for use in correlational analyses. Surveys of the attitudes of the population are sometimes evidence that a change in venue for a trial is appropriate. *Quasi-experimental studies* try to approximate the true experiment in a setting in which manipulation of all the variables is not possible. It is not always possible, for example, to randomly assign subjects to groups. One is left to study the groups as they already exist. Many studies of human behavior that are referred to as experimental are really quasi-experimental because many of the critical variables are impossible to control. There are also *analog studies* that attempt to simulate in the laboratory events in real life. The specifics of street sign design can be presented to subjects in the laboratory to see which signs are easiest to perceive and the various reaction times of subjects to different colors and shapes. *Behavioral research* has also been conducted with animals to discover general rules about behavior (which could ultimately apply to humans) as well as the particular aspects of that species behavior. Only about 7 percent of psychological research is conducted with animals, and of this, more than 90 percent is done with rodents or birds. *Animal research* has contributed much to the understanding of human conditions and disorders. Psychologists also extend their concern for ethical principles in research to their own species and address issues such as risk to participants, the right to privacy, the limitation of deception, and the need for debriefing subjects.

Chapters 4, 5, 6, and 7 focus on the measurement of psychological dimensions such as intelligence or personality. A compendium of many (but not all) of these tests (*Ninth Mental Measurements Yearbook*, 1986) contained over fourteen hundred listings. The scientific development of these measures is an enterprise using the methods reviewed in this chapter to establish two standards: *reliability* and *validity*.

Reliability refers to the consistency between testings. There are several ways to test reliability. The most common is test-retest reliability. This is the correlation between the outcome of two successive applications of the same test. If the result of an aptitude test given one week is dramatically different from that obtained the following week, the reliability of the measure is in question because we know that these personal attributes are relatively stable. Sometimes two forms of a test are developed so that they can be repeated in a short period of time with no carry-over or practice effect. If a memory test is given one week and the same test is given the following week, the subject may improve because of the first testing. Alternate forms attempt to eliminate this effect but can only work if they are fairly consistent in their scores. If one test is more difficult, then the retest is not a fair mirror of the first. A correlation between the two forms of the test should be high to ensure this equivalence. Finally, a test of a behavioral dimension (e.g., anxiety) should have internal reliability. This is usually tested by dividing the items in a test into two equal parts (e.g., alternate questions) and correlating them. This is referred to as a *split-half coefficient*.

Validity shows the extent to which a test measures what it is intended to measure. It is not enough that a test consistently measures a dimension—the dimension may not be the one you intended to measure. If a test is designed to measure depression, does the content of the test really reflect the reality of this disorder? Does it correlate with other already established tests of depression? How do people with high and low scores on your test really differ in their mood? All of these questions need to be addressed empirically before a test can be accepted as valid. Sometimes in the early stages of constructing a test, questions that, on their face, appear to measure the trait or behavior you desire do not do so. Validity must be shown, not assumed.

CHAPTER **FOUR**

Personality Tests

WHAT IS PERSONALITY? If you were asked to describe the personality of an individual you knew well, could you do it? Of course you could. Behavior is not random; it follows predictable patterns over time. Personality can be defined conveniently as an individual's *characteristic* pattern of thoughts, behaviors, and emotions. With people whom we know well, we use our understanding of them and their personality to make practical predictions about them. We know what they would like to eat, wear, read, do for recreation, and many other things. These persistent characteristics on which we make predictions are called *traits*. We can identify common traits in others (and ourselves) and place each person somewhere along a continuum—is the person shy or outgoing? Is she passive or aggressive? Is he trusting or suspicious? These traits tend to be enduring qualities for most people, often from childhood onward. This is not to say that a passive person will not act aggressively on occasion. Sometimes the situational demands are so strong that they override the characteristic way of behaving. Both the person and the situation are important in predicting how an individual will respond.

Types of Personality Tests

Why do people respond in characteristic ways? Again a host of theories have been offered to answer this question. Are you a socially outgoing person because you were raised in an environment that reinforced this behavior? Is it reflective of unconscious needs? Is it simply a biologically determined predisposition for you to behave in this way? As the review of models of behavior in chapter 2 showed, we cannot say for sure which of these is the true or strongest explanation of your behavior. Beyond the theoretical debate is the need to scientifically measure aspects of personality. These needs include the clinical purposes of diagnosis and determination of treatments, as well as the measurement of progress in the forms of treatments. Most nonpsychologists assess personality on a regular basis. We assess potential friends, partners, employees, salespeople, and the like. Formal personality assessment uses a variety of techniques to arrive at judgments such as the ones we make informally every day. The format of the testing will vary, depending on the theoretical model underlying it. It will vary from direct to indirect methods. (See Table 4.1.) These methods are not necessarily contradictory, and a combination of techniques to assess personality is considered to be the norm. The assessment of personality using the techniques described in this chapter should always be coordinated with a proper clinical interview of the individual being assessed and, ideally, combined with other independent sources of information about the person and his or her history. The goal of personality assessment is to generate hypotheses for the clinician to weigh: What is the pattern of abnormal symptoms in this person? What are his or her enduring patterns of behavior? What are his or her main difficulties today? How likely is the person to respond to particular forms of treatment? How compliant or cooperative will he or she be? How do this person's problems compare with those of others with similar symptoms?

TABLE 4.1 Direct and Indirect Methods of Personality Assessment

Direct (Behavioral)	1. Observation of behavior (frequency, duration, etc.)
	2. Rating scales (impressions based on observation)
	3. Objective personality tests (self-report)
Indirect (Psychoanalytic)	4. Projective personality tests

Observational Techniques

The position of behavioralists on assessment is that it is not a static process to be conducted to produce an appropriate category in which to place a person, but a process to generate information that will be useful in understanding behavioral patterns and changing troublesome ones.

Even clinicians from orientations other than behaviorism will rely upon direct observational assessment during initial contact with their patients, but those with the behavioral orientation will go beyond simple observation to probing theoretical bases for the behavior. The strength of behavioral observation is that it emphasizes that a person's behavior, despite some stability, does change over time and between settings. Therefore, this form of assessment is ongoing and self-corrective. It is a live-action study rather than a "snapshot" taken by "tests." While it assesses excess behaviors (e.g., eating), it also identifies strengths and the contexts in which behavior occurs. Additionally, it should be *ecologically valid,* indicating that it is the measurement of real behavior in real settings rather than indirect measures taken in the offices of professionals.

If you wanted to stop biting your nails it would be appropriate to assess this specific behavior first. You may record each time you bite your nails (frequency) and where and when you do this (context). You may note specifically the events preceding and following this behavior. This may provide clues as to why you are maintaining the behavior, even if you profess not to want to do it. This approach is sometimes called the ABC assessment because it measures the *Antecedent* conditions of the behavior, the *Behavior* itself, and the *Consequences* of the behavior. With this knowledge the behavior therapist can set about to change the antecedents or consequences to alter the behavior.

Behavior, particularly that of a child, may be observed by a third party and recorded objectively. As the observer watches, she records aspects of behavior that have been determined to be important. If a child is observed in a playground, the observer might code whether he played alone or with others or if he teased or hit other children. The observer might also make some account of how others reacted to the child. There are several problems with this approach. The first is that there is sometimes a reaction by the person being watched. The use of less-intrusive methods (e.g., video cameras) may still cause the behavior to be less than natural. As well, some less-public behavior is not suitable to observer recording. The alternative of self-recording of unwanted or critical behavior has a long history: Ben Franklin kept a diary of his undesirable behaviors as an index of his success in ridding himself of them. Almost any behavior or thought is countable by the person keeping the diary. The diary approach, however, is vulnerable to intentional or unintentional distortion of the record. Lawyers will frequently ask their personal-injury clients to keep a daily diary of a particular problem (e.g., headaches and number of analgesics consumed). Yet the accuracy of this record certainly can be challenged. Often the mere act of self-observation will change the frequency of occurrence of the behavior. For example, people who begin monitoring their food intake may begin to reduce the intake because they realize how much food they have been consuming.

Rating Scales

Rating scales are one step removed from direct recording of behavior. Instead of counting behaviors as they occur, the observer renders an estimate of frequency or severity at the end of a specified period. Rating scales exist for a wide range of behaviors and thoughts, including pain, depression, eating, self-esteem, anxiety, and sexual excitement. These scales are easy to construct—you simply define the dimension and then create a self-anchored scale on which a person makes a judgment. At one end of the scale you present the most intense judgment and at the other end, the least intense. The scale can extend from many points, but it usually ranges from 1 to 5 or from 1 to 7 points, with the understanding that there are equal intervals between these points. It is best to assign verbal anchors to the numbers to help the judge make a decision (e.g., 7 equals intense depression: thoughts of suicide, constant tearfulness, severe sleep disturbance). The scale can be scored (add up all the ratings for each observed behavior) to provide a numerical judgment that can then be compared to previous periods (e.g., before treatment) to see if any changes have occurred.

This technique of assessment has some problems. First it requires the individual making the judgment to rely on memory, which is always vulnerable to various influences. The rater also may be influenced by other forces such as his or her attitude toward the person being rated or, in the case of self-ratings, the purpose of the rating. A person who is rating her or his own pain in the context of a suit for damages certainly is aware of the purpose for which information will be used and may distort it. Some of these scales have been well developed and standardized (development of comparison scores), but others have been quickly constructed and may have no data on reliability or validity.

Objective Personality Tests

During World War I an attempt was made to develop a questionnaire (the Woodworth Personal Data Sheet) to locate individuals who might develop shell shock that would interfere with their duties and to screen out draftees who were otherwise unsuitable. This early attempt to develop a personality inventory asked the respondent to answer yes or no to questions such as "Do you get tired of people quickly?" This project ended before it could be evaluated properly, but it provided a model for others to develop questionnaires to assess normal and abnormal personality features. Since this effort hundreds of personality inventories have been developed—some to measure many aspects of personality, others to measure a single problem or trait.

The most widely used objective personality inventory is the Minnesota Multiphasic Personality Inventory (MMPI). The scales of this test were first published separately. However, a complete omnibus version of the test appeared in 1946. In 1989 a revised version of this test appeared. It is referred to as the MMPI-2. A form to be administered to adolescents is also now available called the MMPI-A. In 1937 a psychologist (Starke R. Hathaway) and a psychiatrist (J. Charnley McKinley) set about to develop an instrument that would assist in the diagnosis of mental disorders. The main breakthrough of the test they developed was that items were included on particular scales (e.g., Depression) only if they clearly differentiated one clinical group from a normal population. The content was unimportant. If a question such as "I like peanut butter sandwiches" distinguished schizophrenia from normal populations, then it was kept as an item on the Schizophrenia scale. In effect, each item was selected for demonstrated validity and not by an intuitive or rationale method. The items Hathaway and McKinley selected covered wide content such as physical symptoms, emotional reactions, and attitudes. They wrote items so that minimal educational levels were required of subjects taking the test. An innovative feature of the test was the inclusion of validity scales that measure the test-taking attitude of the subject. Especially in legal contexts, one may have the desire to present oneself in a positive or a negative light. Some psychopathic individuals will attempt to portray themselves as mentally ill when they face serious criminal charges. Plaintiffs in personal-injury suits may try to present themselves as morally virtuous (and really not launching the suit because of the money).

More research has been conducted on the MMPI than on any other psychological test, and it is a mainstay in most forensic assessments. Hundreds of scales have been developed for the MMPI and MMPI-2. Table 4.2 contains the basic clinical and validity scales.

TABLE 4.2 MMPI, MMPI-2 Basic Clinical and Validity Scales

Scale	Content
? (Cannot say)	This is the number of questions not completed. A high score may indicate evasiveness or misunderstanding of the questions. When many questions are not answered, the clinical scales will be lowered. A rule of thumb is that the profile should not be interpreted if more than 30 items are omitted.
L (Lie)	A high score indicates that the individual does not admit to minor faults and character flaws. This may indicate that the individual is attempting to create a favorable impression. It sometimes reflects a rigid and moralistic view of life.
F (Infrequency)	These are items infrequently endorsed by normal individuals. This score is higher in persons who are psychotic, or "faking bad" by feigning unusual mental symptoms.
K (Correction)	The fourth basic validity scale measures defensiveness. Unlike L, it is a more subtle measure of whether a person is willing to acknowledge personal issues.
1. (Hs—Hypochondriasis)	These 32 items measure a variety of both specific somatic complaints and general bodily preoccupation. High scorers tend to be complaining, demanding, and self-centered.
2. (D—Depression)	These 57 questions measure the main features of depression: feelings of discouragement, hopelessness, and pessimism, as well as somatic symptoms often related to depression (sleep and appetite problems).
3. (Hy—Hysteria)	Some of these 60 items reflect somatic difficulties that are frequently linked to anxiety and stress. Hy also measures some tendency to deny psychological difficulties and the connection that these have to reported physical problems.

TABLE 4.2 MMPI, MMPI-2 Basic Clinical and Validity Scales *(continued)*

Scale	Content
4. (Pd—Psychopathic Deviance)	This scale measures antisocial/amoral conduct often found in the psychopathic personality. These 50 items cover many topics, including family problems, difficulties with authorities, acting out, and criminal behavior.
5. (Mf—Masculinity/ Femininity)	For both genders this scale measures acceptance or rejection of stereotypic sex roles. It is correlated with educational level and other cultural factors.
6. (Pa—Paranoia)	These 40 items deal with paranoid symptoms such as suspiciousness, excessive sensitivity, and rigid opinions and attitudes, along with feelings of persecution and grandiosity.
7. (Pt—Psychasthenia)	The label on this scale reflects an out-of-date term that suggested weakening of a person's mental control over thoughts and behaviors similar to obsessive-compulsive conditions. The 48 items gauge generalized anxiety and distress, self-blame, and general malaise.
8. (Sc—Schizophrenia)	While the items on this scale were originally drawn from psychotic patients and reflected strange beliefs and unusual experiences, it became apparent that elevations on this scale were found in many clinical populations (e.g., drug and alcohol abusers, brain-injured).
9. (Ma—Hypomania)	These 46 items measure behavior indicative of manic symptoms (e.g., over-ambitious, extroverted, grandiose, and hyperactive). It gauges degree of psychological and physical *energy*.
0. (Si—Social Introversion)	These 69 questions measure the tendency to withdraw from or approach social interactions with others. High scorers tend to avoid social participation and are often self-depreciating.

After the subject completes the true or false questions on the MMPI–2, scores for each scale are calculated and are placed on a profile that compares that subject to developed norms. Figure 4.1 shows a profile of the basic scales.

In reading the MMPI–2 profile we begin at the left and review the validity scales. The norm for the scales is indicated as a *T*-score (or standard score) of 50 and a statistically significant elevation on a scale is a *T*-score of 65. Only 8 percent of the population would score as high as this. *T*-scores of 50 and 65 are indicated by the two horizontal lines running across the profile. There are no lines to signify a significant low score, but these may also be clinically significant and interpretable. The sample profile is of a twenty-eight-year-old Caucasian male, who was assessed on a forensic unit as he was awaiting a charge of robbery. We see that the validity scales show no overt distortion in general test-taking attitude and that two scales (D and Pd) are above the significant cutoff. In interpreting the validity scales, it is necessary to understand the individual who completed the test. Individuals who have a severe psychosis or who are in the midst of a personal crisis will likely have a high F score. Even though it is above the cutoff mark, the F score would not indicate an invalid profile because it is measuring aspects of thought often seen in disturbed individuals. However, if the same F score were produced by a person with no overt symptoms of mental disorder, it may indicate malingering. Two other basic validity scores (L and K) must also be interpreted in light of personal information about the subject.

Several newer validity indices are being used with the MMPI–2, but the basic indicators remain the most useful. Sophisticated clinicians will not just report the results of the basic scales; they will add information from other scales. For example, the Harris-Lingoes scales are subscales of the basic scales that can give additional diagnostic information. The main D scale is divided into five Harris-Lingoes subscales, acknowledging that depression can include different symptoms such as subjective feelings of sadness, avoidance of others, somatic complaints (e.g., poor appetite, sleep problems), and difficulties with memory, concentrating, and brooding. Two "depressed" individuals may have the same score on the main D scale but very different symptoms from each other. These symptoms are reflected in the Harris-Lingoes scales.

Profiles can be interpreted by an analysis of scores on single scales or on profile type. In the above case two scales (number 2 or D and number 4 or Pd) are prominently elevated, so this would be referred to as a 2-4 profile. An accumulation of information on profile types is available

FIGURE 4.1 Profile for MMPI-2 Basic Scales

MMPI-2™
S.R. Hathaway and J.C. McKinley
Minnesota Multiphasic Personality Inventory-2

Profile for Basic Scales
Minnesota Multiphasic Personality Inventory-2
Copyright © by THE REGENTS OF THE UNIVERSITY OF MINNESOTA
1942, 1943 (renewed 1970), 1989. This Profile Form 1989.
All rights reserved. Distributed exclusively by NATIONAL COMPUTER SYSTEMS, INC.
under license from The University of Minnesota

"MMPI-2" and Minnesota Multiphasic Personality Inventory-2" are trademarks owned by The University of Minnesota. Printed in the United States of America.

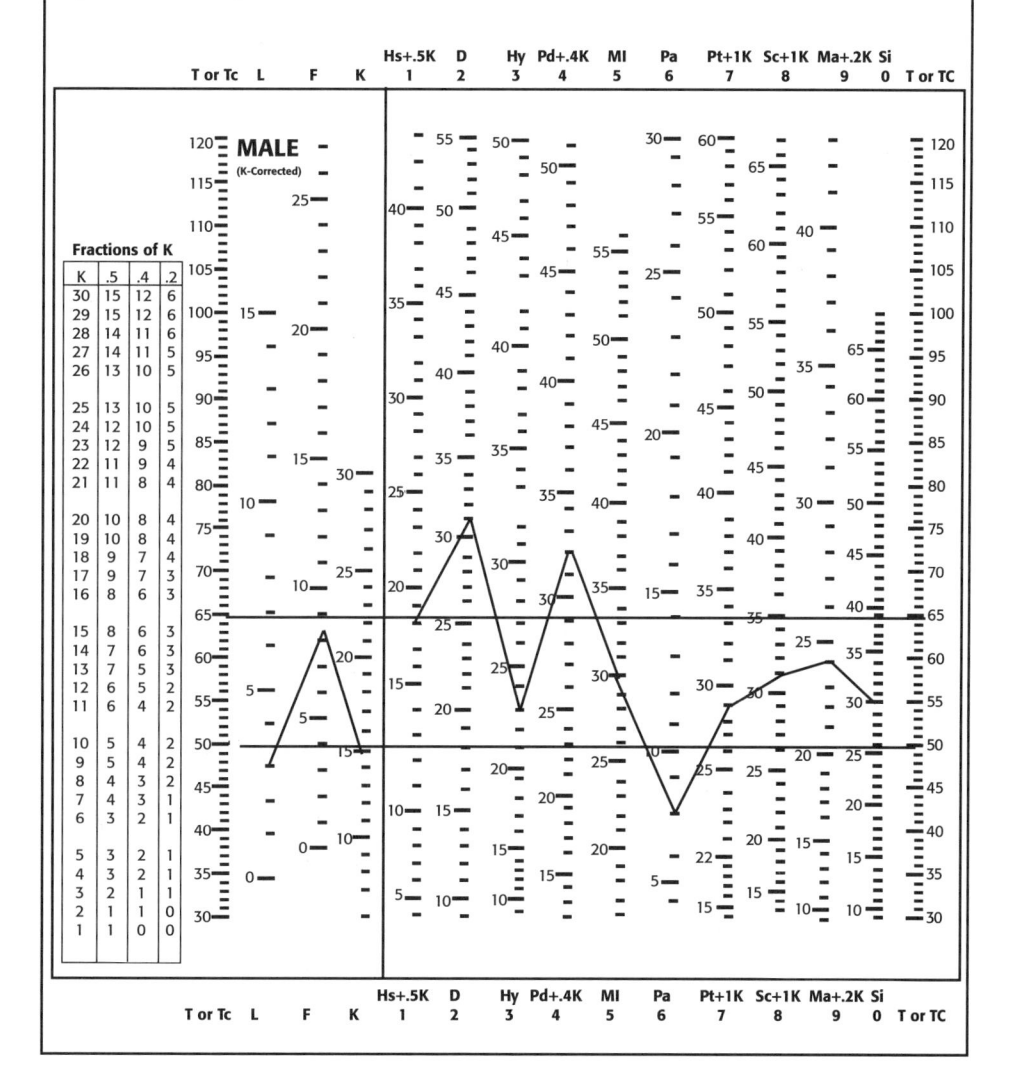

for the clinician to consider in interpretation. Graham (1993, p. 88) provides some of these descriptions and says of this profile:

> When persons with the 24/42 code come to the attention of professionals, it usually is after they have been in trouble with their families or with the law. They are impulsive and unable to delay gratification of their impulses. They have little respect for social standards and often find themselves in direct conflict with societal values. Their acting-out behavior is likely to involve excessive use of alcohol, and their histories often include alcoholic benders, arrests, job loss and family discord associated with drinking.... They may report feeling depressed, anxious and worthless, but these feelings do not seem to be sincere.

In the past fifteen years the scoring and interpretation of personality profiles such as the MMPI–2 increasingly have been carried out by computers. Computer scoring is an effective and efficient way of obtaining the basic scales and many of the extra scales a clinician may want to see in assessing a person. Computer-generated interpretations, on the other hand, are potentially hazardous for they may be accepted in courts as indicating conditions that are not valid for the person who completed the test. The computer can generate only *hypotheses* about what an elevated score *might* mean and the well-trained clinician uses all of the previous information he or she has obtained to extract useful interpretations. A computer program may suggest that a person's score indicates a particular diagnosis (e.g., schizophrenia) that is incorrect. Computers *cannot* diagnose or clinically interpret for individual cases. The presumed esteem of the computer's printout must be challenged, and the computer-generated score must not be placed in the hands of unqualified personnel. Unfortunately, the use of computer interpretations has made it easier for poorly trained clinicians to parrot seemingly scientific methods. When these computerized interpretations are presented to the courts, the caveats I have given should be highlighted and perhaps read from the printout (they usually appear on the front page).

A number of sources provide questions for lawyers who wish to challenge an MMPI–2 interpretation (e.g., Pope, Butcher, and Seelen, 1993, who provide eighty basic questions to ask the expert witness). The obvious way to challenge an interpretation, however, is to have a psychologist skilled in this instrument develop the questions. Was the test supervised? Is the test identified correctly (is the subject's signature on the test form)? What is the psychologist's (or on rare occasions, psychiatrist's) training and experience with the MMPI–2 (a weekend workshop)? How many protocols has she or he interpreted? What literature on this instrument did the psychologist rely on in the interpretation? Has she or he published any articles on the test? Why did the psychologist interpret each scale in a particular way (there are different interpretive possibilities for each of the clinical scales)? How confident is the psychologist in the interpretation of the test?

Another personality test gaining popularity since its first version was published in 1977 is the Millon Clinical Multiaxial Inventory. The third edition of this test was published in 1994, and it is typically referred to as the MCMI–III. This test is much shorter than the MMPI–2 (only 175 questions), and it has a strong theoretical base on personality structure. In the diagnoses of personality disorders it generally outperforms the MMPI–2, as its items are closely tied to the latest diagnostic dimensions in the *Diagnostic and Statistical Manual of Mental Disorders* (DSM-IV). It, too, has validity indicators that can assist in judging the attitude of the respondent to the test items. Compared to the MMPI–2, however, the MCMI–III is more limited in its scope of assessment across diagnostic categories. The two tests overlap in the area of DSM-IV Axis I disorders (see chapter 7) such as depression, psychosis, and drug abuse, with the MMPI–2 usually thought to be superior to the MCMI-III in assessing these conditions.

In assessing personality one may want to know not only what is *wrong* with the patient or client, but what his or her normal personality structure is like. Focusing only on pathology is a flaw in many clinical assessments. Objective personality tests, such as the 16 Personality Factors Questionnaire (now in its fifth edition), examine normal personality structure and place each respondent on a continuum for each dimension. Is the person reserved or outgoing, easily perturbed or calm, submissive or dominant? By combining this information with that obtained from a test measuring mental pathology, such as the MMPI–2, we get a complete and individualized picture of the person. Two patients may both show severe depression, but their personalities may be very different independent of this disorder. Assessment of normal personality is also important in child-custody cases where the *fit* between a parent and child may be a central issue. Personality traits also figure prominently in cases involving suitability of an individual for particular types of work. In many administrative law actions (e.g., employment disciplinary hearing), a clinical examination may reveal that a person has no identifiable disorder but that his or her personality is such that he or she is "difficult"—rigid, aloof, incommunicative, not open to change, stern—and a person whom others do not like. This may provide an explanation of the employment conflict not dependent on viewing the person as "disordered." A competency evaluation of elderly persons who are making their wills may show them to be extremely independent of influence in their personality structure and not acting erratically, as some potential beneficiaries may protest.

Projective Personality Tests

These tests begin from the hypothesis that when people try to understand or interpret an ambiguous stimulus such as cloud formations, their ideas will reflect their own internal makeup more than the stimulus itself. They, in essence, *project* onto the stimulus inner aspects of themselves. The idea is an old one—Leonardo da Vinci used the technique to evaluate the minds of his art students. For the psychoanalytically oriented professional, projectives offer a means of assessing unconscious personality drives and conflicts.

In 1911 the Swiss psychiatrist Hermann Rorschach began conducting experiments by presenting ambiguous stimuli to patients to better understand their hidden thoughts. He dropped ink onto a piece of paper, folded the paper in half, and then unfolded it. This produced bilaterally symmetrical forms on a white background. He had patients observe the inkblots and report what images they saw. Over time he became convinced that individuals with certain disorders reported seeing similar images, and he published his test (consisting of ten inkblots, half in color and the others in black, gray, and white) in 1921. The test, which became known as the Rorschach, is individually administered. The clinician presents each card to the subject and asks him or her to say what the image might be. No restrictions are placed on the responses of subjects and no clues are provided. After the subject responds to all cards, the clinician asks her or him to tell where specifically in the blot the images were seen and to explain what features of the blot suggested those associations. The responses are scored on criteria of location in the stimuli (small or large part), which property of the blot evoked the image (color, form, or texture), content (subject matter such as animals or humans), and originality.

The scientific community has severely criticized the Rorschach test for its lack of validity and reliability and for its highly subjective interpretations. It is often said that the interpretations reveal more about the interpreter than the subject. In 1974 John Exner attempted to increase the reliability of the Rorschach scoring system by redefining the dimensions that were to be evaluated. One of these dimensions was called *fabulized combination*, in which the subject describes an implausible relationship between two or more blot details (e.g., two dogs playing hockey). Although Exner's system helped increase reliability, it was not a breakthrough in increasing the validity of what these responses might indicate about the individual.

The Holtzman Inkblot Technique was an attempt to improve the Rorschach. It consists of two parallel sets of forty-five cards to which the subject is only allowed one response per card. Each response may be scored on twenty-two dimensions (e.g., location, content, and so forth). For each category or dimension, norms have been developed for different age samples. Again, although this may assist in determining whether a response is unusual, it does not suggest validated meanings of responses.

Another projective test is the Thematic Apperception Test (TAT). This test was devised in 1935 by two psychologists at Harvard University. Unlike Rorschach's, this test was not touted as a tool to diagnose mental disorders but as a way of understanding normal personality characteristics.

In its administration the TAT is more structured than the Rorschach; it consists of thirty pictures and one blank card. Some cards are designed for males, others for females, and some are appropriate for individuals of different ages. A card is presented to a subject, who is told, "I am going to show you some pictures. I want you to tell me a story about each picture. Tell me what led up to the story, what is happening, what characters are thinking and feeling, and what the outcome will be." Typically about ten or twelve cards are administered to each person. The examiner records responses and reaction times. Each card is designed to elicit *themes*, needs, and other personality features, and a subject's delay in responding may be interpreted as indicating difficulties.

The scoring systems for the TAT are numerous and include both quantitative and qualitative methods, with most users employing the less-rigorous qualitative interpretations. Most of these attempt to make some sense out of the hero in the story, the needs expressed, the press (environmental forces that interfere with or facilitate satisfaction of needs), theme, and outcome of the scene. Frequency, duration, and intensity of aspects of the story are assessed.

The examiner finds a wide range of responses by individuals to the same cards. Because the stimulus is the same, the responses do reflect individual differences in subjects. In interpreting these responses, however, there are many assumptions that may not hold. Does the storyteller identify with the hero? Are all stories of equal importance? Do recurrent themes really mirror characteristics of the storyteller? Are sociocultural factors reflected in the stories? Do the stories reflect momentary or enduring experiences of the storyteller? We really do not know the answers to these questions, let alone the fundamental premise of whether people project any of their strivings, dispositions, or conflicts into these stories.

The psychometric properties of the TAT are quite unsound, with little established validity and a completely subjective base for interpretation.

The use of freehand drawings has also been employed by psychologists to delve into the depths of the patient's psyche. A person (often a child) is asked to draw a person or tree or house and the psychologist then deciphers the product for its projective insight. The drawings are evaluated on their quality and shape, placement and relative size of figures, features of the figures, use of background, and other dimensions. Interpretations are rarely based on empirical findings but rather the clinical intuition (i.e., guess) of the psychologist. Studies of reliability and validity have repeatedly found projective drawing tests to have neither. This is not to say that drawing tasks with children cannot be useful vehicles for discussion, rather that their interpretation as *meaning* certain things is unfounded. Although used mostly with children, drawing analyses for adults may still be proffered and are open to the same critique.

Personality Tests in the Court

Personality tests, particularly objective tests such as the MMPI, have become standard features of courtroom presentations. Because of their rather shaky reliability and validity, projective tests are used much less often. Cross-examination can dismantle these interpretations when they are presented in court. Measures of direct observation of behavior have appeared only infrequently in courts because their development was closely tied to behavioral treatment of conditions and not to a diagnosis. Rating scales are gaining in popularity in psychological reports to the courts. Because a wide range of tests is included in this group, however, you should be critical of the status of individual scales.

There are restrictions on the transmission of the raw data obtained in personality assessments (or from other psychological tests). In personal-injury litigation cases a court order or subpoena is sometimes necessary to obtain such information. The American Psychological Association in its recent revision of Ethical Principles (see appendix B) prohibits the release of raw test results and data to unqualified persons. When I resisted the release of data that would be easy to misinterpret, one judge reminded me that I would release the data to whomever he designated. And with humility I acknowledged that I would follow the directive of the court, but that I assumed the court would also like the data to be exchanged in a professional manner. With the power differential clearly established, the judge accepted my proposal for the exchange of the psychological test data. The recommended course of action is for the side that seeks the data to retain a qualified psychologist of its own, and the raw data can then be transmitted directly to him or her. The psychologist could then interpret the data to counsel.

CHAPTER FIVE

Cognitive and Neuropsychological Assessment

INTELLIGENCE IS ARGUABLY THE MOST CHERISHED trait of our species. We even have the narcissistic audacity to refer to ourselves as *Homo sapiens* (wise or intelligent man). The use of tasks to gauge this precious commodity is certainly not of modern origin. Most games that pit the talents of one person against those of another are measures of intelligence or specific ability. In ancient Greece, China, and the Ottoman Empire, tests of intelligence were devised to assist in the selection of students for formal learning. This was also one of the primary purposes of the development of modern intelligence quotient or I.Q. tests, first devised by the French psychologist Alfred Binet at the turn of the century. Thousands of ability tests are administered daily in North America and it is very likely that you have taken one of these tests, such as the test required for admission into professional schools.

Most of us would agree that we can readily differentiate a "smart" from a "not-so-smart" person. But what do we really mean by smart? For the past one hundred years psychologists have attempted to quantify objectively the dimension of intelligence. When various tests were given to individuals it was noted frequently that the scores from different measures were correlated. For some this gave rise to the idea that a general ability factor or *g* underlies most tests of cognitive ability. Others resisted the idea that we possess general intelligence. They insisted that intelligence was a collection of separate independent abilities. The real truth, as is typical in similar debates, falls in the middle, with both general abilities and specific talents defining most persons' intelligence. Recent theoretical developments in this field have broadened the concept of intelligence to include different styles of problem solving and creativity. It is probably fair to say that there are a variety of *intelligences* that could be identified. As you read the following examination of intelligence tests, you should understand that the idea of general intelligence underlies most of these standard measures.

The I.Q. is based on the principle that intelligence follows a normal distribution (a *bell curve*). That is, most people cluster around an *average*, with fewer people toward the extreme of very high or very low intelligence. (See figure 5.1.)

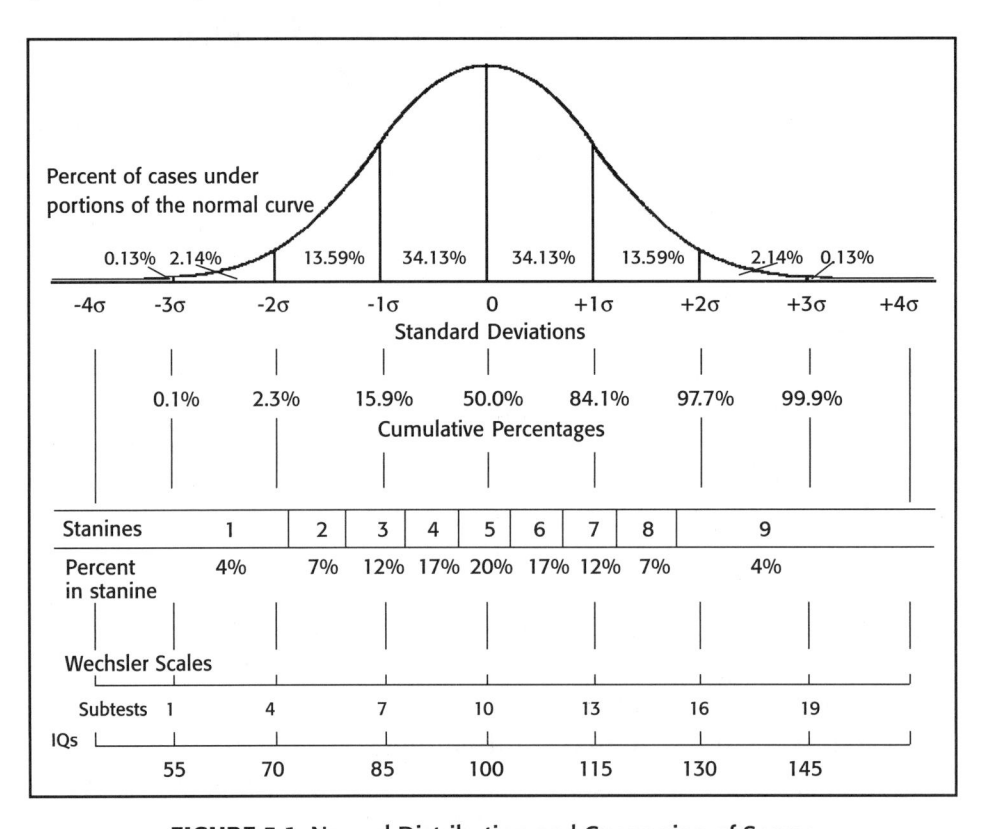

FIGURE 5.1 Normal Distribution and Conversion of Scores

The average or mean I.Q. of the population is 100, and the different categories of intelligence are defined on how deviant they are from the norm. The average range of intelligence (between 90 and 109) encompasses 68 percent of the population. The further a score deviates from this norm, the fewer the number of people who will be described.

Individual scores on the Wechsler scales (described later in this chapter) follow the same pattern, with 10 representing the mean.

As part of this discussion of the bell curve and test scores, it is instructive to examine a few other ways test scores are noted by their relationship with the normal distribution. A *standard deviation* is a way of describing how the scores are spread from the center of the bell curve. A small standard deviation means that many of the scores are clustered around the mean and are not spread very widely. A large standard deviation indicates that the curve is flat, with the scores spread from the mean. Percentiles are a good way of describing where on the curve an individual falls in comparison with his peers. Looking at the bell curve diagram you can see that if a person has an I.Q. of 130, then her score will be higher than almost 98 percent of the rest of the population, and that this score is two standard deviations above the mean score of 100. A few psychological tests are scored in terms of *stanines* (short for *standard nines*). This is a common method of comparing performances in school tests, and you will come across this method of standardization when you read school records. Again this is simply another way of breaking down the bell curve into segments. Stanine scores can be converted to other descriptions of the bell curve, such as percentiles.

The most widely employed tests of intelligence are the series developed by David Wechsler at New York's Bellevue Hospital. In 1944 Wechsler defined intelligence as "the aggregate or global capacity of the individual to act purposefully; to think rationally and to deal effectively with his environment." He developed a family of tests that have withstood the critics and continue to be the standard. The current version of his test for adults (1981 revision) comprises six tests that measure aspects of verbal ability (verbal I.Q.) and five tests that measure nonverbal or performance I.Q. The sum of the eleven tests produces a Full Scale I.Q. On the verbal tests the subject is asked to give word definitions, provide common-sense explanations of social situations, give abstract reasons for similarities between two word pairs, solve oral arithmetic problems, and recall a series of digits both forward and backward. The performance measures ask a subject to identify missing features of pictures, arrange a proper sequence of pictures as in cartoon strips, copy designs with blocks, assemble jigsaw puzzles, and quickly copy symbols associated with numbers. There are different versions of this test for preschool children (Wechsler Preschool and Primary Scale of Intelligence or WPPSI) and school-aged children (Wechsler Intelligence Scale for Children–III or WISC–III).

Intelligence tests have broad application in society and in clinical psychology. They are used widely in educational settings to assist in the diagnosis of mental retardation, giftedness, or learning disorders. In adult settings they are routinely administered as parts of a neuropsychological assessment of brain-injured patients and provide insight into the current functioning of individuals with psychotic disorders. In vocational assessment they also are used in predicting success of potential employment. In the courts they may be seen as generally descriptive, but they also have special applications in determining an accused's competency to stand trial or to direct one's estate.

There are many other tests that purport to measure intelligence—most of which promote themselves as highly correlated with the Wechsler tests but less onerous to administer, less time-consuming to administer, or suitable for group administration. The Wechsler tests are individually administered by a trained psychologist or psychometrist and require up to an hour and a half to complete. This is also the case with other comprehensive I.Q. tests (Stanford-Binet and Kaufman Assessment Battery for children). Most alternative quick I.Q. tests do not assess the range of specific abilities that the Wechsler tests provide, but they may give an estimate of g.

Many factors can influence performance on I.Q. and other ability tests: motivation, persistence, anxiety, fatigue, and the nature of the test-taker's relationship with the examiner. However, when administered properly to a motivated individual, the tests are highly reliable—that is, scores do not vary greatly over time. A person who has a true I.Q. of 85 and who scores 85 one year will not score an I.Q. of 108 next year. Small changes with retesting (110 to 108 I.Q.) should not be overinterpreted and usually reflect expected, nonsignificant variance. I.Q. tests are rich sources of information to the skilled clinician, but they have inherent limitations: They do not measure all aspects of intelligence, and they contain culturally biased tasks. An I.Q. test is unlikely to reflect the optimal performance of an individual from other than a Western culture. Even a person who has developed good functional skills in English as a second language may not completely understand many of our verbal concepts. As well, although most of us in North America now have some experience with I.Q. measures, people from other cultures may not have the same level of experience. Having a test administered by a person of another ethnic background may cause some discomfort in the test-taker and adversely affect his or her performance. Some test developers have tried to develop tests that are not culturally loaded, but the understanding of cultural expectations and standards is considered a good index of some forms of *intelligence*. We may develop instruments that determine intelligence in a technically rigorous fashion. In the end, however, it is the exercise of skilled judgment as to whether this information is applied in a fair and useful way.

Intelligence arises from a functioning brain. Having developed objective means to measure this facility, the next obvious step to take is to draw conclusions about the brain that are based on cognitive testing. This is the task of the field of clinical neuropsychology. The human brain is highly specialized in terms of its geographical representation of abilities. By administering a large battery of tests that measure specific skills (e.g., oral language, motor strength), we can create a functional map of the brain and its strengths and weaknesses and then correlate this map with brain injury or disease that the individual may have suffered. To appreciate this concept it is necessary to review the fundamental architecture of the human brain.

The basic building block of our nervous systems is the *neuron*, of which we each have about 100 billion. Each neuron has hundreds (sometimes thousands) of connections with other neurons. By communicating through chemical and electrical means, they produce all of our behaviors and thoughts. In clinical practice we do not have the capability (or necessity) of examining single neurons; instead, we analyze groups of neurons located in regions of the brain. The human brain consists of three main divisions: the *hindbrain*, which is the lowest and historically most primitive level of the brain; the *midbrain*, which is situated above it; and, lastly, the *forebrain*, which contains the cerebral cortex, the largest level of the brain. (See figure 5.2.)

The *hindbrain* is composed of the brainstem and the cerebellum. As the spinal cord enters the base of the skull, it swells and forms a body referred to as the brainstem. The lowest part of the brainstem is referred to as the *medulla*, which governs many critical automatic functions of the body such as heart rate, blood pressure, respiration rate, and some facial movements. Above this area is the *pons*, which integrates movement between two sides of the body and controls some stages of sleep. To the rear of the brainstem is the *cerebellum* (*little brain*), which plays a key role in control of voluntary movement of the skeletal muscles and the regulation of balance. Damage to this area of the brain may produce *ataxia*, jerky, uncoordinated, and inaccurate movements. A person with damage to the cerebellum may exhibit motor behavior that mimics that of a drunken person with tremors and lack of balance.

The *midbrain* is the upper portion of the brainstem. All information passing between the upper regions of the brain and the spinal cord

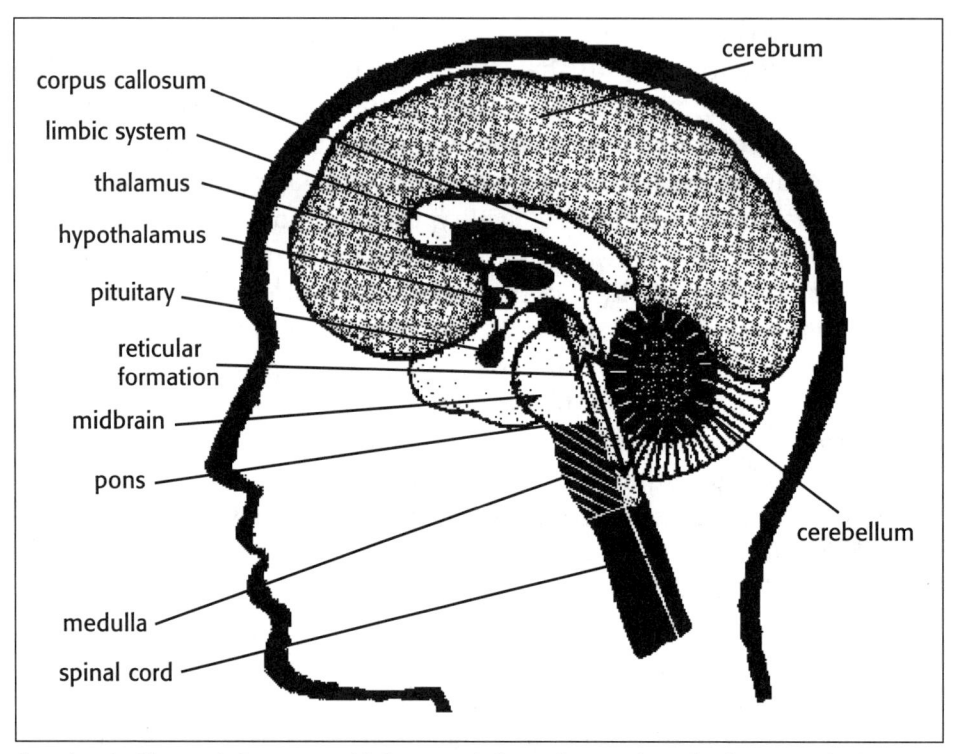

(Reprinted with permission. R.E. Smith from Psychology: The Frontiers of Behavior, *3rd Edition 1986, Harper & Row.)*

FIGURE 5.2 Basic Divisions of the Brain

passes through this body. It is responsible for the "startle" reflex and controls movements involved in fighting and sexual behavior. It also reduces sensitivity to pain in emergency situations.

Running through the middle of the hindbrain and the midbrain is a collection of nerve fibers known as the *reticular formation*. It is a sentry system arousing the higher centers of the brain when information critical to survival must be processed and sustained for long periods. Damage to this formation in the lower brain can disrupt the natural wake-sleep cycle and can result in a coma.

The *forebrain* is composed of the cerebral cortex (cortex means *bark*) and a number of small brain structures buried in the center of the brain. The *thalamus* looks like two small eggs lying on their sides on the top of the brainstem. Parts of the thalamus receive information from most sensory organs (eye, ear, skin), conduct some preliminary analyses of the information, and pass it along to the cortex for full processing. The thalamus is an important way station for sensory information coming to the brain and motor commands going from the brain to the body.

The *hypothalamus* (meaning *below the thalamus*) is the size of a grape and is involved in the regulation of complex activities such as eating, drinking, temperature regulation, and sexual and aggressive behavior. It also controls the *pituitary gland* located adjacent to it. The pituitary gland is often referred to as the "master gland," as it exerts control over the rest of the glands in the body that influence behavior through the release of hormones. The hypothalamus is often considered part of the *limbic* (meaning *bridge*) system located at the border between the cerebral cortex and the brainstem. The limbic system is involved in the regulation of *instincts*—behaviors that seem hard-wired into each species and include fighting, fleeing, feeding, and reproducing. The necessity of these behaviors for the species probably explains why they are not left to the discretion of the individual. The limbic system (with structures such as the *amygdala* and *hippocampus*) is sometimes thought of as the *old cortex* because in evolution it appeared before the *new cortex* or cerebral cortex. So-called "lower" animals such as fish and reptiles do not even have a cerebral cortex. The more developed the cerebral cortex of an animal, the more complex and flexible (less *instinctive*) its behavior is. As the cerebral cortex increases in size across species, the limbic system declines proportionately.

In a picture of the human brain, it is the convoluted cerebral cortex that is prominent. Indeed, it makes up over 70 percent of all the neurons in the central nervous system, and it is here that we must look for the physiological basis of human nature and the source of behavioral dysfunction. The cerebral cortex is composed of two halves, with the left side slightly longer and wider in most right-handed people. The folds and fissures of the brain allow more cortical surface without the need for a skull as big as that of Zoltar from the planet Zivron. Most of our *thinking* (such as what you are doing at this moment) takes place in the outer layer of the cortex (which is about the width of a credit card) called *gray matter*, while the rest of the cortex is composed of *white matter*—covered axons that are like cables carrying the information to other parts of the brain or body.

Each side of the cortex is composed of four lobes: frontal, parietal, occipital, and temporal. (See figure 5.3.)

These different regions are divided conventionally, using naturally occurring geographic features (like countries divided by a river). However, individual differences in brain structure sometimes make it difficult for even an experienced anatomist to tell precisely where one lobe ends and another begins. The lobes hold specialized functions within their borders. Sensory pathways for our eyes terminate within the

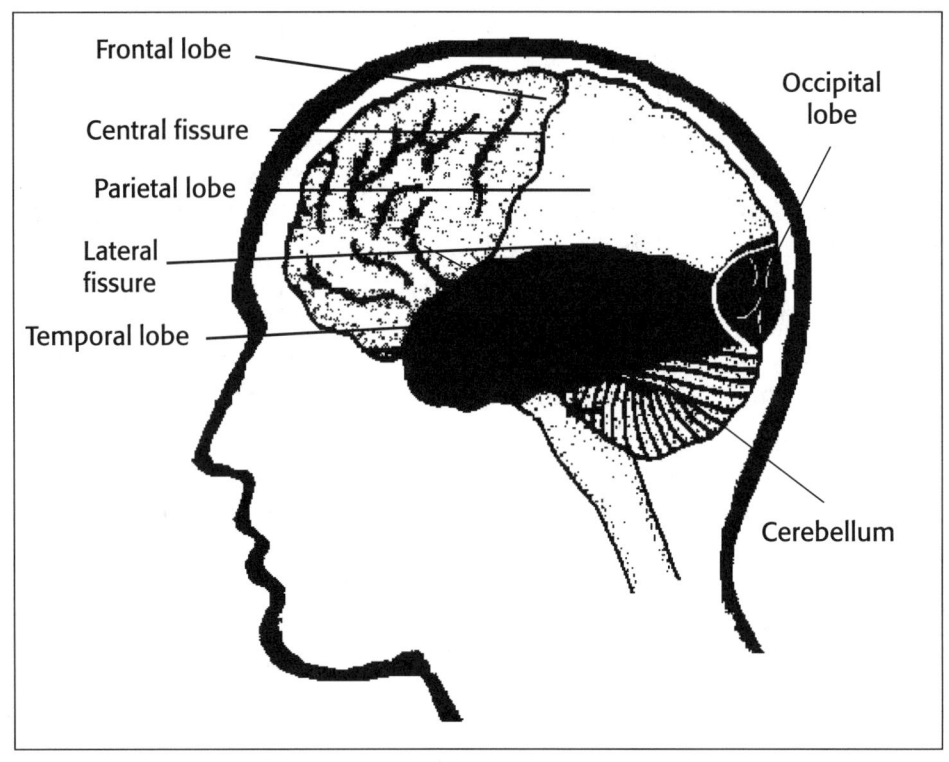

(Reprinted with permission. R.E. Smith from Psychology: The Frontiers of Behavior, *3rd Edition 1986, Harper & Row.)*

FIGURE 5.3 Four Lobes of the Cortex.

occipital region; from our ears, within the temporal lobe; and from our skin, within the parietal zone. This gives a clue to what processes will be conducted there. The relative size of these four regions also can tell us a little about the lifestyle of the different species. Primates (such as humans) are visually dependent and have relatively larger occipital lobes than do cats, who are dependent on their sense of hearing more than vision. These different areas of the brain, however, are located in the same places across different animal species.

On each side of the cortex there is a vertical strip that controls specific body areas and their movement. At the top of the strip are groups of neurons that control the feet. Moving down the strip, we find areas that control the trunk, then the hands, the fingers, the face, the lips, and the tongue. Right behind this strip is another strip with parallel functions. It receives sensory information from the same sites. Both the movement of and sensation from the body are decussated (*crossed*). This means that the area of the cortex that controls the fingers of the *right* hand is located in the *left* cerebral cortex.

As we saw, information coming into the brain from the senses is sent to primary processing stations in the various lobes. However, the simple processing of sight, sound, and touch requires only a small amount of cortex. What happens in the vast amount left? Much of the remainder is referred to as *association cortex*. It is here that learning, planning, memory, and more complex thinking occur.

The two sides of the cerebral cortex in humans are not mirror images with all functions. Complex functions such as language are lateralized to one side of the brain. Look at each lobe on both sides of the brain:

Occipital lobe. The occipital lobes contain the processing areas for visual information. Although damage to primary processing areas will produce some specific blindness, damage to the association areas will not. People with the latter kind of damage may display interesting difficulties such as seeing an object perfectly but being unable to recognize it. People looking at an apple may describe the object but not know what it is. When they pick it up, they will recognize it as an apple because the tactile sense is not impaired. This deficit (called *visual agnosia*) is described in Oliver Sacks's *The Man Who Mistook His Wife for a Hat* (1986), referring to a patient who saw but did not perceive.

Temporal lobe. The temporal lobes receive and process sounds. Damage to the left temporal association cortex may cause severe language deficits. Depending on the precise area of damage, the patient may not comprehend speech. In the right hemisphere damage to the temporal lobes does not usually produce language problems, but it disrupts the patient's understanding or recognition of other environmental sounds, including patterns of rhythm and tone. A patient's ability to locate a sound in the environment may also be impaired. Damage to the inside segments of the temporal lobe may also produce severe memory impairments.

Parietal lobe. These areas of the brain perceive sensation from the body but many other functions also reside here. Damage to the left parietal region may impair reading or writing or comprehension of speech without disturbing the ability to speak. Drawing difficulties are also related to the parietal lobe. Damage to the left side impairs people's ability to guide their hands, whereas damage to the right side is perceptual—in drawing a bicycle they may include many of the individual parts, but the parts may not be proportional or coherently organized. Left parietal lobe damage may also cause people to have severe difficulty telling left from right. Right-side damage also may result in sensory neglect, that is, people will only pay attention to the left side of space in front of them.

Frontal lobe. The frontal lobe contains many of the motor functions and is also critical to speech and language production. In front of the motor strip there is a large amount of cortical tissue. The *executive* functions of the human brain are considered to reside in this region—the acts of planning, strategizing, self-awareness, and understanding emotional stimuli among others.

In confronting a patient who possibly has suffered an insult to the brain, a neurologist will observe the individual's behavior and perform behavioral screening tests. For the assessment of more complex processes, such as language, perception, and memory, the neurologist may make a referral to a clinical neuropsychologist. The neurologist will want to examine the *structure* of the brain by ordering a computed axial tomography (CAT) scan or magnetic resonance imaging (MRI), which will provide pictures of the brain. To gauge the electrical activity of the brain (another way of testing the brain's integrity), the neurologist may order an electroencephalograph (EEG). However, just as you cannot always tell how well a car's engine is working just by looking at it, the neuropsychologist will examine the various *functions* of the human brain.

The following questions often precipitate a neuropsychological assessment:

1. Does a functional brain deficit exist and, if so, what is its nature and severity?
2. What is the probable relationship between the deficit and preceding events (e.g., motor vehicle accident)?
3. What is the prognosis for this individual's recovery to a premorbid state?
4. What rehabilitative methods are recommended to assist an uncovered deficit?
5. Are there other factors beside brain injury that could account for the individual's problem?

The basic format of a neuropsychological assessment is to interview the individual, observing his or her behavior closely for *pathognomic* signs (i.e., characteristic indicators of abnormality) of brain injury, and, at the same time, record the history of the individual (developmental, educational, occupational, substance abuse, mental health, physical health). A history is an essential element in proper assessment and diagnosis of changes in behavior that may unfold because of a brain injury. This history may be supplemented from other sources such as a spouse or parent. Following the gathering of this information a formal series of tests is administered to quantify objectively various aspects of brain-behavior relationships:

1. lateral dominance (handedness, eye and foot preference)
2. motor functioning (strength, dexterity, speed, graphic ability on both sides of the body)
3. auditory functioning (perception of speech and non-speech sounds)
4. spatial ability
5. language skills (speaking, comprehending, repeating)
6. general intelligence
7. memory functions
8. executive functions (planning, developing hypotheses, problem solving)
9. academic skill

A personality assessment is often added to this broad assessment of cognitive and motor ability, because some brain injuries can cause direct personality change or indirect reactive changes (e.g., depression). Interpretation of this battery of tests requires extensive knowledge of the research in brain-behavior relationship and the specific areas of the brain that each test administered is designed to assess. The administration of a neuropsychological battery may take from six to ten hours and may need to be spread over several days.

A single psychological test will not have a great deal of use in a neuropsychological examination. It is the pattern presented by a large battery of tests that will show which skills are deficient and which are preserved in the patient. Organized batteries of tests have been developed, the oldest of which is called the Halstead–Reitan Neuropsychology Battery, named after its originators. A more recently developed battery is the Luria–Nebraska Neuropsychology Battery. Few neuropsychologists will administer a *pure* battery but will borrow from these and add specific tests from a large compendium available. In the following section, I review some of the methods and specific tests given. Special neuropsychological tests and adaptations of adult batteries are available for children who require assessment of their brain functioning.

Lateral dominance. The importance of knowing if an individual is right- or left-handed and how strongly so is important in the interpretation of other tests. Some left-handed individuals (about 30 percent) have reversed cerebral asymmetry, meaning that their language functions are on the *right* side of the cerebral cortex. Eye and foot dominance can also be assessed by using simple tests (look through a telescope, kick a ball).

Motor skill. Checking both hands for motor ability is a way of assessing the large regions of the motor strip controlling the hands. Right-handed individuals should do much better on motor tests with their right hand. If they do not, and there has been no injury to that hand or arm, then the possibility of damage to the motor region is raised. Some right-handed individuals will retain better strength with their left hand. Under questioning they may say that they were forced to write with the right hand as a child even though they were natural southpaws. This practice has abated substantially. Some left-handed people may perform better with the right hand. This finding may indicate *pathological left-handedness,* meaning that the individuals were genetically set to be right-handed but in early development (probably due to damage in the left hemisphere) they switched. Motor abilities (such as strength and dexterity) are measured by a hand-dynamometer, which an individual squeezes; a pegboard, in which he or she places pegs as quickly as possible; and a telegraph key, which the individual taps as quickly as possible.

Auditory functioning. Auditory tests examine the functions of the parietal lobes. The Rhythm Test presents the patient with two rhythm patterns of beep sounds, and the patient must respond if the sounds are the same or different. The Speech Perception Test presents nonsense speech sounds (e.g., *leeng*), and the patient must identify them from a list of printed words. Spelling skill must remain intact for this test to be valid.

Spatial ability. The copying of figures gauges an individual's spatial conceptualization and motor control. The Tactual Performance Test requires the patient, while blindfolded, to place differing shapes in their right holes on a board. The patient uses each hand separately, then both in unison.

Language skills. Many language skills are measured in general intelligence tests because so much of our intelligence rests on our language skill. Specific analyses of discrete aspects of language are often necessary in cases of *aphasia* that results from damage to areas of the brain controlling language. Some aphasia tests include the Aphasia Screening Test and the Boston Diagnostic Aphasia Test.

General intelligence. Tests such as those designed by Wechsler are some of the most important components of a neuropsychological examination. The WAIS–R by itself is considered to be a neuropsychological test in that it measures many discrete cognitive skills, and the verbal/performance difference in I.Q. may be related to left- versus right-sided cerebral damage.

Memory. Some of the most frequent complaints received by the neuropsychologist are related to memory. Memory functions are quite diverse and require a range of individual tests to cover most of the skills casually referred to as *memory*. Memory consists of registering information, putting it into storage, retaining it, and retrieving it from storage. Problems can occur at any point in this process. As well, our brains seem to process various kinds of information differently. Memory for facts, dates, and events seems to be processed in the left cerebral cortex. Memory for patterns, designs, and external spatial relationships is processed in the right cerebral cortex. Many of the other tests given (e.g., WAIS–R) do measure aspects of short- and long-term memory. Wechsler also designed a battery of memory tests that have now been revised. This test, the Wechsler Memory Scale, surveys many aspects of memory from recall of verbal stories to learning pairs of objects. It is important to survey memory for different types of material (verbal and nonverbal) because these skills are not located in the same brain regions. Many patients who complain of memory problems actually have problems in concentration and attention, which are common after a head injury. Specific tests can separate some memory functions from simple attention.

Executive functions. Tests such as the Category Test present the patient with a complex changing task that requires problem solving, hypothesis testing, reasoning, and the ability to abandon unsuccessful strategies. The Trail-Making Test requires the patient to connect circles on a piece of paper, some containing numbers and some containing both letters and numbers. In the latter case the patient must oscillate between numbers and letters (e.g., 1-A-2-B). Both of these tests are reasonably strong indicators of frontal lobe functioning, although damage to other brain areas may affect them as well.

Academic skill. Various tests of reading, spelling, and arithmetic are often administered to individuals with brain damage. If the area of injury is not in the left-parietal area, then it is unlikely that these skills will be compromised by injury because they are so entrenched in our cognitive repertoire. Reading and spelling ability often serve as a good indication of premorbid or preaccident cognitive ability. By contrasting reading and spelling ability with the measure of general intelligence, a rough measure of intellectual "loss" can be obtained.

Neuropsychologists increasingly are becoming involved in the rehabilitative aspect of brain damage. The previous strong emphasis on assessment and diagnosis has modified to include the development and evaluation of training strategies for specific brain impairments.

The most widely used legal application of neuropsychology is the assessment of individuals who have been injured. Every year, over five hundred thousand people in the United States suffer head injuries, most of whom are males between the ages of sixteen and twenty-five. The majority of these injuries occur in motor vehicle accidents. The estimated loss is $25 billion in direct and indirect costs and thirty-five thousand worker-years of productive labor. As most of these injuries are the result of human negligence, the direct relevance to law is obvious.

Another legal application for neuropsychology is the diagnosis of mental conditions in the elderly or other individuals who have their competency challenged. I am often amazed at how intact and cognitively sharp aged individuals are who are supposedly "demented." Odd how the potential benefits of a legal action can warp an individual's perception of another—even when the other person is a parent. Apparently many older people do not heed Samuel Butler's advice that, when you have told someone that you have left him a legacy, the only decent thing is to die at once.

Neuropsychology is often introduced in criminal matters. Many individuals who find themselves before the criminal courts have a lifestyle that involves dangerous conduct and exposure to substances that can lead to brain dysfunction. This is rarely a full defense to a charge, but it is sometimes used in mitigating responsibility for illegal acts.

CHAPTER **SIX**

Other Tests

THE NEED TO DEVELOP TOOLS TO MEASURE human assets, deficits, and dimensions has led to an exponential proliferation of psychological tests. Each test must be weighed on its own merits to determine whether it meets the standards of reliability and validity discussed. Among this collection of psychological questionnaires and inventories, I will focus on those that may find their way into psychological reports destined for the courts. This smorgasbord is obviously incomplete, but it covers topics of interest to lawyers in their everyday practice.

Pain

In 1837, the High Court in England recorded its first case of an employee seeking compensation for a work injury. Since that time a proliferation of suits have sought financial relief for pain resulting from injuries. Contrary to myth, pain is not cured by a verdict. Pain, particularly when it is chronic, is a complex condition affected by a variety of factors—biological, environmental, physiological, behavioral, and social. The International Association for the Study of Pain produced a classification scheme in 1986 based on five axes: the region of the body that is experiencing pain, the physiological system involved, temporal characteristics of the pain, the patient's assessment of pain intensity, and the cause of the pain. This classification scheme has not been placed into general use because only two of the five axes demonstrated sufficient reliability.

Other attempts have tried to measure aspects of pain. These have included pain-rating scales, behavioral observations of pain, and constructs associated with pain. The most widely used scale to measure pain is the McGill Pain Questionnaire, which has appeared in several hundred studies of pain and has spawned similar instruments. Although we cannot directly measure pain, we do know that each kind of pain is characterized by a distinctive verbal expression. The McGill Pain Questionnaire taps into this phenomenon by asking patients to peg their experience of pain on a word (e.g., shooting, cramping, throbbing). Different types of pain (childbirth, toothache, bone fracture) not only show different overall levels of pain but are described differently. The questionnaire also separates pain into sensory, affective, and evaluative components. It requires only five minutes to administer.

The Multidimensional Pain Inventory (MPI) is a more complex instrument that has scales to assess interference with activity, social support from others, pain intensity, and emotional distress. Four distinct profiles of pain patients have emerged using this test: the disabled, the dysfunctional, the interpersonally distressed, and adaptive copers.

Many professionals use a form of structured interview to assess pain in their patients, matching the patient's description of pain duration, sensation, intensity, location, and time course with known descriptions of pain and the cause of pain syndromes. Classical descriptions of headaches provoked by psychological tension, for example, are dramatically different from the pattern seen in migraine or cluster headaches.

Parenting

Batteries of psychological tests are often given to parents seeking custody of their children in family courts. The rationale for giving this large battery of tests is sometimes difficult to follow. It does not matter if one parent has a specific MMPI–2 score two points higher than the other parent. The essential information about parenting skill should be front and center in any assessment for this purpose.

Parenting is assessed clinically by observing the parent and child interacting in the home. However, the very act of observation may affect the conduct of both parent and child. Several tests have been developed to supplement general clinical assessment and observation of the parent. The Parental Awareness Skills Survey presents the parent with eighteen child-care dilemmas and the parent is asked what he or she would do or say in response to each situation. The two parents can be compared to each other, or if only one parent is assessed, the general quality of his or her knowledge of appropriate conduct can be assessed. This test measures knowledge that is a requisite of appropriate action, but it cannot actually test whether the parent would carry out the response to the hypothetical situations.

The child's perception of each parent is an additional need in custody evaluations. During interviews with the child alone her or his perceptions are explored. However, perception is a difficult aspect for even experienced clinicians to gauge, especially in the dynamics of the divorce/custody environment. An interesting test developed by Barry Bricklin (Bricklin Perceptual Scales: Child Perception of Parent Series) measures a child's verbal and nonverbal perception of each parent in the areas of competence, supportiveness, follow-up consistency, and the possession of admirable traits. Parents can be compared on these dimensions or changes in parents can be measured before and after therapeutic intervention. A child responds to each of sixty-four questions (Does this parent [mother or father] do something *well* or *not so well*?), and the child responds by placing a pinhole mark along a continuous line, with *well* and *not so well* as the poles on either end. The exact place on the line is later quantified for each question and overall for each parent. Many clinicians place more emphasis on these nonverbal responses than on verbal ones because the child may parrot verbal information that ultimately comes from one of the parents. This is less likely to derive from nonverbal responses.

Sexuality

Measuring aspects of sexuality has become important in criminal cases involving sexual assaults. Both indirect and direct forms of assessment have evolved. The indirect measures include questionnaires such as the Derogatis Sexual Functioning Inventory. This test assesses an individual's understanding of the fundamental facts of human sexual anatomy and functioning, range of sexual experience, sexual drive, attitude toward sexual matters, gender role definition, fantasy themes, body image, and sexual satisfaction. Patterns on these factors have been collected for types of sexual offenders.

Direct assessment of sexual arousal is conducted with the aid of a penile plethysmograph. This procedure involves recording a subject's physical responses as he views photographic slides or videotapes or reads stories of a variety of sexual and nonsexual material. Penile reactions are usually recorded with a transducer (a type of hollow elastic tube filled with mercury and connected to a computer that records the expansion and contraction of the subject's penis as he responds to stimulus material. To prevent pretesting masturbation, the subject is often not told when he will undergo the procedure. Prior to presenting the test stimuli, the subject is often given material intended to produce a maximal erection. Test responses are thus measured in percentage of maximal arousal. The subject is often given instructions to arouse and suppress penile responses to gauge his ability to control sexual arousal. A profile of the subject's sexual response pattern is generated by comparing arousal to different stimuli, including sexual scenes with children. It is not the level of sexual response that is important so much as the differences in responses to the stimuli. The degree of response can be influenced by fatigue, masturbation, or drugs, but these do not influence the relative response to stimuli. This procedure was first used to measure sexual responses in humans in 1957, and the procedure has been used increasingly by state hospitals, prisons, and forensic services. Patterns of sexual response are reasonably stable across time.

The procedures and stimuli presented to subjects are not standardized across the hundreds of laboratories that conduct this form of testing. Thus it is difficult directly to compare results across these settings. However, there is general agreement that this procedure can be a useful adjunct in the comprehensive assessment of sexual offenders, particularly in the assessment and treatment of child molesters. It is not appropriate to use the penile plethysmograph to assess the veracity of sexual abuse claims. As well, the use of the test as a single indicator of pathology is not an accepted standard of practice. Some subjects (between 20 and 40 percent) in this procedure show little or no penile response. This is usually interpreted to mean either that the individual exercised very good control over his responses or that the laboratory setting was inhibiting. Some subjects also may experience pretrial anxiety that may influence the procedure. The plethysmograph is not a sexual "lie-detector," with arousal indicative of guilt of a crime.

Testing Validity of Sexual Abuse Complaints

When the accused denies a complaint of sexual assault, a method of measuring the veracity of the complaint may be put in motion. Although there are ways to examine behavior and to suggest that it was probable or improbable to various degrees, there exists no litmus test that definitively determines the truthfulness of the complaint or denial. It was once widely believed that children never lie about such matters, but considerable evidence now shows that they do lie in some situations, or that they act on suggestions by others. The rate of false allegations of child sexual abuse in divorce and child-custody cases is alarmingly high.

The search for validity frequently arises when a child complains of being sexually abused or when an adult recalls a sexual assault in her or his past and brings the assault to the authorities. In the case of an alleged child victim, police and social service agencies commence a host of interviews. Later a psychologist may be asked to judge the veracity of the complaint based on the symptoms of the child and on the impressions from interviewing the child as well. This is a situation fraught with erroneous methodology and assumptions. First, the more times the child is interviewed, the higher the probability that his or her testimony may be contaminated by suggestions (implicit or otherwise) from the interviewers. Second, there are no specific behavior signs that validate that abuse has occurred. The only behavior that has a higher incidence in sexually abused children is sexualized behavior; that is, acts, knowledge, and language that is clearly not age appropriate and therefore must have been learned by exposure to adult sexual behavior. Although depression, anxiety, and school difficulties can accompany sexual abuse of children, they are not specific to this type of abuse and can appear for many different reasons. Lastly, the psychologist or other professional may not follow an appropriate protocol in gaining information from the child.

To gather information properly from a child suspected of being sexually abused, a protocol termed the Step-Wise Interview, developed by John Yuille of the University of British Columbia, has gained considerable respect. The goals of this format are to minimize the trauma of the investigation for the child, to maximize the information obtained about the alleged event, to minimize the contaminating effects of the interview on the child's memory, and to maintain integrity in the investigative process. The interview should be videotaped to reduce the number of interviews with the child. Videotaping also reduces the need to take notes, and it does not depend upon the interviewer's memory to recall what occurred.

The first step in this procedure is to build rapport with the child and to informally observe her or his language, overall ability, and behavior. Then the child is asked to describe two experiences such as a birthday party or school outing, which allows a general gauge of memory for specific events and provides a model for the child when discussing sexual-abuse allegations. The next step involves establishing the need to tell the truth, progressing from a general introduction of the topic to an agreement that only the truth will be told during the interview. The topic of concern is then introduced, beginning with general open-ended questions and proceeding to more specific ones. The interviewer never names the suspect or suggests the nature of the alleged acts. The child is then asked to describe each event from the beginning and without leaving out any details. General questions are then introduced to allow the child to recall further details. More specific questions follow, but multiple-choice questions are avoided whenever possible. Interview aids such as drawings and dolls must be used cautiously. Anatomically detailed dolls should never be used until the child has disclosed details of the abuse. Several jurisdictions have disallowed evidence obtained with these dolls. If concerns about the child's suggestibility have been raised, a test can be applied at the end of the interview by asking leading questions about irrelevant issues ("You came here by bus, didn't you?"). When the information from the Step-Wise Interview is gathered in this systematic fashion, it can be submitted to inspection through Statement Validity Analysis, a technique for gauging the credibility of a child's evidence. An assault interview protocol that has similar goals to the Step-Wise Interview has also been developed for adults.

When adults come forward recalling sexual abuse from the distant past, the issue of "false memory" arises. Can a person block traumatic memories of child abuse only to have them surface in the course of psychotherapy years later? Some clinical advocates say yes, whereas the scientific community has raised serious doubts about its probability. The alternative explanation is that during therapy, the adult constructs false memories, often with the unwitting assistance of a therapist. Once these memories have been established, they are indistinguishable from genuine memories. Elizabeth Loftus, a leading researcher in human memory, has published some of the key reviews in this field, and others have begun to develop guidelines by which genuine and false memories may be distinguished. These issues have been debated in both criminal and civil cases, and several cases exist of psychotherapists being sued successfully for damages arising from false memories created in therapy. Professional organizations have issued warnings to therapists practicing in this area of the need to be cautious when asking about past sexual abuse.

Malingering and Deception

Gauging a person's overt attempt to mislead has become a growth industry in psychology as applied to the courts, especially in personal-injury litigation.

The clinician can measure deception in a number of ways. The first way is the use of behavioral observation. Many clinical signs have been cited as indicating *dissimulation* (our euphemism for lying). These include dramatic presentation, deliberate and careful response to questions, symptoms inconsistent with known disorders, disparities and contradictions in self-reports, and endorsement of blatant but not subtle symptoms. These are all useful observations, but individually or without more objective findings, they can be challenged on their nonempirical base.

I have shown that objective personality tests such as the MMPI–2 can be quite useful in detecting dissimulation—both defensiveness and malingering. Other methods have been developed for detecting specifically malingered cognitive deficits. The most common of these is a forced-choice recognition memory test. The subject is shown a series of pictures, one at a time, and asked later to remember the item (e.g., face). If the subject's memory were completely absent (a very improbable event even with genuine brain-damaged individuals), the hit rate would be 50 percent. If a subject's performance falls below this chance level, it is assumed that he for she recognizes the right stimulus but gives the opposite answer. Thus, the subject overdoes the "deficit." Many other neuropsychological tasks are the same; we know a great deal about how people with genuine deficits (and no deficits) perform on these tests, and the subject attempting to malinger is unaware of how to portray these disorders genuinely. The subject gives near misses, gross discrepancies from the norm, inconsistencies between similar tests, resistance to some tests, and inconsistencies between reported and observed deficits. The probability of successfully malingering a cognitive deficit, in face of a comprehensive neuropsychological examination, is understandably slim. I should also point out that sometimes it is not a case of having a genuine condition or faking symptoms. Even with very genuine injuries, some subjects "add" deficits to ensure that their claim is seen as legitimate. In doing so, they jeopardize the entire claim.

Other methods advocated for "getting to the truth" are drug-assisted interviews, hypnosis, and the use of the polygraph. The sodium amytal interview has the reputation of forcing truthfulness from a person through the administration of a "truth serum." A short-acting barbiturate is given to a subject. Many of the overt changes that occur are similar to those seen in individuals under the influence of alcohol. In the early stages of the drug, the subject may show increased euphoria and verbosity; in later stages, slurring of speech and motor impairment. Like alcohol this drug's effects are highly variable, depending on the individual consuming it and the circumstances under which it is consumed. Because of the complexity of this technique and the many variables that can affect it, little scientific justification exists for its use. Even its advocates argue that the subject should be properly informed of the purpose of the interview, and that the interview should only be used as an extra method of investigating dissimulation after other techniques have proved unsuccessful.

The polygraph has a long history and continuing wide use in the field of "lie detection." Recent estimates suggest that up to 4 million Americans are given polygraph tests every year. The tests are given by police forces, private polygraphists, private businesses, and government agencies. Although few polygraphists are trained as psychologists, the technique falls clearly within the scientific purview of psychology. The basic premise of the polygraph is that when a person lies, he or she responds physiologically, and that these responses can be measured by such indices as heart rate, respiration rate, and skin resistance. The premise is faulty, for it fails to account for the fact that most strong emotions (fear, anxiety, anger, guilt) have physiological correlates, and they are often indistinguishable. There is no specific physiological pattern of response, although the technique relies on trying to impress upon the subject that indeed there is a distinct pattern. The polygraph procedure is a complex one that involves lengthy interviews with the subject and the structuring of individualized questions, often followed by an old-fashioned attempt to extract a confession from a person who has been told previously that the machine is infallible and that there is little to fear from it. Abundant reasons exist for the inadmissibility of polygraph evidence!

Hypnosis is another technique touted to gain access to hidden memories and unspoken truths. Since mesmerism was renamed hypnosis (for Hypnos, the Greek god of sleep) in 1842, the phenomenon has been understood as a state entered because of highly concentrated attention rather than mystical forces. It has a long history of use in medical and dental procedures, as well as in the treatment of mental disorders. In the 1920s scientific work began on this state. Prior to this a number of ideas had accumulated about the conditions one could cause in subjects through hypnosis. With 75 years of research it is now known that most of these unusual behaviors (e.g., age regression) are due not to hypnotic conditions but to the willingness of the subjects to cooperate in a task, expectations that they might have about hypnosis, and the guiding characteristics of the situation in which they find themselves. When memories are constructed under hypnosis, the subjects may feel very confident of them, but no accepted evidence exists to show that the memories are any more accurate (often they are more inaccurate) than memories produced without this technique. Hypnosis is sometimes used to validate claimed amnesia. Again, the validity of this purpose is uncertain. When legal evidence is based on results of hypnotic interviews, strict scientific criteria (see Orne, 1979) should be used in conjunction with relevant jurisdictional statute.

The important question to ask is: What is the clinical relevance of the dissimulation or distortion in clinical presentation of the legal client? This will vary with the degree and type of distortion as well as the referral question. On the MMPI–2 a parent in the middle of a custody dispute may provide evidence from the validity scales that he or she is attempting to be seen in a favorable light. Does this mean that he or she is thus the less suitable of two parents to assume responsible care of their child? Of course not! The parent is so motivated to achieve a goal that he or she has intentionally or otherwise tried to put the best foot forward and simply went too far. Yet when presented in court, the elevated *Lie* score would have negative connotations. Little weight may be placed appropriately on this finding. Attempts to present psychological or cognitive injury in the middle of a personal-injury suit or feigned mental disorder in a criminal trial carry more serious implications for the professional assigned to investigate the veracity of these presentations.

Dangerousness

In criminal proceedings and other legal venues (e.g., labor arbitration matters) the issue sometimes arises of whether an individual is dangerous. Although there is no definitive test to answer this question, much research has been compiled to provide a clinician, trained in the prediction of dangerousness, to offer reasoned opinions. When such opinions are offered in legal forums, it is important to scrutinize closely the method of how such conclusions were reached.

A recent advance in the assessment of dangerousness and risk to others is the HCR–20 Scheme. This rating scheme incorporates the advances of risk prediction from the scientific literature into a practical format. It is a checklist of known important variables needed in the formulation of risk prediction that the clinician reviews and weighs with each case. The acronym HCR stands for historical, clinical, and risk variables. Beginning with history, we know that previous violent acts, the age at which they first presented, and other past behaviors are strong predictors of future violent conduct. This glimpse into the past is often taken from objective sources (past files) as well as from the person being evaluated. The second component is the examination of current clinical features and behaviors—does the person have "insight" or recognize that his behavior is irrational or inappropriate? Is his attitude pro- or anti-social? What active symptoms of mental disease is he displaying? Finally, the individual's future is examined. How compliant with guidelines is the person likely to be? What support and supervision of his behavior will be in place? What stressors will he be facing in the future? When the clinician has completed this checklist, he or she produces a summary of scores and provides an estimate of high, medium, or low risk. Currently the instrument is a research guide without an established database, but this is likely to change in the near future. The instrument is based on demonstrated scientific principles drawn from many empirical studies of violence.

The conclusion regarding dangerousness and risk should specify not only the degree of risk, it should also specify conditions under which risk is highest (e.g., when the subject is impaired by alcohol), the type of dangerous behavior the subject is most likely to display (e.g., sexual assault), and the potential pool of victims (e.g., females between the ages of fifteen and thirty).

A widely heralded instrument in the assessment of dangerousness is the Psychopathy Check List–Revised (PCL–R), developed by Robert Hare. This instrument quantifies dimensions of the psychopathic personality such as lack of remorse, conning, callousness, impulsiveness, and criminal versatility. The PCL–R has emerged as a strong predictor of recidivism in criminal samples.

Vocational Assessment

An individual has suffered an accident that may limit his future employment and wants redress for this limitation. A long-time employee has been dismissed from her job and seeks compensation. A man claiming he can best provide for his children's material needs applies for sole custody of them. All of these are situations that may require a vocational assessment to be placed in a legal forum.

When looking at a match between an individual and a particular career, usually three dimensions are considered: ability, personality, and interests. Some jobs require a certain level of education, training, and intelligence; some require personality assets such as the ability to interact easily with other people and not become easily frustrated. These dimensions can be measured with cognitive or specific ability tests and personality tests. It has been demonstrated empirically that certain personality profiles or sets of traits are more common in particular professions and trades.

The final dimension of vocational analysis is interests. Measurement of interests is more complex than it might appear. The assessment of interests in a formal psychometric format dates back over sixty years. The early test instruments were pragmatic gauges but had little theory to explain their findings. The most widely held theory of vocational interest was developed by John Holland, who postulated six basic occupational personality types. The first type is *Realistic,* people who like outdoor pursuits and mechanical work. Often their social skills are not highly developed. Realistic jobs for these people include automobile mechanic, surveyor, farmer, and electrician. This type has the lowest prestige and educational level of the six basic types. The next type is *Investigative,* which emphasizes ideas rather than people. This type is characterized by abstract intelligence and is perceived by others to be cold and distant. These individuals have strong mathematical and scientific skill but often lack leadership ability. Some investigative jobs include biologist, geologist, and medical technologist. This has the highest prestige level of the six types.

The next occupational type is the *Artistic,* people who are creative in orientation and who work with ideas and materials to express themselves. Some of these occupations include writer, musician, interior decorator, and actor.

The *Social* occupational type enjoys working with others and displays social skills and talents but often lacks scientific or mechanical ability. Nurturance and support, not leadership, are common characteristics. Examples of this work type include teachers, counselors, speech therapists, and religious workers.

The *Enterprising* type is also oriented toward people but seeks to control or dominate others. This type is task oriented and prefers well-defined and unambiguous goals. Salespersons, buyers, promoters, and managers are some examples of this type.

Finally the *Conventional* type likes working with numbers and performing clerical tasks. This type does not aspire to high-level positions within organizations and is content to maintain orderly adherence to structure and authority. Some examples include bookkeeper, banker, stenographer, and cost estimator.

There is consensus on this type of model in defining occupational interest, even if not all of these types are found in every study. In measuring interests most people show a combination of these traits (Realistic-Investigative-Enterprising). The model also proposes that the work environment can be categorized using the same six descriptors. A realistic environment is populated in large part by realistic personality types. People will also search for the environments that will allow them to exercise their skills and preferred roles. Repeated testing has revealed that individuals' occupational interests remain stable over time. What *type* do lawyers generally fall into, taking into account that specific specialists in law may fall into different employment categories? As it turns out, lawyers, judges, and politicians all share the same code—ESA—or are primarily Enterprising, Social, and Artistic. With more specific subgroups, the groupings would be slightly varied (for tax attorneys it would be ESI).

Many instruments have been designed to measure interest/occupational types, including the Vocational Preference Inventory and the Self-Directed Search. Other widely used interest inventories include the Strong Interest Inventory and the Jackson Vocational Interest Inventory.

A widely used test for both public and private sector skilled and semi-skilled workers is the General Aptitude Test Battery (GATB). It tests general cognitive, perceptual, numerical, and psychomotor skills and is often viewed as a screening tool for employers.

CHAPTER SEVEN

Diagnosis: Understanding the Diagnostic and Statistical Manual of Mental Disorders (DSM–IV)

WHAT IS THE PROBLEM? This central question is posed in every field when trouble arises. When malfunctions occur in automobiles or computers or in people, a diagnostic mission is undertaken to accurately and reliably describe or define the problem so that sound remedial steps can be taken. In mental health distinguishing anxiety from depression, for example, is important in understanding, predicting, and changing behavior. In law a solid diagnostic opinion of mental disorder is often the single pivotal issue in a case. To invoke an insanity defense, a specific set of mental disorders qualify as a necessary, if not sufficient, condition. In personal-injury claims specific diagnoses related to causative events are necessary to advance suitable compensation and to predict losses to future earnings and quality of life. Decisions in family law often rest on the mental stability of parents. A diagnosis of a mental disorder in one parent can be very influential. Similarly, competency in probate must rely on diagnosis (e.g., types of dementia) and not simply on a casual reference to a dysfunction or a disability. Many administrative and insurance claims require a definable mental condition (with standard criteria) prior to approval of benefits. A comprehensive understanding of the diagnostic process and the range of categories is thus fundamental to lawyers in these fields.

In the early stages of investigation, all sciences seek to classify the phenomena under study. In biology animals and plants are arranged in naturally related groups based on some factor common to each, such as their structure, embryology, or biochemistry. Classes are subdivided in descending order from large groupings to smaller, increasingly homogeneous ones. The rationale for these classifications is that nature has endowed the world with patterns. Describing these patterns leads frequently to understanding and prediction of natural events. Although this is a widely accepted principle of classical science, there is certainly an appreciation that nature has an erratic side, occasionally disrupting the orderly progress of scientific advancement. The further science strays from the controlled environment of the laboratory, the more nature displays its erratic puzzles. It is with this appreciation of the limitations of classification that I approach the complexities of categorizing human behavioral abnormalities.

History of Diagnosis

History reflects attempts to classify abnormal behavior from the earliest records. During the ascendancy of the Greek and Roman civilizations (from approximately 500 B.C. to A.D. 400) philosophers/physicians described discrete conditions such as *melancholia* (profound sadness), *mania* (euphoric frenzy), and other conditions. The father of medicine, Hippocrates, theorized that human behavior was influenced by the balance of four fluids, or *humors*, that flowed through the body: yellow bile, black bile, blood, and phlegm. This system revealed another aspect of behavior classification—the continuum. One tended toward sadness in a graded manner, depending on the amount or balance of bodily fluid. Excessive yellow bile resulted in manic activity.

Eighteen hundred years later these seeds of early diagnosis were revisited in Germany, where modern diagnostic systems for mental disorder were born. In 1883 Emil Kraepelin published the first influential system for classifying abnormal behavior. An astute German physician, Kraepelin collected thousands of case studies of patients in mental hospitals and began sorting them into *syndromes*, or clusters of *symptoms*.

A *symptom* or sign is typically a narrow description. An elevated temperature is a physical sign or symptom that is easily quantified. In itself, however, it is not diagnostic of a specific problem. When certain symptoms cluster together with regularity and follow a predictable course, general agreement on a syndrome develops. When an individual displays a syndrome he or she is placed in that category. Over time a comprehensive list of syndromes developed to catalogue all known afflictions.

Purposes of Clinical Classification Systems

Clinical classification systems have a number of purposes. With the templates of the system, a clinician can *diagnose* (from Greek *to discriminate*) one condition from another. With a diagnosis in place, a body of accumulated general information can be referenced (e.g., what treatments work best, how common the condition is in the general population, whether it is equally distributed between the sexes). Classification systems also assist the *investigation* of abnormality by developing the body of knowledge on the disorders, such as possible causes. Finally a classification system allows for more efficient *communication* between researchers and clinicians. A symptom-by-symptom listing is unnecessary in that a diagnosis will convey a general picture and understanding of the patient's difficulties.

Two Systems: ICD and DSM

From Kraepelin's work two primary classifications or diagnostic systems of mental disorders arose. The first work is a part of the *International Classification of Diseases* employed by the World Health Organization. This work covers the full range of physical and mental diseases and is now in its tenth edition, known as *ICD–10*.

The other system to evolve from Kraepelin's ideas is the *Diagnostic and Statistical Manual of Mental Disorders*, which deals only with mental conditions. This work has strong parallels with the mental disorder section of the ICD–10, but it dominates the clinical classification system in North America and is the most widely used diagnostic system in the international scientific literature. The fifth revision of this work has been published (1994) and is commonly referred to as the *DSM–IV* (following the third edition, a revised third edition was released). These two classification systems of mental disorder, ICD and DSM, have come increasingly to overlap to a considerable degree. Because the science of abnormal psychology is constantly accumulating information, one can anticipate updated compendiums at least every decade. The first DSM was released in 1952, with DSM–II published in 1968 and DSM–III and DSM–III–R appearing in 1980 and 1987. Although published by the American Psychiatric Association, the progress in classification is assisted by scientists from other disciplines, and the diagnostic system is not exclusive to any particular group. Indeed, the text of the manual refers generically to *clinician*, recognizing that qualified professionals from a number of disciplines have the ability to diagnose mental disorders.

DSM–IV

The proper use of the diagnostic system does require specialized clinical training in both the scientific literature on abnormal behavior and assessment techniques. Although a disorder may appear in the DSM–IV, this does not imply that there is universal agreement among clinicians that the disorder exists or is defined in precisely the way described in the text. With some conditions (e.g., schizophrenia, substance use disorders) there is a very high level of agreement or reliability. With a limited number of mental conditions (e.g., dissociative personality disorder, or what was formerly called multiple personality disorder) there is disagreement concerning whether the disorder exists at all. This level of debate fortunately is rather uncommon in this classification system.

Some notions that diagnoses of mental disorder are unreliable stem back to studies using early diagnostic systems, when one clinician would diagnose a patient as schizophrenic and the next one would suggest depression. For most categories of mental disorder the use of clear behavioral descriptors has reduced these incidents. The diagnostic reliability for most mental disorders now exceeds that for most physical disorders.

The DSM–IV recognizes more than two hundred mental disorders. Each entry describes the diagnostic features, subtypes of the condition, and associated features (though not essential) that may appear. Each entry also includes other information for each disorder, including specific culture, age, and gender features; prevalence; course; familial pattern; and conditions with similar features from which the clinician must differentiate the disorder. DSM–IV focuses on verifiable symptoms rather than attempting to infer underlying causes. The following DSM–IV entry for posttraumatic stress disorder illustrates the kind of information provided on each disorder.

309.81 Posttraumatic Stress Disorder
(Reprinted by permission of the American Psychiatric Association)

Diagnostic Features

The essential feature of Posttraumatic Stress Disorder is the development of characteristic symptoms following exposure to an extreme traumatic stressor involving direct personal experience of an event that involves actual or threatened death or serious injury, or other threat to one's physical integrity; or witnessing an event that involves death, injury, or a threat to the physical integrity of another person; or learning about unexpected or violent death, serious harm, or threat of death or injury experienced by a family member or other close associate (Criterion Al). The person's response to the event must involve intense fear, helplessness, or horror (or in children, the response must involve disorganized or agitated behavior) (Criterion A2). The characteristic symptoms resulting from the exposure to the extreme trauma include persistent reexperiencing of the traumatic event (Criterion B), persistent avoidance of stimuli associated with the trauma and numbing of general responsiveness (Criterion C), and persistent symptoms of increased arousal (Criterion D). The full symptom picture must be present for more than 1 month (Criterion E), and the disturbance must cause clinically significant distress or impairment in social, occupational, or other important areas of functioning (Criterion F).

Traumatic events that are experienced directly include, but are not limited to, military combat, violent personal assault (sexual assault, physical attack, robbery, mugging), being kidnapped, being taken hostage, terrorist attack, torture, incarceration as a prisoner of war or in a concentration camp, natural or manmade disasters, severe automobile accidents, or being diagnosed with a life-threatening illness. For children, sexually traumatic events may include developmentally inappropriate sexual experiences without threatened or actual violence or injury. Witnessed events include, but are not limited to, observing the serious injury or unnatural death of another person due to violent assault, accident, war, or disaster or unexpectedly witnessing a dead body or body parts. Events experienced by others that are learned about include, but are not limited to, violent personal assault, serious accident, or serious injury experienced by a family member or a close friend; learning about the sudden, unexpected death of a family member or a close friend; or learning that one's child has a life-threatening disease. The disorder may be especially severe or long-lasting when the stressor is of human design (e.g., torture, rape). The likelihood of developing this disorder may increase as the intensity of and physical proximity to the stressor increase.

The traumatic event can be reexperienced in various ways. Commonly the person has recurrent and intrusive recollections of the event (Criterion B1) or recurrent distressing dreams during which the event is replayed (Criterion B2). In rare instances, the person experiences dissociative states that last from a few seconds to several hours, or even days, during which components of the event are relived and the person behaves as though experiencing the event at that moment (Criterion B3). Intense psychological distress (Criterion B4) or physiological reactivity (Criterion B5) often occurs when the person is exposed to triggering events that resemble or symbolize an aspect of the traumatic event (e.g., anniversaries of the traumatic event; cold, snowy weather or uniformed guards for survivors of death camps in cold climates; hot, humid weather for combat veterans of the South Pacific; entering any elevator for a woman who was raped in an elevator).

Stimuli associated with the trauma are persistently avoided. The person commonly makes deliberate efforts to avoid thoughts, feelings, or conversations about the traumatic event (Criterion Cl) and to avoid activities, situations, or people who arouse recollections of it (Criterion C2). This avoidance of reminders may include amnesia for an important aspect of the traumatic event (Criterion C3). Diminished responsiveness to the external world, referred to as "psychic numbing," or "emotional anesthesia," usually begins soon after the traumatic event. The individual may complain of having markedly diminished interest or participation in previously enjoyed activities (Criterion C4), of feeling detached or estranged from other people (Criterion C5), or of having markedly reduced ability to feel emotions (especially those associated with intimacy, tenderness, and sexuality) (Criterion C6). The individual may have a sense of a foreshortened future (e.g., not expecting to have a career, marriage, children, or a normal life span) (Criterion C7).

The individual has persistent symptoms of anxiety or increased arousal that were not present before the trauma. These symptoms may include difficulty falling or staying asleep that may be due to recurrent nightmares during which the traumatic event is relived (Criterion Dl), hypervigilance (Criterion D4), and exaggerated startle response (Criterion D5). Some individuals report irritability or outbursts of anger (Criterion D2) or difficulty concentrating or completing tasks (Criterion D3).

Specifiers

The following specifiers may be used to specify onset and duration of the symptoms of Posttraumatic Stress Disorder:

Acute. This specifier should be used when the duration of symptoms is less than 3 months.

Chronic. This specifier should be used when the symptoms last 3 months or longer.

With Delayed Onset. This specifier indicates that at least 6 months have passed between the traumatic event and the onset of the symptoms.

Associated Features and Disorders

Associated descriptive features and mental disorders. Individuals with Posttraumatic Stress Disorder may describe painful guilt feelings about surviving when others did not survive or about the things they had to do to survive. Phobic avoidance of situations or activities that resemble or symbolize the original trauma may interfere with interpersonal relationships and lead to marital conflict, divorce, or loss of job. The following associated constellation of symptoms may occur and are more commonly seen in association with an interpersonal stressor (e.g., childhood sexual or physical abuse, domestic battering, being taken hostage, incarceration as a prisoner of war or in a concentration camp, torture); impaired affect modulation; self-destructive and impulsive behavior; dissociative symptoms; somatic complaints; feelings of ineffectiveness, shame, despair, or hopelessness; feeling permanently damaged; a loss of previously sustained beliefs; hostility; social withdrawal; feeling constantly threatened; impaired relationships with others; or a change from the individual's previous personality characteristics.

There may be increased risk of Panic Disorder, Agoraphobia, Obsessive-Compulsive Disorder, Social Phobia, Specific Phobia, Major Depressive Disorder, Somatization Disorder, and Substance-Related Disorders. It is not known to what extent these disorders precede or follow the onset of Posttraumatic Stress Disorder.

Associated laboratory findings. Increased arousal may be measured through studies of autonomic functioning (e.g., heart rate, electromyography, sweat gland activity).

Associated physical examination findings and general medical conditions. General medical conditions may occur as a consequence of the trauma (e.g., head injury, burns).

Specific Culture and Age Features

Individuals who have recently emigrated from areas of considerable social unrest and civil conflict may have elevated rates of Posttraumatic Stress Disorder. Such individuals may be especially reluctant to divulge experiences of torture and trauma due to their vulnerable political immigrant status. Specific assessments of traumatic experiences and concomitant symptoms are needed for such individuals.

In younger children, distressing dreams of the event may, within several weeks, change into generalized nightmares of monsters, of rescuing others, or of threats to self or others. Young children usually do not have the sense that they are reliving the past; rather, the reliving of the trauma may occur through repetitive play (e.g., a child who was involved in a serious automobile accident repeatedly reenacts car crashes with toy cars). Because it may be difficult for children to report diminished interest in significant activities and constriction of affect, these symptoms should be carefully evaluated with reports from parents, teachers, and other observers. In children, the sense of a foreshortened future may be evidenced by the belief that life will be too short to include becoming an adult. There may also be "omen formation"—that is, belief in an ability to foresee future untoward events. Children may also exhibit various physical symptoms, such as stomachaches and headaches.

Prevalence

Community-based studies reveal a lifetime prevalence for Posttraumatic Stress Disorder ranging from 1% to 14%, with the variability related to methods of ascertainment and the population sampled. Studies of at-risk individuals (e.g., combat veterans, victims of volcanic eruptions or criminal violence) have yielded prevalence rates ranging from 3% to 58%.

Course

Posttraumatic Stress Disorder can occur at any age, including childhood. Symptoms usually begin within the first 3 months after the trauma, although there may be a delay of months, or even years, before symptoms appear. Frequently, the disturbance initially meets criteria for Acute Stress Disorder (see p. 429) in the immediate aftermath of the trauma. The symptoms of the disorder and the relative predominance of reexperiencing, avoidance, and hyperarousal symptoms may vary over time. Duration of the symptoms varies, with complete recovery occurring within 3 months in approximately half of cases, with many others having persisting symptoms for longer than 12 months after the trauma.

The severity, duration, and proximity of an individual's exposure to the traumatic event are the most important factors affecting the likelihood of developing this disorder. There is some evidence that social supports, family history, childhood experiences, personality variables, and preexisting mental disorders may influence the development of Posttraumatic Stress Disorder. This disorder can develop in individuals without any predisposing conditions, particularly if the stressor is especially extreme.

Differential Diagnosis

In Posttraumatic Stress Disorder, the stressor must be of an extreme (i.e., life-threatening) nature. In contrast, in **Adjustment Disorder,** the stressor can be of any severity. The diagnosis of Adjustment Disorder is appropriate both for situations in which the response to an extreme stressor does not meet the criteria for Posttraumatic Stress Disorder (or another specific mental disorder) and for situations in which the symptom pattern of Posttraumatic Stress Disorder occurs in response to a stressor that is not extreme (e.g., spouse leaving, being fired).

Not all psychopathology that occurs in individuals exposed to an extreme stressor should necessarily be attributed to Posttraumatic Stress Disorder. **Symptoms of avoidance, numbing, and increased arousal that are present before exposure to the stressor** do not meet criteria for the diagnosis of Posttraumatic Stress Disorder and require consideration of other diagnoses (e.g., a Mood Disorder or another Anxiety Disorder). Moreover, if the symptom response pattern to the extreme stressor meets criteria for **another mental disorder** (e.g., Brief Psychotic Disorder, Conversion Disorder, Major Depressive Disorder), these diagnoses should be given instead of, or in addition to, Posttraumatic Stress Disorder.

Acute Stress Disorder is distinguished from Posttraumatic Stress Disorder because the symptom pattern in Acute Stress Disorder must occur within 4 weeks of the traumatic event and resolve within that 4-week period. If the symptoms persist for more than 1 month and meet criteria for Posttraumatic Stress Disorder, the diagnosis is changed from Acute Stress Disorder to Posttraumatic Stress Disorder.

In **Obsessive-Compulsive Disorder,** there are recurrent intrusive thoughts, but these are experienced as inappropriate and are not related to an experienced traumatic event. Flashbacks in Posttraumatic Stress Disorder must be distinguished from illusions, hallucinations, and other perceptual disturbances that may occur in **Schizophrenia, other Psychotic Disorders, Mood Disorder With Psychotic Features,** a **delirium, Substance-Induced Disorders,** and **Psychotic Disorders Due to a General Medical Condition.**

Malingering should be ruled out in those situations in which financial remuneration, benefit eligibility, and forensic determinations play a role.

■ **Diagnostic criteria for 309.81 Posttraumatic Stress Disorder**

A. The person has been exposed to a traumatic event in which both of the following were present:

   (1) the person experienced, witnessed, or was confronted with an event or events that involved actual or threatened death or serious injury, or a threat to the physical integrity of self or others
   (2) the person's response involved intense fear, helplessness, or horror. **Note:** In children, this may be expressed instead by disorganized or agitated behavior.

☐ **Diagnostic criteria for 309.81 Posttraumatic Stress Disorder** *(continued)*

B. The traumatic event is persistently reexperienced in one (or more) of the following ways:

   (1) recurrent and intrusive distressing recollections of the event, including images, thoughts, or perceptions. **Note:** In young children, repetitive play may occur in which themes or aspects of the trauma are expressed.
   (2) recurrent distressing dreams of the event. **Note:** In children, there may be frightening dreams without recognizable content.
   (3) acting or feeling as if the traumatic event were recurring (includes a sense of reliving the experience, illusions, hallucinations, and dissociative flashback episodes, including those that occur on awakening or when intoxicated). **Note:** In young children, trauma-specific reenactment may occur.
   (4) intense psychological distress at exposure to internal or external cues that symbolize or resemble an aspect of the traumatic event
   (5) physiological reactivity on exposure to internal or external cues that symbolize or resemble an aspect of the traumatic event

C. Persistent avoidance of stimuli associated with the trauma and numbing of general responsiveness (not present before the trauma), as indicated by three (or more) of the following:

   (1) efforts to avoid thoughts, feelings, or conversations associated with the trauma
   (2) efforts to avoid activities, places, or people that arouse recollections of the trauma
   (3) inability to recall an important aspect of the trauma
   (4) markedly diminished interest or participation in significant activities
   (5) feeling of detachment or estrangement from others
   (6) restricted range of affect (e.g., unable to have loving feelings)
   (7) sense of a foreshortened future (e.g., does not expect to have a career, marriage, children, or a normal life span)

D. Persistent symptoms of increased arousal (not present before the trauma), as indicated by two (or more) of the following:

> ☐ **Diagnostic criteria for 309.81 Posttraumatic Stress Disorder** *(continued)*
>
>   (1) difficulty falling or staying asleep
>   (2) irritability or outbursts of anger
>   (3) difficulty concentrating
>   (4) hypervigilance
>   (5) exaggerated startle response
>
> E. Duration of the disturbance (symptoms in Criteria B, C, and D) is more than 1 month.
>
> F. The disturbance causes clinically significant distress or impairment in social, occupational, or other important areas of functioning.
>
> *Specify* if:
>
>   **Acute:** if duration of symptoms is less than 3 months
>   **Chronic:** if duration of symptoms is 3 months or more
>
> *Specify* if:
>
>   **With Delayed Onset:** if onset of symptoms is at least 6 months after the stressor

Formulating a Diagnosis

In formulating a diagnosis the clinician evaluates the patient's condition on five separate axes or elements. This practice compels the clinician to consider a broad range of information about the patient rather than to just consider whether he or she has a single disorder. The patient is seen as a multidimensional individual. All persons with alcohol dependence are not the same. Yet providing only this classification gives prominence to the condition and not to the person. By including less obvious information about the patient, a fuller picture of the individual is achieved. The information that the clinician uses to diagnose the patient comes from the variety of sources I have described in previous chapters. Often observing and interviewing the patient will be sufficient. For other diagnoses psychological tests and collateral interviews with individuals who have known the patient will be necessary or will validate observational findings.

In legal contexts a higher standard of information often is sought than is used in clinical settings. Convergent validity is a useful tool to convince a third party that an individual has a mental disorder. This approach uses information from a variety of sources to cross-validate the diagnostic formulation. Relying simply on the patient's own version of his or her history or behavior can invite attack in many legal forums. The psychologist experienced in legal work will be aware of this, but many well-trained nonforensic clinicians may neglect the broader approach until it is too late.

The primary diagnostic consideration is to decide whether a patient meets the descriptive criteria for a disorder that is recorded on Axis I or Axis II or both. Axis I lists florid or more prominent conditions such as posttraumatic stress disorder, described previously. Axis II disorders are usually enduring conditions that begin in childhood or adolescence and persist into adulthood. The separation criteria on two axes is intended to ensure that consideration is given, in adults, to the presence of disorders that may be buried or masked by the more vivid conditions on Axis I. In many instances there are disorders recorded on both Axis I and Axis II.

In the following section I examine briefly the main categories of mental disorder as listed in the DSM–IV. The complete listing is found at the end of this chapter.

Disorders Usually First Diagnosed in Infancy, Childhood, or Adolescence

The disorders in this category are distinguished by usually being evident early in life. They include *attention-deficit/hyperactivity disorder*, which is characterized by inattention, impulsiveness, and hyperactivity; *conduct disorder*, a persistent pattern of conduct in which an individual violates the basic rights of others and major age-appropriate norms; *learning disorders*; and *mental retardation*. Many children who come to the attention of mental health professionals, however, do not have a definable mental disorder and may be manifesting problems in relationships with their parents or other family circumstances.

Delirium, Dementia, and Amnestic and Other Cognitive Disorders

The problems in this category are caused by known physical disorders or conditions (e.g., brain damage). Organic mental syndromes include *delirium*, which is a reduced ability to maintain and shift attention and disorganized thinking as seen in rambling, irrelevant, or incoherent speech; *dementia,* an impairment in memory that is associated with difficulties in abstract thinking, impaired judgment, or personality change. Dementia may become relevant in matters in which an individual's competency to manage funds is contested. The DSM–IV outlines methods of differentiating the normal process of aging from a pathological process. Frequently the diagnosis requires the kind of formal neuropsychological testing I described previously. Some of the conditions in this category arise from abuse of substances such as alcohol or other drugs. Others may be described and measured with the cause remaining unknown.

Mental Disorders Due to a General Medical Condition Not Elsewhere Classified

For the conditions in this category it is judged that the presence of mental symptoms results directly from a medical condition (e.g., congestive heart failure, vitamin deficiency, viral infections).

Substance-Related Disorders

The highly recognizable disorders in this category reflect the symptoms and maladaptive behavioral changes associated with regular use of drugs that affect the central nervous system. The changes are thought to be undesirable in almost all cultures. The drug classes range from alcohol to street drugs to prescription medications. By specifying the particular drug or drugs abused, the typical known behaviors associated with them can be presented in a legal forum as a way to comprehend the user's conduct.

Schizophrenia and Other Psychotic Disorders

The group of disorders in this category is characterized by loss of contact with reality and includes symptoms such as hallucinations, delusions, and disturbances in emotional expression. *Schizophrenic disorders* follow a typical pattern and course and are the largest group of psychotic conditions. Approximately 1 percent of the North American population suffers from this serious mental condition.

Other psychotic disorders may show a more limited range of symptoms than schizophrenia. The essential feature is persistent, nonbizarre delusions, often with paranoid themes. There are a number of types of *delusional disorders*, including erotomania, which can involve the delusion of idealized love (sometimes with a famous person) and stalking the object of this attraction. Other delusion types include bodily processes, imagined unfaithfulness in a lover, and grandiose ideas. Psychosis may also result from substance abuse.

Mood Disorders

Mood is defined as a prolonged emotion that colors an individual's entire perspective and typically involves depression or elation. The group of disorders in this category defines the variation in abnormalities of mood including *major depressive episode* and *bipolar disorder* (manic-depression). Depression is a widespread disorder, and one of the more well-studied of the mental disorders. Many specific subclassifications of depression have been developed that contribute to more exact treatment strategies and predictions of outcome.

Anxiety Disorders

The most common mental disorders involve anxiety and often subsequent avoidance. Feelings of anxiety can be broad and free-floating (as found in *generalized anxiety disorder*) or focused on irrational fear (phobia) of a specific object or situation (e.g., open spaces or *agoraphobia*). Included in this grouping is *posttraumatic stress disorder*.

Somatoform Disorders

The conditions in this category are defined by the emergence of physical symptoms that are not fully explained by physiological mechanisms. Such disorders include *hypochondriasis*, in which those afflicted are preoccupied with the fear of having, or the belief that they have, a serious disease based on the person's interpretation of physical signs or sensations. These symptoms are not under voluntary control.

Factitious Disorders

Factitious disorders are characterized by symptoms (physical or psychological) that are produced intentionally or feigned to assume the role of the patient. They are distinct from *malingering*, in which the symptoms are also produced intentionally but with the clear intent of secondary gain (for monetary compensation or to avoid work or other responsibilities).

In factitious disorders it is thought that the individual has a need to assume the sick role rather than external incentives to do so. This differs from hypochondriasis in that the factitious patient knows that he or she does not have physical disease, whereas the hypochondriacal individual is convinced he or she has a disease for which there is no medical evidence. Usually the judgment that a person has a factitious disorder is made after excluding all other possible causes of the behavior. Malingering may be thought of as an adaptive response, whereas factitious disorders often signal a very serious personality disturbance.

Dissociative Disorders

Ordinarily an individual's identity, memory, and consciousness are integrated. Under some circumstances (after severe stress) a person may suddenly and unexpectedly travel away from home, assume a new identity, and be unable to recall her or his previous identity. This is *dissociative fugue*. Related but controversial categories of *dissociative personality disorder* (formerly multiple personality disorder) and *dissociative amnesia* are also placed in this category. Dissociative personality disorder (DPD) is probably the most debated category in DSM–IV, with a small group of vocal adherents and a much larger group of skeptics. The exponential growth of the diagnosis of multiple personality disorder (MPD) has led many to be wary of this diagnosis. Indeed, when many of the patients diagnosed as having this condition are studied intently they are found to have other disorders that account for their overinterpreted symptoms. Disorders such as substance abuse and borderline personality disorder are some of the more common disorders erroneously (but enthusiastically) diagnosed as MPD (now DPD). Many mental health professionals with a more conservative approach to this controversy suggest that this disorder is iatrogenic—that is, caused or suggested by the therapist, with the patient acquiescing. MPD has been offered in the courts as a defense in criminal trials and as a liability in domestic cases. Whenever it is presented it must be examined rigorously and alternative explanations explored. Dissociative amnesia is the inability to recall important personal information, usually of a traumatic nature, that is too extensive to be explained by ordinary forgetfulness.

Sexual and Gender Identity Disorders

Sexual disorders are divided into three groups. The *paraphilias* include arousal to sexual objects or situations that are not part of normal arousal-activity patterns (e.g., nonhuman objects, suffering or humiliation of oneself or others, or children/nonconsenting adults). *Sexual dysfunctions* are defined as inhibitions in sexual desire or the psychophysiologic changes that characterize the sexual response cycle. *Gender identity disorders* indicate strong and persistent cross-gender identification (the desire to be or insistence that one is of the other sex). Also there is evidence in this classification of persistent discomfort about one's assigned sex or a sense of inappropriateness in the gender role of that sex.

Eating Disorders

This category of mental disorders describes severe disturbances in eating behavior. Included are *anorexia nervosa*, the resistance to maintaining a minimally normal body weight, and *bulimia nervosa*, which is characterized by repeated episodes of binge eating followed by inappropriate compensatory acts such as fasting, excessive exercise, or induced vomiting. Simple obesity (without any compulsive characteristics) is not considered a mental disorder, for it is not associated consistently with psychological or behavioral syndromes.

Sleep Disorders

The disorders in this category are chronic dysfunctions (greater than a month in duration) rather than the transient sleep disturbances that are a part of ordinary experience.

The conditions may be *dyssomnias*, in which the main disturbance is the amount, quality, or timing of sleep, or *parasomnias*, which describe abnormal events (e.g., nightmares, sleepwalking) during sleep.

Impulse-Control Disorders Not Elsewhere Classified

As part of the symptom array of some disorders (substance abuse, paraphilias, schizophrenia) some individuals display problems with inhibiting impulses. This separate category recognizes that even without these predisposing problems, some people are unable to resist impulses, drives, or temptations to perform some act that is harmful to them or others. These disorders include *intermittent explosive disorder*, in which a person's angry outbursts far exceed the precipitant; *kleptomania; pyromania*; and *pathological gambling*. The acts carried out by individuals with these disorders may or may not be planned and are frequently chronic in nature.

Adjustment Disorders

Stressors such as divorce or business losses often lead to expected emotional reactions. *Adjustment disorder* is diagnosed when the reaction exceeds that expected or impairment in occupational or social functioning occurs. The severity of the reaction is not always predictable from the intensity of the stressor. The reaction can be acute or chronic

Personality Disorders

When personality traits are inflexible and maladaptive and cause either significant functional impairment or distress, they are considered to be *personality disorders*. The characteristics must be long-term manifestations of behavior rather than acute aberrations that can appear in many other disorders (e.g., adjustment disorders). The DSM–IV recognizes ten distinct personality disorders. An additional category exists for personality deviations that do not fall into these delineations. One deviation encountered frequently in the criminal courts is *antisocial personality disorder*, which is characterized by irresponsible and antisocial behavior that begins in childhood or early adolescence and continues into adulthood. These disorders are highly resistant to change.

Other Conditions That May Be a Focus of Clinical Attention

This adjunctive listing shows other conditions or problems that clinicians may want to deal with in treatment. These include psychological factors that may affect a medical condition (e.g., symptoms of anxiety influencing recovery from surgery). These additional areas of clinical concern do not have to reach the level of a mental disorder. Also this section records medication-induced movement disorders, relational problems (e.g., partner relational problem), and other problems that do not meet the full criteria for a mental disorder (e.g., occupational or academic problems).

In addition to the recognized mental disorders, the DSM–IV includes as guidelines to researchers a number of types of problems that were proposed for listing as a mental disorder but did not have sufficient empirical support. This recognizes that knowledge of mental conditions is not static and that other criteria for disorders and other categories of disorder should continue to be investigated for possible inclusion. Some of these extra categories include *postconcussional disorder* (acquired impairment in cognitive functioning and other neurobehavioral symptoms that follow a closed head injury), *premenstrual dysphoric disorder* (in common terms, PMS), and *passive-aggressive personality disorder.*

In the DSM–IV classification system Axis III records any general medical conditions that the patient may suffer. Typically this includes only conditions relevant to the understanding or management of the individual's mental disorder. For example, a person with cardiac disease may suffer a concurrent major depression. There need not be a causative association between the two conditions, but the treatment of the depression may be altered by the presence of the physical disorder.

Axis IV provides an opportunity for the clinician to report psychosocial and environmental problems that may affect the existing mental disorder. These may be negative life events (death of family member), interpersonal stresses, or inadequacies of social support or personal resources. Often, affected individuals will have more than one psychosocial or environmental problem, and as many as are relevant should be coded. Usually these are judged to have affected the person in the previous year.

Axis V allows the clinician to rate a person's overall functioning in terms of psychological, social, and occupational functioning on a scale ranging from 1 (e.g., persistent danger of severely hurting self or others) to 100 (superior functioning in a wide range of activities/no symptoms). The quantitative index may be called into question for its subjective nature (although behavioral *pegs* are provided for number ranges). This scale may be useful for comparing the patient at different times (current

TABLE 7.1 Example of a DSM–IV Diagnosis

Axis I:	305.00 Alcohol Abuse
Axis II:	301.6 Dependent Personality Disorder
Axis III:	None
Axis IV:	Estrangement from spouse, threat of job loss
Axis V:	GAF = 55 (current)

and after a period of prescribed treatment), although there currently is little in the way of empirical evidence that it has either validity or reliability for this purpose.

Validity and Reliability

Like the various assessment instruments I have discussed in previous chapters, the value of a diagnostic system is judged by its validity and reliability. Reliability in this context refers to the agreement between different clinicians on the patient's condition at a particular time. If one clinician diagnoses schizophrenia while another diagnoses cannabis abuse, the diagnostic system does not meet the test of reliability. Reliability is dependent on both the system and the skills of the clinician. It is not possible to gauge the overall reliability of the DSM–IV, only individual categories. In research the skill of the diagnostician is usually controlled by employing a number of experienced judges. Some diagnostic categories (e.g., antisocial personality disorder) have very high reliability among experienced clinicians. Reliability suffers in the categories of DSM–IV that are vaguely defined (e.g., anxiety disorder not otherwise specified). These categories are still required because on occasion a patient appears to have a disorder, but the disorder does not quite fit the definition of a primary category. The impression of reliability from notorious court cases is that categories of mental disorder are very unreliable. An expert on one side presents his or her diagnosis, whereas the expert on the other side presents a conflicting formulation. All this demonstrates is that two professionals disagree. If the same patient is presented to one hundred clinicians, it is extremely unlikely that a 50-50 split on diagnostic impression will occur. Rather most clinicians (in the order of 80 to 90 percent) will likely agree on the general category of the disorder. It is wise for lawyers to have a copy of the diagnostic information (such as that for posttraumatic stress disorder) and to review with their expert which criteria they felt the person being assessed had or did not have. This strengthens the preparation, and asking experts under cross-examination exactly which criteria they felt were met can be an effective tool for challenging an expert's diagnostic opinion.

The issue of validity of diagnosis is complex. A physical diagnosis of disease sometimes can be validated by the use of biological tests such as blood tests or CAT scans. These objective indicators are not widely available for mental disorders. Often validity is estimated by the predictive accuracy of a diagnostic category. If the diagnosis of depression is valid, then predictions follow about what one expects of the patient (e.g., sleep and appetite disturbance). The more accurate the predictions, the more valid the diagnosis is thought to be. Validity may be suggested if consistent information is obtained from diverse sources (family members, psychological tests), as I have suggested.

Despite the significant advances in the last several editions of the DSM, criticism of the system remains. Some psychologists have argued against the medical model of classification of abnormal behavior. They have suggested that behavior is too complex to view as merely symptomatic and externally observed. Others comment that the DSM places too much emphasis on categorizing persons rather than on exploring behavioral strengths and weaknesses. A behavioral model that emphasizes what people do rather than what they "have" has been touted as an alternative to the "medical" model of psychodiagnosis. This model has withered against the strengthening scientific foundation connected with modern diagnosis of mental disorders. Even the second version of DSM (1968) was used by over 90 percent of professional clinical psychologists, and DSM–IV will be used by virtually all clinicians for a host of scientific and economic reasons.

Despite occasional criticisms of this evolving classification system, the DSM is a well-entrenched part of the mental health system of North America and will continue to enjoy strong recognition in all legal arenas.

DSM-IV Classification

From the American Psychiatric Association: *Diagnostic and Statistical Manual of Mental Disorders, Fourth Edition,* Washington, DC, American Psychiatric Association, 1994. Reprinted by permission.

(All categories are on Axis I except those indicated otherwise.)

DISORDERS USUALLY FIRST DIAGNOSED IN INFANCY, CHILDHOOD, OR ADOLESCENCE

Mental Retardation
Note: These are coded on Axis II.
Mild mental retardation
Moderate mental retardation
Severe mental retardation
Profound mental retardation
Mental retardation, severity unspecified

Learning Disorders
Reading disorder
Mathematics disorder
Disorder of written expression
Learning disorder NOS*

NOS - Not otherwise specified

Motor Skills Disorder
Developmental coordination disorder

Communication Disorders
Expressive language disorder
Mixed receptive-expressive language disorder
Phonological disorder
Stuttering
Communication disorder NOS*

Pervasive Developmental Disorders
Autistic disorder
Rett's disorder
Childhood disintegrative disorder
Asperger's disorder
Pervasive developmental disorder NOS*

Attention-Deficit and Disruptive Behavior Disorders
Attention-deficit/hyperactivity disorder
    Combined type
    Predominantly inattentive type
    Predominantly hyperactive-impulsive type
Attention-deficit/hyperactivity disorder NOS*
Conduct disorder
Oppositional defiant disorder
Disruptive behavior disorder NOS

Feeding and Eating Disorders of Infancy or Early Childhood
Pica
Rumination disorder
Feeding disorder of infancy or early childhood

Tic Disorders
Tourette's disorder
Chronic motor or vocal tic disorder
Transient tic disorder
Tic disorder NOS

Elimination Disorders
Encopresis
    With constipation and overflow incontinence
    Without constipation and overflow incontinence
Enuresis (not due to a general medical condition)

Other Disorders of Infancy, Childhood, or Adolescence
Separation anxiety disorder
Selective mutism
Reactive attachment disorder of infancy or early childhood
Stereotypic movement disorder
Disorder of infancy, childhood, or adolescence NOS

DELIRIUM, DEMENTIA, AND AMNESTIC AND OTHER COGNITIVE DISORDERS

Delirium
Delirium due to... *(indicate the general medical condition)*
Substance intoxication delirium
Substance withdrawal delirium
Delirium due to multiple etiologies
Delirium NOS

Dementia
Dementia of the Alzheimer's type, with early onset
Dementia of the Alzheimer's type, with late onset
Vascular dementia

Dementia due to Other General Medical Conditions
Dementia due to HIV disease
Dementia due to head trauma
Dementia due to Parkinson's disease
Dementia due to Huntington's disease
Dementia due to Pick's disease
Dementia due to Creutzfeldt-Jakob disease

Dementia due to... *(indicate the general medical condition not listed above)*
Substance-induced persisting dementia
Dementia due to multiple etiologies
Dementia NOS

Amnestic Disorders
Amnestic disorders due to... *(indicate the general medical condition)*
Substance-induced persisting amnestic disorder
Amnestic disorder NOS

Other Cognitive Disorders
Cognitive disorder NOS

MENTAL DISORDERS DUE TO A GENERAL MEDICAL CONDITION NOT ELSEWHERE CLASSIFIED
Catatonic disorder due to... *(indicate the general medical condition)*
Personality change due to... *(indicate the general medical condition)*
Mental disorder NOS due to... *(indicate the general medical condition)*

SUBSTANCE-RELATED DISORDERS

Alcohol-Related Disorders
Alcohol Use Disorders
Alcohol dependence
Alcohol abuse

Alcohol-Induced Disorders
Alcohol intoxication
Alcohol withdrawal
Alcohol intoxication delirium
Alcohol withdrawal delirium
Alcohol-induced persisting dementia
Alcohol-induced persisting amnestic disorder
Alcohol-induced psychotic disorder
  With delusions
  With hallucinations
Alcohol-induced mood disorder
Alcohol-induced anxiety disorder
Alcohol-induced sexual dysfunction
Alcohol-induced sleep disorder
Alcohol-related disorder NOS

Amphetamine (or Amphetamine-Like) -Related Disorders
Amphetamine Use Disorders
Amphetamine dependence
Amphetamine abuse

Amphetamine-Induced Disorders
Amphetamine intoxication
Amphetamine withdrawal
Amphetamine intoxication delirium
Amphetamine-induced psychotic disorder
  With delusions
  With hallucinations
Amphetamine-induced mood disorder
Amphetamine-induced anxiety disorder
Amphetamine-induced sexual dysfunction
Amphetamine-induced sleep disorder
Amphetamine-related disorder NOS

Caffeine-Related Disorders
Caffeine-Induced Disorders
Caffeine intoxication
Caffeine-induced anxiety disorder
Caffeine-induced sleep disorder
Caffeine-related disorder NOS

Cannabis-Related Disorders
Cannabis Use Disorders
Cannabis dependence
Cannabis abuse

Cannabis-Induced Disorders
Cannabis intoxication

Cannabis intoxication delirium
Cannabis-induced psychotic
  disorder
    With delusions
    With hallucinations
Cannabis-induced anxiety disorder
Cannabis-related disorder NOS

Cocaine-Related Disorders
Cocaine Use Disorders
Cocaine dependence
Cocaine abuse

Cocaine-Induced Disorders
Cocaine intoxication
Cocaine withdrawal
Cocaine intoxication delirium
Cocaine-induced psychotic disorder
    With delusions
    With hallucinations
Cocaine-induced mood disorder
Cocaine-induced anxiety disorder
Cocaine-induced sexual dysfunction
Cocaine-induced sleep disorder
Cocaine-related disorder NOS

Hallucinogen-Related Disorders
Hallucinogen Use Disorders
Hallucinogen dependence
Hallucinogen abuse

Hallucinogen-Induced Disorders
Hallucinogen intoxication
Hallucinogen persisting perception
  disorder (flashbacks)
Hallucinogen intoxication delirium
Hallucinogen-induced psychotic
  disorder
    With delusions
    With hallucinations
Hallucinogen-induced mood
  disorder
Hallucinogen-induced anxiety
  disorder
Hallucinogen-related disorder NOS

Inhalant-Related Disorders
Inhalant Use Disorders
Inhalant dependence
Inhalant abuse

Inhalant-Induced Disorders
Inhalant intoxication
Inhalant intoxication delirium
Inhalant-induced persisting
  dementia
Inhalant-induced psychotic
  disorder
    With delusions
    With hallucinations
Inhalant-induced mood disorder
Inhalant-induced anxiety disorder
Inhalant-related disorder NOS

Nicotine-Related Disorders
Nicotine Use Disorder
Nicotine dependence

Nicotine-Induced Disorders
Nicotine withdrawal
Nicotine-related disorder NOS

Opioid-Related Disorders
Opioid Use Disorders
Opioid dependence
Opioid abuse

Opioid-Induced Disorders
Opioid intoxication
Opioid withdrawal
Opioid intoxication delirium
Opioid-induced psychotic disorder
    With delusions
    With hallucinations
Opioid-induced mood disorder
Opioid-induced sexual dysfunction
Opioid-induced sleep disorder
Opioid-related disorder NOS

Phencyclidine (or Phencyclidine-Like) -Related Disorders
Phencyclidine Use Disorders
Phencyclidine dependence
Phencyclidine abuse

Phencyclidine-Induced Disorders
Phencyclidine intoxication
Phencyclidine intoxication delirium
Phencyclidine-induced psychotic disorder
    With delusions
    With hallucinations
Phencyclidine-induced mood disorder
Phencyclidine-induced anxiety disorder
Phencyclidine-related disorder NOS

Sedative-, Hypnotic-, or Anxiolytic-Related Disorders

Sedative, Hypnotic, or Anxiolytic Use Disorders
Sedative, hypnotic, or anxiolytic dependence
Sedative, hypnotic, or anxiolytic abuse

Sedative-, Hypnotic-, or Anxiolytic-Induced Disorders
Sedative, hypnotic, or anxiolytic intoxication
Sedative, hypnotic, or anxiolytic withdrawal
Sedative, hypnotic, or anxiolytic intoxication delirium
Sedative, hypnotic, or anxiolytic withdrawal delirium
Sedative-, hypnotic-, or anxiolytic-induced persisting dementia
Sedative-, hypnotic-, or anxiolytic-induced persisting amnestic disorder
Sedative-, hypnotic-, or anxiolytic-induced psychotic disorder
    With delusions
    With hallucinations
Sedative-, hypnotic-, or anxiolytic-induced mood disorder
Sedative-, hypnotic-, or anxiolytic-induced anxiety disorder
Sedative-, hypnotic-, or anxiolytic-induced sexual dysfunction
Sedative-, hypnotic-, or anxiolytic-induced sleep disorder
Sedative-, hypnotic-, or anxiolytic-related disorder NOS

Polysubstance-Related Disorder
Polysubstance dependence

Other (or unknown) Substance-Related Disorders

Other (or unknown) Substance Use Disorders
Other (or unknown) substance dependence
Other (or unknown) substance abuse

Other (or unknown) Substance-Induced Disorders
Other (or unknown) substance intoxication
Other (or unknown) substance withdrawal
Other (or unknown) substance-induced delirium
Other (or unknown) substance-induced persisting dementia
Other (or unknown) substance-induced persisting amnestic disorder
Other (or unknown) substance-induced psychotic disorder
    With delusions
    With hallucinations
Other (or unknown) substance-induced mood disorder
Other (or unknown) substance-induced anxiety disorder
Other (or unknown) substance-induced sexual dysfunction
Other (or unknown) substance-induced sleep disorder
Other (or unknown) substance-related disorder NOS

SCHIZOPHRENIA AND OTHER PSYCHOTIC DISORDERS
Schizophrenia
- Paranoid type
- Disorganized type
- Catatonic type
- Undifferentiated type
- Residual type

Schizophreniform disorder
Schizoaffective disorder
Delusional disorder
Brief psychotic disorder
Shared psychotic disorder
Psychotic disorder due to... *(indicate the general medical condition)*
- With delusions
- With hallucinations

Substance-induced psychotic disorder
Psychotic disorder NOS

MOOD DISORDERS

Depressive Disorders
Major depressive disorder
- Single episode
- Recurrent

Dysthymic disorder
Depressive disorder NOS

Bipolar Disorders
Bipolar I disorder
- Single manic episode
- Most recent episode hypomanic
- Most recent episode manic
- Most recent episode mixed
- Most recent episode depressed
- Most recent episode unspecified

Bipolar II disorder
- Most recent episode hypomanic
- Most recent episode depressed

Cyclothymic disorder
Bipolar disorder NOS
Mood disorder due to... *(indicate the general medical condition)*
Substance-induced mood disorder
Mood disorder NOS

ANXIETY DISORDERS
Panic disorder without agoraphobia
Panic disorder with agoraphobia
Agoraphobia without history of panic disorder
Specific phobia
Social phobia
Obsessive-compulsive disorder
Posttraumatic stress disorder
Acute stress disorder
Generalized anxiety disorder
Anxiety disorder due to... *(indicate the general medical condition)*
Substance-induced anxiety disorder
Anxiety disorder NOS

SOMATOFORM DISORDERS
Somatization disorder
Undifferentiated somatoform disorder
Conversion disorder
Pain disorder
- Associated with psychological factors
- Associated with both psychological factors and a general medical condition

Hypochondriasis
Body dysmorphic disorder
Somatoform disorder NOS

FACTITIOUS DISORDERS
Factitious disorder
- With predominantly psychological signs and symptoms
- With predominantly physical signs and symptoms
- With combined psychological and physical signs and symptoms

Factitious disorder NOS

DISSOCIATIVE DISORDERS
Dissociative amnesia
Dissociative fugue
Dissociative identity disorder
Depersonalization disorder
Dissociative disorder NOS

SEXUAL AND GENDER IDENTITY DISORDERS

Sexual Dysfunction
Sexual Desire Disorders
Hypoactive sexual desire disorder
Sexual aversion disorder

Sexual Arousal Disorders
Female sexual arousal disorder
Male erectile disorder

Orgasmic Disorders
Female orgasmic disorder
Male orgasmic disorder
Premature ejaculation

Sexual Pain Disorders
Dyspareunia (not due to a general medical condition)
Vaginismus (not due to a general medical condition)

Sexual Dysfunction Due to a General Medical Condition
Female hypoactive sexual desire disorder due to... *(indicate the general medical condition)*
Male hypoactive sexual desire disorder due to... *(indicate the general medical condition)*
Male erectile disorder due to... *(indicate the general medical condition)*
Female dyspareunia due to... *(indicate the general medical condition)*
Male dyspareunia due to... *(indicate the general medical condition)*
Other female sexual dysfunction due to... *(indicate the general medical condition)*
Other male sexual dysfunction due to... *(indicate the general medical condition)*
Substance-induced sexual dysfunction
Sexual dysfunction NOS

Paraphilias
Exhibitionism
Fetishism
Frotteurism
Pedophilia
Sexual Masochism
Sexual Sadism
Transvestic Fetishism
Voyeurism
Paraphilia NOS

Gender Identity Disorders
Gender identity disorder
    In children
    In adolescents or adults
Gender identity disorder NOS
Sexual disorder NOS

EATING DISORDERS
Anorexia nervosa
Bulimia nervosa
Eating disorder NOS

SLEEP DISORDERS

Primary Sleep Disorders
Dyssomnias
Primary insomnia
Primary hypersomnia
Narcolepsy
Breathing-related sleep disorder
Circadian rhythm sleep disorder
Dyssomnia NOS

Parasomnias
Nightmare disorder
Sleep terror disorder
Sleepwalking disorder
Parasomnia NOS

Sleep Disorders Related to Another Mental Disorder
Insomnia related to... *(indicate the Axis I or Axis II disorder)*
Hypersomnia related to... *(indicate the Axis I or Axis II disorder)*

Other Sleep Disorders
Sleep disorder due to... *(indicate the general medical condition)*
Substance-induced sleep disorder

IMPULSE-CONTROL DISORDERS NOT ELSEWHERE CLASSIFIED
Intermittent explosive disorder
Kleptomania
Pyromania
Pathological gambling
Trichotillomania
Impulse-control disorder NOS

ADJUSTMENT DISORDERS
Adjustment disorder
    With depressed mood
    With anxiety
    With mixed anxiety and depressed mood
    With disturbance of conduct
    With mixed disturbance of emotions and conduct
    Unspecified

PERSONALITY DISORDERS
Note: These are coded on Axis II.
Paranoid personality disorder
Schizoid personality disorder
Schizotypal personality disorder
Antisocial personality disorder
Borderline personality disorder
Histrionic personality disorder
Narcissistic personality disorder
Avoidant personality disorder
Dependent personality disorder
Obsessive-compulsive personality disorder
Personality disorder NOS

OTHER CONDITIONS THAT MAY BE A FOCUS OF CLINICAL ATTENTION

Psychological Factors Affecting Medical Condition
... *(Specified psychological factor)* affecting... *(indicate the general medical condition)*
Choose name based on nature of factors.
Mental disorder affecting medical condition
Psychological symptoms affecting medical condition
Personality traits or coping style affecting medical condition
Maladaptive health behaviors affecting medical condition
Stress-related physiological response affecting medical condition
Other or unspecified psychological factors affecting medical condition

Medication-Induced Movement Disorders
Neuroleptic-induced Parkinsonism
Neuroleptic malignant syndrome
Neuroleptic-induced acute dystonia
Neuroleptic-induced acute akathisia
Neuroleptic-induced acute dyskinesia
Medication-induced postural tremor
Medication-induced movement disorder NOS

Other Medication-Induced Disorder
Adverse effects of medication NOS

Relational Problems
Relational problem related to a mental disorder or general medical condition

Parent-child relational problem
Partner relational problem
Sibling relational problem
Relational problem NOS

Problems Related to Abuse or Neglect
Physical abuse of child
Sexual abuse of child
Neglect of child
Physical abuse of adult
Sexual abuse of adult

Additional Conditions that May Be a Focus of Clinical Attention
Noncompliance with treatment
Malingering
Adult antisocial behavior
Child or adolescent antisocial behavior
Borderline intellectual functioning
Age-related cognitive decline
Bereavement
Academic problem
Occupational problem
Identity problem
Religious or spiritual problem
Acculturation problem
Phase-of-life problem

CHAPTER **EIGHT**

Treatment

IF YOU READ IN THE NEWSPAPER that a person had lived an entire life without suffering a single physical malady or injury, you would be amazed. In like manner, it will be virtually impossible to achieve optimal mental health throughout your life. Yet there is a persisting, irrational belief that mental disorders are of concern only to a few. If we take only the categories of anxiety disorders, depression, schizophrenia, and substance abuse—one in every three of us will experience these conditions. Add the several hundred other disorders listed in DSM–IV and you begin to realize that we, our families, our friends, and our colleagues *will* experience some contact with mental disorder. Recent surveys in the United States have suggested that in the course of a year between 16 million and 22 million people receive therapy for psychological problems.

The task of treating mental disorders will fall to a variety of clinicians: psychiatrists, clinical psychologists, social workers, psychiatric nurses, and counselors. Their abilities, orientations, and suitability to a particular patient or client will vary immensely.

To the lay person a mystique surrounds therapists, who may be seen as individuals who are able to *analyze* others rapidly and to prescribe magical advice to solve their problems. This is a distorted image. It is important that a level of trust exist between the patient and the therapist. Beyond that, the methods of behavior change can be demystified easily.

The two fundamental types of treatment for behavioral or mental dysfunction can be subsumed under psychotherapy or biological treatments. The choice of which treatment a person receives is not always an objective decision. A physician may provide a depressed patient with a prescription for an antidepressant medication, whereas a psychologist presented with the patient may offer one of a variety of forms of treatment, based on his or her talks with the individual. Which treatment is better? This is a difficult question to answer. In some situations and with some patients one form of treatment may have advantages (more rapid action, longer-lasting benefits) than the other. With many disorders (e.g., depression) we have a large and varied armamentarium of effective treatments. With others (e.g., personality disorders) fewer effective treatments exist, and even when these treatments are rendered by expert clinicians they often have very modest effects on behavior. Some psychological therapies rendered to men with antisocial personality disorders can actually make them worse (i.e., better psychopaths). In this chapter I will review types of treatment that in most cases spring from the models of behavior reviewed in chapter 2.

Biological Treatments

Drug Treatment

The use of substances such as opium and alcohol to alter behaviors in disordered individuals dates to ancient Greece. However, the wide-scale use of drugs in the treatment of psychological disorders began in the early 1950s. In that period there was an explosion of technology, with the general public accepting that the fruits of technological advances would be preferable over less modern approaches. Most scientists saw the emergence of drugs to alter unwanted behavior as the gateway to a modern way to treat mental disease. Today psychoactive drugs are widely used as the dominant or adjunct form of treatment for a variety of mental and behavioral conditions (see Table 8.1).

In psychopharmacology drugs are classified in a number of ways. They are classed primarily by their clinical or main behavioral action (e.g., antidepressants). Past this general description, however, there may be a more specific classification that is based on the chemical structure or action of the drug (e.g., tricyclic antidepressants). Drugs are often described by other variables such as their potency, latency of onset, and the length of effect. The rate of absorption and speed of action of a drug is in part determined by how it is administered. The usual ways to administer a drug are by mouth, intramuscularly, and intravenously—listed in increasing order of speed of action. *Dosage* refers to the amount

Drug Category	Drug Class	Generic Name	Trade Name
Anxiolytics (Antianxiety)	Benzodiazepine	Diazepam	Valium
		Chlordiazepoxide	Librium
		Oxazepam	Serax
		Lorazepam	Ativan
	Triazolobenzodiazepine	Alprazolam	Xanax
	Propanediol	Meprobamate	Miltown, Equanil
	Hypnotics	Flurazepam	Dalmane
Neuroleptics (Antipsychotic)	Phenothiazines	Chlorpromazine	Thorazine
		Thioridazine	Mellaril
		Mesoridazine	Serentil
		Perphenazine	Trilafon
		Trifluoperazine	Stelazine
		Fluphenazine	Prolixin
	Thioxanthene	Chlorprothixene	Taractan
	Butyrophenone	Haloperidol	Haldol
	Dibenzoxapine	Loxapine	Loxitane
	Dibenzodiazepine derivative	Clozapine	Clozaril
	Benzisoxazole derivative	Risperidone	Risperidal
Antidepressants	Tricylics	Imipramine	Tofranil
		Desipramine	Norpramin
		Doxepine	Sinequan
		Nortriptyline	Pamelor
		Protriptyline	Vivactil
	MAO inhibitor	Pheneizine	Nardil
	Serotonin reuptake inhibitor (SSRI)	Fluoxetine	Prozac
		Fluvoxamine	Luvox
		Paroxetine	Paxil
Antimanic		Lithium carbonate	Lithane
Stimulants		Methylphenidate	Ritalin
		Dextroamphetamine	Dexadrine

TABLE 8.1 Major Types and Names of Drugs

(expressed conventionally in milligrams) of the active ingredient of the drug (not the overall size of the drug compound, which may contain many inactive ingredients). The action of a drug, however, is not always predictable. It is dependent upon the drug history of the individual, the physical state of the individual prior to drug ingestion, the individual's environment, and a myriad of idiosyncratic physiological variables (e.g., hypersensitivities). As dosage increases, however, variables such as environment become less powerful in modifying the effect of the drug.

The first class of psychoactive drugs are the *hypnotics/sedatives*, which all act to depress the activity of the central nervous system. These drugs reduce arousal and motor activity and, in higher doses, draw the patient toward sleep. They tend as well to reduce anxiety. These agents carry the liability of inducing tolerance (requiring more and more of the drug to produce the desired effect) and dependence. Stopping the drug abruptly may result in withdrawal symptoms in dependent patients.

The original tranquilizer was alcohol, which has an eight-thousand-year history. Substances naturally derived from plants (opium and cannabis) also have long histories. In the late nineteenth century a variety of synthetic compounds emerged from the laboratory and in clinical practice found wide use for diverse conditions. Their use has narrowed today, and their main clinical applications include detoxification, sedation, and as anticonvulsants.

Anxiolytics or antianxiety drugs also depress the central nervous system, but they are considered less potent than hypnotics/sedatives, and they have a higher margin of safety. However, these drugs still can be misused with overdose or when combined with alcohol. The volume for prescriptions of these agents reached 100 million in 1973 in the United States alone. Today they still constitute over three-quarters of all prescriptions for psychoactive medications. Because anxiety is the most common clinical condition, it follows that a drug treatment would be equally prevalent. There are strong challenges to this wide use. Little evidence supports the long-term benefits of drug treatment compared to psychotherapy or behavior therapy. Use of anxiolytics is justified when the anxiety level of the patient is too high to permit effective nondrug treatment to take effect. Maintenance on low doses may be useful in patients who do not respond well to the therapeutic alternatives. Unfortunately, their use to treat the chronic minor anxiety that accompanies our everyday lives is too common.

Neuroleptics, commonly called *antipsychotics* (and somewhat incorrectly *major tranquilizers*), ushered in a new era in 1954, when they proved to combat many of the main symptoms of psychotic disorders. This therapeutic breakthrough directly affected the restructuring of the mental-health system with dramatic reductions in the number of beds in mental hospitals. Community treatment of the seriously mentally ill grew proportionately thereafter. All of these neuroleptic agents produce sedation, but their main behavioral action is the reduction of bizarre perceptual and cognitive experiences in the psychotically ill. The responsive patient typically becomes less agitated and excited, exhibits less social withdrawal, and reports fewer hallucinations and delusions. The use of the drugs with patients such as schizophrenic individuals is long-term. Some agents are injected and have a life span of several weeks. Although they are usually used with the schizophrenic population, neuroleptics can also be beneficial in treating psychosis that arises from drug reactions and some incidents of psychosis from brain injury. Treatment is often initiated on an inpatient basis and follow-up continued through an outpatient service. The psychopharmacology industry is aggressively seeking new neuroleptics, and some very effective agents are being investigated further. As with most drugs the improvements brought about by neuroleptics often carry a liability of side effects.

Lithium is a naturally occurring salt that was introduced in 1949 in Australia and soon became widely used in most countries, except the United States, which delayed approval until 1970. It is effective in many cases in the treatment of bipolar disorder (manic depression) and the prevention of relapse of this condition. It does not have an effect on behavior until four to ten days after it is administered.

Antidepressants are employed when an individual's depressive feelings become more than transient reactions to losses or are out of proportion to the precipitating event. A range of different agents have been proven effective in lifting moods in depressed individuals, particularly those with severe forms of depression who have *vegetative* symptoms (sleep disturbance, poor appetite, weight loss, psychomotor retardation). Some antidepressants are also effective in treating obsessive-compulsive behavior, agoraphobia, and even some types of headaches.

Stimulants are the reverse of sedating drugs; they activate or excite the central nervous system. Stimulants such as caffeine and nicotine are ubiquitous in their use. More powerful agents such as amphetamines promote alertness, decreased feelings of fatigue, and increased physical activity. Stimulants have been used to treat morphine addictions, obesity, and depression. The advent of safer, more effective treatments has eclipsed these uses. Current useful applications of stimulants are for narcolepsy (an uncontrollable tendency to sleep) and attention-deficit hyperactivity disorder (ADD). The use of stimulants to treat ADD children has provoked some controversy, but the empirical results clearly support some positive effects of this type of drug for a large percentage of ADD children.

Electroconvulsive Therapy (ECT)

In 1939 Italian physicians Ugo Cerletti and Lucio Bini introduced the technique of administering electric shock to patients with mental conditions. They had seen electric shock used in slaughterhouses and observed that the animals often convulsed after the procedure. With others Cerletti and Bini believed that convulsions were incompatible with schizophrenia. Following this logic, they believed that the induction of seizures in psychotic patients might cure or ameliorate the symptoms of schizophrenia. The technique was widely used during the decade that followed its introduction. With the advent of psychoactive drugs in the early 1950s, however, its use diminished. Its use shifted as well from the treatment of schizophrenia (for which it was virtually useless) to the treatment of severely depressed patients. This application remains, and most modern psychiatric facilities still retain an ECT suite. Approximately fifty thousand individuals in the United States receive this treatment every year from psychiatric practitioners, which is much reduced from past figures. In a recent survey of three thousand psychiatrists, 86 percent responded that they considered ECT an appropriate treatment; yet only 22 percent actually had used it. ECT remains controversial. First, the very idea seems primitive and brutal. The procedure involves attaching two electrodes to a patient's head (usually the right side) and briefly passing an electrical charge of 50 to 140 volts through the brain. For the procedure the patient receives anesthesia and muscle relaxants and is restrained. The patient undergoes an average of seven to nine sessions, usually spaced several days apart.

The overriding question is: Is ECT effective? There seems to be little doubt that its short-term effects can include dramatic and rapid relief from severe depression in 60 to 70 percent of those who receive it. Its more long-term effects, however, are equivocal. ECT has been shown to cause at least temporary and in some cases significant long-term memory problems. Since its introduction the voltage used has been greatly reduced, and recent Magnetic Resonance Imaging (MRI) scans of patients who had received ECT failed to show structural damage of the brain. A rare side effect can be the induction of cardiac arrest in susceptible patients. Most clinicians would argue that the risks of this procedure are minimal when they are compared to the possibility of death by suicide of the depressed patient who has not responded positively to other treatment methods.

Psychosurgery

Surgical intervention is a rarely used form of intervention to alter behavior, but one that is still practiced in North America. Brain surgery to alter behavior recalls Frankenstein images of dark laboratories and stormy nights. The formal genesis of psychosurgery was with the Portuguese neurologist Antonio de Egas Moniz, who operated on the frontal lobes of a schizophrenic woman without benefit of any scientific research to support the radical procedure. He first drilled two holes in her skull and then injected alcohol to damage the lobes that he believed were the source of her disorder. He altered the technique soon after, using a scalpel to sever parts of the frontal lobes. Perhaps because of the status he had earned for his internationally recognized diagnostic work, other physicians accepted this radical and untested procedure and the sparse theory that accompanied it in the late 1930s. He was awarded the Nobel Prize in medicine in 1949, at the height of the psychosurgery era. First named a *leucotomy*, the surgery was renamed *lobotomy* in America. The standard technique was justified as a treatment of highly agitated patients suffering from anxiety or depression or forms of psychosis. By June 1951, over eighteen thousand of these operations had been performed in the United States, with some estimates quadrupling this number. The early clinical reports of the surgery's effectiveness were robust, but later scrutiny of these patients showed dreadful and permanent effects such as seizures, severe listlessness, stupor, and occasional death. Psychosurgery is still performed, however, in rare cases of severe depression, anxiety, and obsessive-compulsive disorders.

Another form of surgery to alter behavior is concerned with the removal of tissue in another region of the body. Judicial castration of sexual offenders has been advanced as an alternative to the use of drugs to suppress sexual urges. In Indiana in 1899 a Dr. Sharp used castration on prisoners convicted of sexual crimes, with the first "therapeutic" castration conducted by Forel in Switzerland in 1892. In the early years of the twentieth century, the treatment became more widely accepted, particularly in the Scandinavian region. In Denmark between 1929 and 1959, 738 castrations were completed—and apparently only ten of these men (1.4 percent) relapsed in offending, a remarkable success compared to other forms of treatment at the time. The findings were also confirmed in Germany and Norway. Despite its success, however, the use of this procedure has greatly been reduced, largely replaced by drug treatment.

Other physical treatments

We experience many biological events or changes (e.g., diet) that have potentially powerful influences on our behavior and that have not been studied systematically. These may gain more prominence in the future.

Psychotherapies

Psychoanalysis

Freud's contribution to the general enterprise of psychotherapy cannot be disputed. He and his followers were the first to demonstrate that a system of treatment could be offered in opposition to biological intervention. Thus all psychotherapies owe Freud a debt of gratitude. Generations of research, however, have failed to support the scientific effectiveness of his particular theory in bringing measurable positive change in human behaviors. Given the need to demonstrate efficacy of treatment in many settings, it is understandable that this form of treatment is no longer as popular as it was in the past. Still, in 1994, 11 percent of therapists identified themselves as principally Freudian psychoanalytic therapists.

As I noted in chapter 2, the treatment of individuals with classical psychoanalysis assumes that the individuals have a history of reducing their anxiety by using defense mechanisms to avoid issues rather than by directly confronting problems. The unconscious becomes the depository for these developmental conflicts. The therapist using psychoanalytic techniques tries to facilitate *insight* into these conflicts and the subsequent emotional difficulties that result. Moving information from the unconscious to the conscious mind is a main goal of the psychoanalytic process. This is accomplished by using free association, dream analysis, therapeutic interpretation, and patient reactions of resistance and transfer.

One of the techniques for uncovering unconscious motives is the exploration of dream content. Freud called dreams the "royal road to the unconscious." Because sleep reduces the effectiveness of the sentry stationed at the border of the unconscious, many unconscious needs, desires, wishes, and fears may manifest themselves in dreams. The content of the dream is still disguised, and the therapist must interpret what the dreams truly mean.

Free association entails the expression of thoughts and feelings as freely and uninhibitedly as possible. The therapist is then responsible for linking these associations or making sense of them as possible expressions of the unconscious. The therapist shares the interpretation with the patient when she or he is prepared to absorb these insights. In therapy it is often necessary to overcome the resistance of the patient. The patient's hesitancy or avoidance is generally thought to be not a conscious but rather an unconscious way of avoiding anxiety. Changing the subject in conversation or suggesting that she or he cannot think of a response are often considered signs of patient resistance. Another element of treatment is the relationship between the patient and therapist. Psychoanalytic therapists believe that patients may come to behave and feel toward their therapists as they would feel toward important figures in their lives. The interpretation of this transference phenomenon is thought to assist in understanding the patient's relationships with others. Therapists, who also have human anxieties, may have unintentional countertransference or inject their own personal issues into the therapy process. Thus the analyst also must assess his or her feelings and thoughts toward the patient and the therapy.

In the movies, the process of psychoanalysis reflects long-term contact between patients and therapists. Recently psychoanalytic therapists have explored ways to shorten therapy. This move has been driven by cost-conscious consumers but also by a lack of empirical support for the benefits of long-term analysis.

Cognitive Therapy

In the early 1960s a New York psychologist, Albert Ellis, proposed that emotions did not flow mysteriously from the unconscious or psychic desires but directly from people's ideas, thoughts, attitudes, and beliefs. Ten years later Ellis's ideas, which the academic community of psychologists had ignored, were being referred to as the "cognitive revolution." Ellis proposed three main insights: (1) that you mainly disturb yourself; (2) that your current self-defeating thoughts are the problem, not past conflict; (3) that it will require active work and practice for the rest of your life to overcome mental health problems and maintain these gains. His form of cognitive therapy, called *rational-emotive therapy,* calls upon the therapist to help patients discover their irrational thoughts that cause emotional responses and to show them how to construct and use more positive ways of thinking. The therapist's job is that of a teacher, with much hard work done by the client.

Irrational thoughts are common daily occurrences for all of us. Some common irrational thoughts include: It is horrible when things are not the way one would like them to be; one should be thoroughly competent, intelligent, and achieving in all possible aspects; and it is easier to avoid than to face life difficulties and self-responsibilities. The rational-emotive therapist will challenge these irrational ideas and help the patient replace them with rational thoughts.

A similar form of therapy was developed by Aaron Beck in the late 1960s, with special emphasis on the treatment of depression. In this condition many people hold negative thoughts, make errors in logic, and overgeneralize their faults, which fuel their mood disturbance. Both Ellis's and Beck's forms of cognitive therapy have been widely studied, and there is strong support for their effectiveness in improving a variety of emotional disturbances. The percentage of clinicians using these techniques continues to grow exponentially.

Humanistic Therapies

Humanistic therapists attempt to have clients (rather than patients) examine themselves and their life situation in an accepting and accurate manner. This treatment typically is offered to individuals who are looking for enrichment rather than to individuals with clear definable mental disorders. Much of the dialogue in humanistic therapy relates to the client's subjective experience of the world. The emphasis is on current stresses, relationships, and goals rather than on the client's history. Humanistic therapies began in the late 1940s with Carl Rogers's *client-centered* therapy. Rogers and his followers tried to create a climate in which the clients would feel supported in examining themselves. Rogers emphasized that the therapist assisted the client through the display of unconditional positive regard, empathy, and genuineness. The goal was to have clients value their emotions, thoughts, and behaviors, and thereby reduce their insecurities. This treatment approach was the first alternative to psychodynamic therapy.

Other forms of humanistic therapies are *gestalt therapy*, which has some of the aims of client-centered therapy but challenges and frustrates clients instead of accepting them, and *existential therapy*, which practitioners define as encouraging clients to take responsibility for their lives, to realize their ability to choose different paths, and to live an authentic life that has meaning and values. Percentages of therapists reporting use of these treatment approaches are 3 percent for client-centered, 1 percent for gestalt, and 5 percent for existential treatments.

Behavior Modification

As we saw in chapter 2, the behaviorist model assumes that many of our actions and our abnormalities are based on the principles of learning.

Therapy that is based on the behaviorism model uses this theory to understand the symptoms that people display. The goal of behavior therapy or modification is to identify an individual's specific and objectively defined behaviors, manipulate the environmental variable that has produced the behavior, and replace the behavior with more appropriate actions. The various *forms* of treatments follow the types of learning described in chapter 2.

Classical conditioning techniques are intended to disrupt the dysfunctional reactions that individuals have to particular stimuli. If a lawyer approaches court appearances with dread instead of excitement, a psychologist might apply the technique of *systematic desensitization*. First, the psychologist has the lawyer construct a hierarchy of fears associated with court appearances (thinking about it, driving to the courthouse, entering the courthouse, standing to deliver an opening, etc.). Then the lawyer is taught the skill of deep muscle relaxation. While she or he is in a state of relaxation, the therapist has the lawyer imagine the scene at the bottom of the anxiety hierarchy. Gradually, the lawyer moves up the hierarchy until she or he can remain relaxed and image the most (previously) terrifying scene. Confronting the scenes, rather than just imagining them, is a treatment option as well. This technique has been proven to be quite successful in reducing a range of phobic reactions, as it is impossible to be anxious and relaxed at the same time, and the scenes are thus *reconditioned*.

Aversive therapy works on the opposite principle—that anxiety responses are created to some stimuli that the patient finds attractive (e.g., cigarettes, children for sexual purposes). By pairing presentation of the object or pictures of the object with aversive stimuli (shock, ammonia, nausea-producing drug), the attraction to the objects will be broken or diminished. This treatment has been shown to have positive short-term results but equivocal long-term benefits.

Operant conditioning treatments are based on the principle of providing reinforcements (or rewards) for appropriate behavior and punishment for undesired behavior. Rewards can be linked to behaviors one wants to increase (exercise, work and study habits, positive social interaction) with the expectation that they will increase. Often the plan of operant conditioning is set out in a behavioral contract by keeping track of the behaviors to be altered and the expectations of meeting or falling short of goals. A member of your firm may be a champion procrastinator. How can you change this specific behavior? First, by recording the sequence of behaviors exactly, you may discover what rewards he is receiving for procrastinating. What does he actually spend his time doing when he is avoiding work on a file? Reviewing his workday in detail might show that he is engaged in so many unproductive activities that he is unable to get to the work he is really supposed to do, and that he is finding some sort of reinforcement for doing this. The goal you set to assist this colleague will not be immediate change but small, specific changes with clearly defined parameters—work on brief X every day from 9:00 to 10:30—and reinforce the conduct through tangible or social means. Gradually the colleague's desire for more productive work habits will increase and his procrastination will decrease.

Modeling is an effective and efficient way to teach new behavior. Shy and unassertive individuals can watch a model act out appropriately assertive conduct and learn the repertoire of skills to succeed in a similar situation. This procedure is effective in reducing a range of anxiety behaviors and other complex activities and can be learned quickly, compared to the slower process of slowly shaping and reinforcing appropriate conduct.

Although most therapy is delivered to individuals, there is also a need for treatment of groups—couples, families, or collections of persons who receive therapy together. In groups with family members the goal is usually to harmonize their relationship past the therapy period. With other groups there is no expectation that the members will have contact with one another afterwards, only that they will join together in the therapeutic process and, through self-revelation, assist the treatment of others while they themselves benefit from the discussion of problems.

Actual therapy or treatment is unlikely to reflect a "pure" variant of the above methods. When surveyed most therapists list themselves primarily or secondarily as *eclectic*, which suggests they are not tied to only one method of approaching a problem. Indeed, most mental disorders have preferred methods of treatment; that is, those that show the highest response rate. However, it is rare for any one treatment to be exclusively appropriate. Additionally, combining a variety of techniques in changing a person's thoughts, emotions, and behaviors may bring optimal results or at least bring results more quickly than a single treatment. With any treatment one can hope for long-lasting effects, but this is more difficult to achieve than short-term change. Therapy then may have to repeated briefly on a periodic basis. In November 1995 *Consumer Reports* published an article that concluded that patients benefitted substantially from psychotherapy, with some suggestion that long-term treatment had some advantages. This poses a problem when insurance or managed-care programs arbitrarily establish a short period of time for treatment.

Can therapy do harm? Undoubtedly this possibility exists through chance, ignorance, or malice. With every drug treatment there are potential side effects that may be more damaging than the initial problem they were supposed to help. Many drug treatments for mental disorders involve the use of multiple drugs, with a potential for adverse interactions among the drugs.

Some unskilled therapists unwittingly may make suggestions to their vulnerable clients that create *false memories*, which may bring cascading devastation to the client and his or her family. Finally therapists may abuse their position over their clients and exploit them for their own personal needs. These are real dangers, but they likely represent a proportionately small problem (but perhaps not so small when the real numbers of people who are harmed are evaluated).

As with most things, the rule of *caveat emptor* reigns. The more qualified the therapist, the more probable that the hoped-for assistance will be achieved. *Therapist* is not a controlled title such as *psychologist* or *psychiatrist*. Having a license in a profession is no guarantee of a therapist's competency in that field. It simply raises the probability of competence.

Some therapy is available through public institutions as well as independent private practitioners. The costs may be borne by the public, by third-party insurers, or by the consumer.

CHAPTER **NINE**

Psychological Testimony

To PRESENT A PSYCHOLOGICAL ARGUMENT in court you need two things: a favorable opinion and a qualified expert to give it. Before you engage an expert witness, however, you should be clear on the purpose and the boundaries of expert testimony. At the heart of the issue is that the opinion of the expert must be helpful to the judge in understanding the evidence or determining a fact at issue in a case. That opinion must extend into an area beyond the knowledge of the nonexpert. Having an expert provide testimony on the obvious will only irritate the judge if the judge allows such testimony at all. Lawyers typically ask the expert to provide an opinion, but this is not necessary. You can elicit a simple discussion of relevant scientific literature without having the expert draw any inference to the specific case you are arguing. That will fall to the judge.

Hiring the Expert Witness

In appendix A I give some advice on how you can find a psychological expert. If you previously have hired experts in other areas, such as engineering, be aware that there is far more variability in skill and training with psychologists. Remember Albert DeSalvo—the type of defense or argument you plan must be matched with the background of the psychologist. Still, with a few telephone calls you will likely have a couple of potential experts from which to choose. Some of the leading and very credible experts in areas of psychological research will not want to appear in fiercely contested legal cases. Take note of an expert's strong reluctance to appear. This reluctance may be a signal that if, with extraordinary effort, you *were* able to persuade the expert to appear, you cannot count on him or her to put in the extra effort you may require. On the other hand, it is even more worrisome if the expert agrees to appear without having heard any of the facts of the case. A credible expert who has experience in providing opinions will want to hear an outline of the case and then provide you preliminary comment on what you are looking for and what she or he has to offer. Very often, a busy forensic psychologist will be unable to accommodate your request for assistance, but he or she will surely have the name of colleagues who might be able to assist. You must also think about the perception of the expert by the court or jury. Sometimes the world's leading academic appearing in a small rural community may not be as well accepted as a local, competent psychologist who shares the language and culture of the community and may be known and trusted by the jury.

Retainer

In the first meeting, you and the expert should deal directly with fees. You should make firm commitments, and fees should not be the focus of any ongoing debate. Be clear—*you* are hiring the expert, and *you* will be responsible for fees unless other, explicit arrangements are being made. Be aware that many psychologists will require a retainer prior to their involvement in a case.

Written Report

Often you will want, and in many instances require, the expert to prepare a written summary of the opinion or a written assessment of your client. Many psychological experts prefer to have the lawyer ask a series of questions to which they provide responses. When the report is received, you can review it with the expert so that you fully understand it and so that you can correct any errors. If you want the psychologist to answer additional questions in the report, this is the time to ask for that information. A psychologist cannot change basic opinions from the draft report, but he or she can augment the opinions with issues that you have raised. The quality of the professional will most likely be reflected in the written document, in which straightforward, objective, and clearly written ideas are communicated. Psychological jargon (which exists in abundance) should be kept to a minimum and most of the information should be explained so that it is interpretable to all participants in the legal process. If the report you receive does not reflect these characteristics, you may be dealing with a forensic novice, but one whose opinion you still need. Seek to have the expert spell out in common terms what she or he is communicating. Interaction between you and the psychologist is a two-way street where there is mutual education of what the pivotal legal and psychological issues are. Often psychologists will not address the ultimate or substantive issue directly, and they will become irritated when you press them to do so. The psychologist who approaches the ultimate question with hesitancy and reserve by deferring to the judge typically will have a more dramatic impact than will the expert who feels that he or she is called to settle the legal argument. Psychologists, unlike experts in other fields, are bound by ethical codes that may restrict the manner in which they express an opinion.

Cicero said that the aim of forensic oratory is to teach, to delight, and to move. The most important task of psychological testimony is to teach—to tell the court what the discipline of psychology has to offer to the case before them. The best experts that I have observed have been psychologists with university or college teaching experience—those used to talking in public about the basic elements of their discipline. On occasion, a good expert should be able to entertain and, in even rarer circumstances, to move the judge, but these skills should be considered bonuses of expert testimony, not a primary goal. If your psychological expert has abundant skill and experience, he or she should need only minimal guidance from you. There are many highly knowledgeable psychologists whose opinion could be beneficial to you but who lack experience as an expert witness. Stanley Brodsky's book *Testifying in Court: Guidelines and Maxims for the Expert Witness* should be mandatory reading for all novices and a good review even for seasoned veterans. In a highly readable and brief form, it offers clear, pragmatic advice that should provide some comfort to those psychologists unfamiliar with the courtroom. Is it your job to train novices on how to be an expert? If your case depends on the testimony of an expert, you'd better be sure the novice is up to the challenge. A little time in review of his or her presentation is time well spent.

When tendering an expert psychologist to the court, you will select a person with specific expertise (e.g., memory) germane to your case. You will desire that the judge and jury perceive the expert as credible. The "hired gun" who is seen by them as an advocate will not advance your cause. Objectivity and openness under cross-examination will raise the expert's trustworthiness. The judge and jury will view the expert as one who is guided by a set of professional ethics, not by the lawyer who retained him. Thus the expert is distanced from any personal motives in appearing at trial.

The psychologist above all must have a specific expertise in the subject by virtue of one or more of the following: knowledge, skill, experience, training, or education. You should enter as an exhibit the full curriculum vitae of the psychologist (be sure to bring multiple copies). Then you should attempt to spell out the most impressive contents of that document. Experienced psychologists who serve as experts may have already developed a set of questions that they prefer to answer.

Admitting an Expert

There are two forms of admitting an expert: the detailed question and answer (Q and A) and the free narrative. The Q and A format proceeds as follows: Do you have a B.A.? Yes. From which university? Stanford. In what year was it awarded? Do you have a master's degree?, etc. I have observed juries and particularly judges roll their eyes at this excessive detail that detracts from the real issue of what information this expert has to offer. It is much better to ask the psychologist: "Doctor, can you outline your university education?" and have the expert briefly summarize her or his past education. This is not to suggest that you should diminish or gloss over areas on which you want to focus particular attention: "Doctor, I note among your many published articles and books a particular piece in the *American Psychologist* on psychological reactions to violence. Can you tell us a little about that article?" Be sure that you know the article and whether it, in turn, has been cited by others in this field. You will lose credibility if the article or study is only peripherally germane to issues in the trial. Often, when you wish to tender a well-known psychologist with impressive credentials, opposing counsel, seeking to avoid a review of those credentials, will stipulate that they have no objection to the expert's qualifications or admission as an expert. Resist the temptation to accept this kind offer and explain that you believe it necessary to point out specifically why your expert is particularly qualified to provide evidence. By increasing the status of your expert, you also boost the expert's persuasive power. If you have entered as an exhibit the curriculum vitae of an expert, the judge can follow along as you highlight sections, and the jury later can peruse the impressive document. At the least you will want to review education (degrees, courses, internships), employment (positions, responsibilities), current license or registration as a psychologist (which states, provinces), memberships and certifications in scientific and professional bodies, publications, special recognitions or awards, and, specifically, experiences in the courtroom (unless this is a first experience).

The psychologist's demeanor in court can have a powerful effect on persuading the judge. A pleasant, nondefensive demeanor will add to credibility as much or even more than level of knowledge. The most desirable experts also have the characteristic of "dynamism"—being energetic, bold, and forceful. They should have the ability to hold the audience's attention.

Preparation and Qualification

Preparation is the key to any case. Early in my career I responded to last-minute calls to court. The lawyer who summoned me would meet me outside the courtroom, brief me while the judge waited, and then examine me in court in an inefficient and ineffective manner. I no longer respond to these hurried pleas because they are the sign of a lawyer who has not done his or her job and who is instead leaning on my skill to "bail them out." In arranging for an expert witness to attend a trial, be realistic in your expectations of time commitment. Remember that you do not control the length of the cross-examination and be generous in estimating time for this as well. A minimum of a half-day should be estimated for any appearance in a courtroom. It will not help your expert's concentration on the stand if she or he is watching the clock and thinking about the important meeting that she or he is scheduled to attend in fifteen minutes. Most forensic psychologists do not bill for court time by the hour but by the day or half-day, reflecting the fact that they must clear this amount of time on their calendar to attend any court function.

After you have qualified your expert, you then proceed to the direct examination. The judge and jury have to follow the sequence of how your expert reached her opinion. First, have the psychologist *describe* the method used in gathering data or forming the basis of the subsequent opinion. Only after the methodology has been described should you have her give the *interpretation* or opinion that resulted. Weight of argument depends upon data and reasons, not simply opinion. Direct examination should not be excessively long—get to the point and make it as strongly as possible.

Cross-Examination

When you prepare with your expert, spend more time on preparing for the cross-examination than the direct examination. Together with the expert you should be able to anticipate most cross-examination questions. The reason that cross-examination is so important is that judges and juries pay more attention to the information derived from cross-examination than from direct. Properly prepared, you can gain, not lose, from this part of the testimony.

It is important to learn how to cross-examine a psychologist. It is always best to retain your own psychologist to review the report you received from opposing counsel and to assist you in the preparation of questions for the opposition's psychologist. This is a cost-effective way of preparing for the cross. Jay Ziskin, a psychologist and a lawyer, published a manual in 1970 (with four subsequent editions) that attacked the scientific basis of both psychology and psychiatry. He provides general principles of cross-examination to discredit experts in these fields. Ziskin suggests that his approach can systematically and methodically reduce the credibility of psychiatrists and clinical psychologists to the point that a judge or jury will not attach much, if any, weight to their testimony. This is a big bill to fill! Any lawyer expecting Ziskin's approach to accomplish this end is very likely to be disappointed. I remember one lawyer who brought the then two volumes of Ziskin into court and laid them conspicuously on the table, knowing that I would recognize them. I did, and I took great comfort in knowing that, if he was relying on Ziskin, I was in for an easy time.

Some of the ideas in Ziskin may have posed troubles for a novice psychologist or psychiatrist back in 1970, but many of his criticisms now are antiquated. Any skilled forensic psychologist can deflect his arguments with ease.

No cookbook of advice on "how to discredit an expert witness" is going to work, because it can pose only general criticisms, not criticisms that are specific to your case. Cross-examination questions for the expert and his or her opinion should be crafted individually by a person as skilled as or, preferably, with more skill than the expert you will be cross-examining. If the opposition's psychologist refers to scientific literature in his or her report or testimony, obtain that document, for he or she may be misrepresenting the information it contains.

With what demeanor should you approach the expert? There is no easy answer to this question, and indeed the style that you start out with may have to shift if you find that it is not working. The aggressive, barrelhouse style of cross-examination is usually ineffective with an experienced expert. It is bound to cause some distress for novices, who are generally anxious about their court appearance. Generally juries do not like all-out attacks on experts who have presented their data in a professional and objective fashion. I have found the most effective cross-examinations of forensically skilled psychologists to be a polite, businesslike (not too friendly) approach that treats the expert with a degree of respect. When they are approached in this way, most experts will be willing to concede more points. When the cross-examination is done properly, I have seen the expert be extremely helpful to the side that is cross-examining him.

The goal of making *their* expert work for you on the stand is, in many cases, achievable. The "hired-gun" expert who is acting as an advocate is unlikely to respond to this professional approach. A more aggressive and direct approach, beginning with a comparative review of his credentials and those of your expert's, will sometimes reveal to the judge or jury the expert's obvious bias and lack of objectivity. Reference to a specific code of ethics may also help with the hired gun. Much has been written on cross-examination techniques and approaches but, as I will point out in chapter 10, the common lore of courtroom tactics has been based on anecdotal evidence rather than scientific scrutiny. A body of research is now building, based on the study of actual cases or, more commonly, with mock jurors, that gives direction to the presentation of psychological information in particular legal situations.

Ethical Issues

In the course of psychological work in the courts, a host of ethical issues arises that you may have to address in testimony. The general principles of ethical conduct for psychologists have been articulated by the American Psychological Association (see appendix B), and some specific ethical guidelines apply to child-custody evaluations (see appendix C). Specific adaptations of these guidelines for individual states and provinces, as well as laws and regulations governing practice, can be obtained using the addresses in appendix A.

The first general principle is *competency*. All psychologists have limitations to their knowledge, experience, and general ability. Even within their areas of expertise it is necessary for psychologists to constantly upgrade to maintain competency. A familiarity with the recent research in the field of expertise should be expected. A psychologist who ventures from her or his area of expertise on the witness stand does so at great peril. When psychologists are asked questions outside of their area of expertise, they should properly say "I don't know." Rather than diminishing their testimony, this acknowledgment of limitations increases their credibility. Inexperienced psychologists may feel that they need to stretch their expertise to cover any and all questions thrown their way.

The next principle of *integrity* extends directly to expert testimony. Psychologists should not make false or misleading statements, and they should not conceal contradictory or disconfirming evidence they discover in their forensic evaluations. In the course of legal work avoid conflicting or dual relationships. For example, in child-custody work it is improper for a psychologist to accept the role of evaluator or mediator for a family when he or she has been engaged previously as a therapist for one of the family members.

Psychologists should not deflect responsibility from the opinions they give in writing or oral testimony. They should make every effort to ensure that the services or products they provide (e.g., test results) are not misused or misrepresented by others.

Often there are ethical dilemmas in servicing the rights of the client in forensic contexts because there is more than one client. Is the client the individual being examined, the lawyer, the court, or society? Offered opinions may have a detrimental effect on an individual's welfare in the case (e.g., criminal defendant, parent seeking custody, or plaintiff seeking compensation). The duty of truthfulness overrides these considerations.

If you are involved in many cases that require psychological evidence, you undoubtedly will develop an ongoing relationship with experts whom you find useful to your work. These experts are good conduits to other experts, both within subspecialties of psychology or in related disciplines. The benefit of an ongoing relationship is that you and the psychologist know what to expect from each other and can work together more efficiently. You will likely begin to use your psychologist experts in diverse ways from your initial introduction to the science.

CHAPTER TEN

Psychological Consultation on Legal Issues

UNTIL RECENTLY, THE BEHAVIOR OF LAWYERS and other participants in the justice system have not received scientific scrutiny. There are endless decisions or questions about specific aspects of legal practice such as: Should criminal trials be joined? How do community standards influence legal decisions? How reliable are eyewitnesses? How should the testimony of child witnesses be weighted? How competent are children to testify? Does "stealing thunder" (presenting negative evidence about your case) help in civil and criminal cases? What are the most effective words to use in opening and closing statements? To respond to these questions lawyers have relied upon folklore from their firms or from their own experience. Now, however, there is a developing alternative that goes well beyond these unreliable techniques. More and more behavioral scientists are studying the trial process, particularly the importance of jury characteristics and trial procedure. This information is then taken out of the laboratory or research setting and applied to a trial. One of the first practical summaries of this work was published by Michael Nietzel and Ronald Dillehay in 1986, and the field has expanded exponentially since that time.

Because of the volume of information now available, I will select representative questions that the trial consultant will face rather than attempt a comprehensive survey. If you have a question about trial

The Jury

> I'd stay away from women. They would have no sympathy for the rapists, but they place a higher value on life. Taking an M-16 and blowing their heads off is something women just don't understand. You and I understand it because we're fathers. It appeals to us. The violence and blood doesn't bother us. We admire him. You've got to pick some admirers on that jury. Young fathers with some education. (John Grisham, *A Time to Kill* [New York: Dell Publishing, 1989], 308-309).

Every lawyer who has participated in jury deselection has used some overt or covert method of reducing perceived bias from the venire. Clarence Darrow advised that he did not want Scotchmen or Scandinavians on a jury, and that the Irish were best for the defense. Other lawyers have cautioned against certain *types* of jurors and championed other types, according to the lawyers' perceived goals. Perhaps a few of these guidelines have merit, but most of them undoubtedly have the validity of a horoscope.

Psychological studies of jury selection and behavior have accumulated for twenty-five years, and specialized social scientists now offer their services in assisting lawyers in this area. There are historic and recent celebrated trial successes (e.g., William Kennedy Smith) that seem to highlight the advantages of scientific jury selection, but these successes amount only to case studies, with very little in the way of strong empirical support for the use of this expensive process.

If you contrast the clinical assessment of an individual by a trained psychologist who uses all the latest personality and ability tests *with* the individual's cooperation to the brief and very incomplete snapshot of the potential juror, the chance of error in deselection is enormous. Most scientists also suggest that the personality variables of jurors account for very little of the variance in outcome. Within the body of information on jury members three characteristics seem worthy of consideration in deselection. The first is *authoritarianism*, that is, individuals who have traditional values and punitive attitudes toward those who violate societal norms. Individuals who have this trait tend to support conviction in criminal trials, along with heavier sentences. However, if the accused also has these traits or has a profession that infers authoritarianism (e.g., police officer), then this trait may be desirable in a juror.

Social psychology has long established that we are generally attracted to individuals possessing similarities to ourselves.

Another long-established psychological dimension is *internal versus external locus of control*. Individuals with internal locus of control believe that their own behaviors are responsible for their outcome or situation, whereas externally oriented individuals believe that forces outside of their control are at work. Thus, persons with internal locus of control are more likely to require others to assume responsibility for their behavior.

Still another belief that may be important in juror selection is referred to as the *just world* belief. This term defines a dimension by which people accept or reject the idea that they get what they deserve in life. This belief, like most beliefs, arises from our experience that life is not a random series of occurrences for ourselves or others and from the almost innate human need to attribute events to some *cause*. Depending on the facts of a case and how it is presented, individuals holding a just world belief can be harsh on the defendant or the alleged victim. The main difficulty in applying this information in jury review is how to gauge these dimensions with any reliability using the limited information available on the potential juries and the limited ability to question them directly. Still, questions can be crafted to attempt at least some indication of these beliefs (see Frederick, 1995, for an excellent and practical approach for jury selection). Some have challenged the very notion of jury selection. The British system, which allows little in the way of deselection, is not often cited for producing juries that are biased. The consensus is that scientific jury selection may play a minor role in most trials and that it is occasionally very important. However, the element of error in juror selection is high, and the field of scientific jury selection is still at an early stage in its development.

In his book, *In Contempt*, Christopher Darden concludes appropriately that the O. J. Simpson jury pool was a nightmare for the prosecution: a collection of bitter and angry black citizens who carried the sum of their experiences and beliefs into the courtroom. Yet to his credit, Darden agreed that to evade this venire for a more favorable one would be another side of "playing the race card." The jury pool had the duty and privilege to serve the community in this way, and the pool must be accepted as representing that voice. Once again we come to realize that the courtroom reflects a myriad of human values and attitudes, and that the scales of justice do not respond to a pure objective evaluation of fact.

The scientific study of the jury includes much more than the psychological dimension of jurors. The process of jury decision making is in many respects more interesting and potentially more useful than the preoccupation with getting the *right* jury. At the heart of the jury deliberation is the fact that the verdict will reflect a group decision that is far different from a simple compilation by an individual. As in all social groups, specific roles will be established among the group. Krauss and Bonora classified individual jury members in the following way:

a) **leader.** In every group a person will emerge, usually based on status, intellectual ability, and prior leadership roles, who will direct the deliberations. These characteristics are often quite evident during selection.
b) **followers.** Passive members of the panel who will support the views of a more dominant member.
c) **fillers.** Individuals who go along with the majority, often because of difficulty in forming their own independent views.
d) **negotiators.** Individuals who operate to reduce conflict in the group and attempt to facilitate compromises. They operate as nondominant leaders.
e) **holdouts.** These individuals reject leadership and authority. Often they cause delays in decisions, but only 6 percent of trials end in deadlock.

Not every jury will contain each of these types. Understanding these roles, however, may influence how you present testimony to them. In jury votes individual members may have different motives for voting in a particular direction on a particular day. It is well known that the minority jurors on a vote do not simply capitulate to the majority. It is equally well known that the minority can influence the rest of the jury to accept their position and to vote unanimously for that position. Group pressures and strong-biased opinions can influence juries, for there is no evidence that juries behave in fundamentally different ways than any other social group. In their deliberations juries spend time discussing their personal experiences, their opinions (on issues not relevant to the finding of fact), the procedural questions of the trial, the instructions of the judge—and only a small amount of time discussing the actual testimony. Consider any group in which you have participated when a decision has to be made. Reflect on the conflict and social influence that tends to take place in making the decision, regardless of the importance of the issue.

Eyewitness Testimony

Eyewitness testimony was one of the earliest forensically relevant issues studied by psychologists. At Columbia University J. McKeenan Cattell quizzed his students on their perceptions as witnesses of everyday events and was awed at how inaccurate and unreliable this group of intelligent subjects was. The year was 1893. Since that time numerous studies have focused on this topic and have, for the most part, reinforced Cattell's early findings that our abilities as eyewitnesses are not as strong as we generally believe them to be. One prosecutor challenged me, when I was reviewing this topic in court, that I was saying that *any* statement by *any* eyewitness could not be believed. Of course this is incorrect, as our perceptions and memory abilities serve us quite well. It is important, nonetheless, to know how these faculties can generate errors so that we are not overconfident of information provided by an eyewitness.

The eyewitness relies on two related processes—perception and memory. Errors in perception have been studied to understand how witnesses to criminal acts perform. Perception, particularly in these situations, is shaped by attention. A frequently reported effect during the commission of a crime is referred to as the "weapon-focus effect," in which the observer's attention is narrowed to this novel and dangerous element and thus drawn away from other elements of the scene (e.g., physical features of the perpetrator). Witnesses' perception of time during a crime also is often distorted in predictable ways. For example, most witnesses overestimate the duration of an observed criminal event.

Memory is the key to the reliability of eyewitness testimony. Many types of memory have been studied, but when we refer to memory we often mean recollections of our own experience or our *autobiographical* memory. If you had to describe how your memory works, you probably would make some analogy to other devices in your world that have *memory*. Our computers have memory—we input information to the computer, which, barring catastrophe, stores it perfectly without altering it and allows us to retrieve the information with little trouble. We also may think of memory as a videorecording of events we experience. When we want to remember the experience, we pop it into our video player and it gives us the exact sequence that we experienced. Human autobiographical memory, however, is very different from these two models. In the first place the amount of information that we encode, or place in memory from our everyday experience is very small—we are highly selective in what we encode, and our emotional arousal (if too low or high) may impair the recording of information as well. Do we have in our memory a record of what we ate for breakfast for the past three years? The answer is no, there is typically no reason to use valuable memory space for useless information. This is not to say that all of our memories are only of functional utility, but this is certainly a consideration that shapes our input of information.

After we have encoded information in memory, it is stored. Unlike the computer or videotape, our memories are not protected from disturbances while they are in storage. It is a maxim that memories fade, often surprisingly rapidly. Everyone who has ever studied for an exam will relate the experience that they have more confidence that their memories will be better if they study the day prior to an exam than if they study the same material even a week earlier. More interesting is the fact that even the information that is retained in memory can be altered while it is in storage. New information can alter old memories. All autobiographical memories, then, are malleable, not static and impervious. Misinformation can be introduced into memory and meshes with true memories. From that point on it would be difficult if not impossible for the person experiencing the memory to differentiate what is real from what was false about the memory. With the right situation people can even come to believe that they have had experiences that they did not have!

How can this happen? For more than sixty years psychologists have agreed generally that autobiographical memory is a highly constructive process. We take out of memory the small fragments of the event that have been stored (often along with other unrelated memories) and reconstruct the event we experienced. This reconstruction is an interesting process that can be shaped by how we view the event now (negatively or positively), as well as what we think *should* have happened on that day. It is expected that two individuals attending the same event will provide different reconstructions of the event. But how can we remember entire events that never happened to us? Elizabeth Loftus and her students have provided a number of examples to support this contention. In one study subjects were convinced by family members that they had been lost in a mall when they were younger. Although they had no initial memories of this (because it never happened), the subjects gradually began to develop vivid memories of the event. Even when they were told about the deception of the experiment, the subjects struggled with the belief because the memories seemed so real.

In chapter 6 I reviewed the importance of proper interviewing of children so that the probability of suggestibility is reduced. Improper questioning and suggestion (even outside of hypnosis) can have a powerful effect on the recall of both children and adults. Stephen Cici of Cornell University has produced a wealth of scientific information on children's testimonial accuracy and their suggestibility from adults. However, from his and other studies it is clear that children are capable of accurately recalling forensically relevant information. We simply have to be aware of the many postevent distortions of information that can take place (particularly with preschool children). Many researchers are now turning to development of optimal conditions for improving recollection by children of events that are important for courts to discover.

Presenting Evidence

In contrast to the amount of attention they gave to jury selection, an event over which small but ambiguous control may be exerted, social scientists for a number of years give little attention to the powerful and controllable aspect of a trial—the method of presenting evidence. In jury trials we know that jurors have difficulty comprehending fundamental issues such as legal probability and, in criminal trials, reasonable doubt. Lawyers can assist them through repetition of these critical issues throughout the trial.

Although it is not part of the formal evidence in a trial, the opening statement can be so important to the perceptions of the jury that it overrides real evidence. The opening is seen as an opportunity of *conditioning* the jury. Studies of jurors' decision making shows that they do not suspend their opinions until all evidence is rendered. Very early in the trial they form strong opinions on the issues, which they tend to maintain throughout. A well-researched phenomenon in psychology is that we tend to distort or ignore information to fit our already formed ideas. The opening statement will form a framework or schema that will influence jurors' interpretation or even perception of data that is presented to them during the course of a trial.

A persuasive argument at the beginning of the jury trial is critical to success. But often you cannot predict exactly how evidence will unfold. Is there danger in promising too much? Yes and no. If you promise evidence that does not materialize, this *evidence* already has had its impact in the opening statement. An unsubstantiated claim can have dramatic impact. However, at closing, if the opposing counsel reminds the jury of the missing evidence that was promised, then this may cause the jury to doubt other aspects of your case. Therefore, if an anticipated witness or piece of evidence fails to materialize for you, it is far wiser to admit that your case would have been stronger if you had been able to supply the witness but that this was out of your control.

You should put more work into the opening statement than into any other part of the trial. It might be argued that part of the opening statement should cover what the judge's instructions to the jury usually encompass, for when the instructions are delivered at the end of the trial, they are often ineffective: The jury is told is to weigh evidence *after* they have already done so!

Procedural law may limit your scope in referring to law rather than the evidence. By joining concepts to the evidence you intend to offer, however, you may achieve this aim. Although you will have much more latitude in closing argument, remember that at that point you will be trying to influence individuals who have made up their mind—a much more difficult task than persuading the uncommitted. Your references to burden of proof and legal probability should use metaphor or analogy, with yourself as an example: "When my child came home from school and told me a story, I didn't know what or who to believe...." To encourage the jurors to try to suspend judgment, tell them how difficult this is—even you have erroneously prejudged a person on the skimpiest of evidence only to discover later how wrong you were. Tell them that when they find themselves uneasy and switching opinion during the trial, this is a good indication that they are doing their job—weighing each piece of evidence as it is presented and withholding a final opinion until the conclusion of the trial. The jury will not only be evaluating evidence, they will be evaluating *you*—are you honest, full of yourself, a bully, or simply dull? Express your confidence and trust in them; you have no choice, but this signals to them your high opinion of their ability. We tend to reciprocate to those who are so perceptive as to acknowledge our excellent abilities. Extending appreciation to jurors for fulfilling their duty is also never a waste of time. Remember that people are attracted to others like them—try not to distance yourself from the jury in your demeanor, vocabulary, or dress.

Although many lawyers consider the closing argument to be the most important aspect of a trial, social scientists have repeatedly assigned it a minor role, as compared to the opening statement. Do not let this last opportunity escape you. In a trial, the evidence on occasion is overwhelming, and the jury's decisions made early. The closing argument is a time to refresh the jury about the opening statement (which may have been given weeks earlier) and to trigger their memories of your persuasive opening: Have you done what you said you were going to do?

Closing tends to be most effective when it is tied closely to the opening. Should you spend some of your last precious minutes before the jury critiquing your opponent? There is some division of opinion about this. If you do want to turn your attention to the shortcomings of your opponent's case, do it quickly and politely. Then leave the jury with your brilliant summation of your case. It goes without saying that you should not expend precious time reviewing the faults in your case and trying to explain them away—this leaves a very weak impression with the jury. During the course of the trial "stealing thunder" can be a good tactic—acknowledging your weak points and thereby not allowing the other side to pound away on legitimate difficulties. However, this expression of your integrity is not advisable on exiting the case.

Given the difficulty that ordinary individuals have in processing the vast amount of information in a trial, how should your closing statement or argument be presented? Recall that all people retain data that are joined together by natural association. You should attempt, whenever possible, to "tell a story" or narrative that will naturally hang together. It has to hang together because of jurors' limited memory skills (in some jurisdictions, note taking by jury members is not allowed).

Even better than telling is showing events—visual demonstrations can leave unforgettable impressions. I once was retained by the prosecution in the murder trial of a man who had killed another by driving several dozen three-and-a-half-inch nails into his head and body with a pneumatic gun. Throughout the trial the air compressor used in the crime sat in the courtroom directly across from the jury. A demonstration of the machine was given early in the trial, the thud of the gun which drove the nails reverberating in the courtroom. Thunk, thunk, thunk. To this day, the jurors no doubt remember those sounds.

The members of a jury do not possess "the cold neutrality of an impartial judge" (one could argue about this description by the eighteenth-century Irish statesman Edmund Burke); nor have they trained themselves to weigh and discard evidence both on its material merits and on its admissibility. Jurors not only weigh inadmissible evidence, but when instructed to disregard it by a judge, they put more weight on it. Jurors also have been found to be influenced by other irrelevant considerations such as a trial participant's demographic variables—age, sex, clothing, and physical attractiveness.

Can you neutralize some of these influences? This remains an empirical question, but it certainly is possible. Most extraneous influences are not overtly perceived by the jury members. They are unaware that they have been influenced, for example, by the baby-faced appearance of the defendant. If you want to counteract these influences (and sometimes you will not want to), make the jury aware that they may be influenced by these factors (as most normal people are apt to be) but that you are confident that they can control these natural biases and render a verdict that reflects their impartial weighing of the facts. Most people, as I discussed earlier, are unaware of the many influences on them in their social environment. The whole notion that these are outside of their control runs contrary to the general wish to self-determine behavior, thoughts, etc.

Using Trial Consultants

To achieve the maximum benefit from consultations with psychologists on trial issues, their early advice and involvement is crucial. The consultant must have a comprehensive scope of the case and the main argument you wish to advance or the theory of your case. It has been my experience, as well as that of other psychologists who act as trial consultants, that lawyers sometimes treat with skepticism the fresh perspective of our discipline. However, this initial skepticism soon reverts to keen interest and acceptance of an alternative approach. A creative suggestion by a party less tied to the case can get you out of the thinking rut that sometimes develops with a difficult trial.

The main resistance or criticism in this field comes not from lawyers but from psychologists not involved in the legal system who question the ethics or fairness of assisting one side in the adversarial system. The trial consultant certainly is not hired as an objective forensic examiner to offer opinion evidence. Rather he or she is hired to provide partisan assistance. Indeed, when you look a little closer it is the very notion of an adversarial legal system that is at the heart of some psychologists' uneasiness. Scientists who seek a representative sample in a population will likely randomly select individuals from the entire population. They certainly will not try to gather subjects who are most likely to behave the way they want them to against a rival scientist who has selected subjects partial to his theory. Trial consultants still are guided by ethics of their profession and by codes of conduct, and they have come to accept the adversarial legal system, however flawed, as they the one in which they have chosen to work.

CHAPTER ELEVEN

Negotiation and Mediation

ONE OF THE FUNDAMENTAL ASPECTS of human socialization is the resolution of opposing preferences. Jurisprudence evolved essentially as a formal way of assisting people in reaching these resolutions. Reaction to disputes is varied. The first reaction is often *struggle* or *contest*, characterized by military battle, political engagement, or sporting events. Most legal conflicts begin this way with threats, affidavits, and the launch of suits. In ages past two combatants would emerge on the field and proceed to cudgel each other until only one limped away victorious. Life is rarely as simply as this. As is readily obvious, struggle carries many disadvantages, including the potential of grievous loss (of life, money, time, etc.), and it endangers the potential future relationship between the parties. The one advantage of struggle over other methods of dispute resolution is that a party can choose to initiate battle independently of action by the other.

Struggle has always been popular with the human species because it frequently arises from an emotional reaction or foundation. It is summarized in one modern word: *war*. This word has a complex etymology with analogies suggesting strife and confusion. Throughout the enlightened ages, however, the use of force was never the preferred but often the necessary last form of action. The much quoted *The Art of War*, compiled by a mysterious Chinese warrior/philosopher over two thousand years ago, has as its main premise the goal of winning without fighting. The chief reason for this fundamental motive in warfare was that very few powers were so foolish as to think that they were invincible. To begin a battle suggests that you are willing to lose. Lawyers who consider that they have a case that they "can't lose" at trial are waiting for a fall. All contests can be lost—even by champions.

When one cannot decide the outcome of a battle independently, an arbitrator or judge is employed to gauge the points made and appraise a "winner." This is the model many people turn to when considering the courtroom as a battleground. The parallels between pretrial and courtroom tactics and military strategy abound—the Blitzkrieg, the siege, the Trojan Horse. Make no mistake about it, the trial has many elements of a battle, and it is your obligation to provide the best services for your client in this contest. The literature on courtroom tactics is abundant, if untidy. It suffers greatly from the lack of empirical substance in its advice to practitioners. Before you don the armor and draw the weapons, is there a better way?

Negotiation

In the past few years there has been a growing attraction to what is casually termed *alternative dispute resolution* (as opposed to traditional litigation). ADR (as the advocates refer to this approach) is certainly not revolutionary, for many of its principles have evolved slowly. With rising costs of litigation, however, the search for different courses has been pursued more vigorously. The preference for conciliatory procedures has been shown to have a strong cultural element, and it might be argued that the last twenty years have seen a change in Western legal culture that has allowed the growth of ADR approaches. The more radical of the approaches is mediation, but this is simply a variation of negotiation, a behavior that we have used since the beginning of civilization and that we each use on a daily basis. What is perhaps more exciting is the recent scientific exploration of what works in negotiating processes and what does not.

Although prohibitive costs and a favorable climate for negotiation of out-of-court dispute settlements have been a catalyst to growth, negotiation has always been a mainstay of the law. Even when preparing for courtroom battle, skilled legal counsel continue to communicate and negotiate settlement or agreement. Ninety percent of litigation settlements are reached through negotiation rather than arbitration, so in some respects it is more important to develop negotiating skills than trial advocacy. In negotiation there is choice in finding an acceptable solution, and this choice evaporates with struggle. Beyond the law, the necessity of successful negotiating is a vital element for almost any social interaction.

The study of negotiation has several traditions. Driven by economists and *game theorists,* a mathematical model of negotiation emerged as early as 1930 and began to flourish in the 1950s. This type of scientific model of negotiation examines a rational solution in competitive situations. It offers a predictive formula for how we *should* resolve or negotiate particular solutions. Game theorists would do quite well on Vulcan, where Mr. Spock and his comrades could easily accept the mathematical solution to a proposed agreement. Unfortunately, on earth humans have a tradition of less rational conduct.

Building on the mathematical models of negotiation, psychologists began to study the actual behavior of negotiators. Their purpose was to develop theory, as well as a way of helping real-world negotiators. In this work behavioral scientists focused upon the characteristics of individual negotiators, studied their motivations in the negotiation process, and analyzed the cognitive processes negotiators displayed in different stages. A comprehensive analysis of this literature has been provided by Leigh Thompson (1990) and Peter Carnevale and Dean Pruitt (1992).

The negotiating situation begins with the following characteristics:

1. the parties believe that they have conflicting interests
2. communication remains possible
3. compromise/agreement remains possible
4. provisional positions are exchanged and counteroffers presented
5. proposals of settlement are not final until acceptable to both parties

Negotiation research has studied the parties approaching negotiation, the interests of the parties, and the negotiation process and outcome. Unfortunately most real-world negotiators do not begin with a full assessment of the negotiation situation. Negotiation should start with a clear understanding of the parties and of the degree of conflict that they have. It is always amazing to discover that two individuals involved in a dispute have fundamentally different perceptions about what the conflict is all about. Too often the assumption that the parties are "too far apart" is drawn before an actual analysis. It is rare that the parties have pure conflict, meaning that to increase one party's benefit subtracts the same amount from the other's. There are also occasions when coordination can occur between parties, in that their goals are actually different and compatible. Negotiations define this reality and work cooperatively to achieve these aims. The most common situation is referred to as an *integrative* one in which the parties' interests are not purely opposed or completely compatible. Gains by one party do not generally represent an equal loss by the other. Parties to a disagreement usually have different priorities that might lead to trade-off tactics. But failure to complete a comprehensive assessment and knowledge of both parties and their interests is the number one mistake in negotiation.

Common Negotiation Strategies

Once a situational analysis is completed the parties, or more commonly their representatives, marshal a strategy. The three most common strategies are *concession making* (or yielding), *contending* (or forcing the other party to yield), and *problem solving* (looking for new options to satisfy both parties). Concession making and contending are simply posturing forms of battle and are the most traditional in negotiating behavior. However, it is commonly found in real negotiating that all three strategies are necessary, even though they are incompatible at a given time. This may mean that a sequence of strategies occurs quickly, oscillating between parties yielding and contending or different members of a negotiating party portraying opposing strategies. Often we see *official* positions and strategies as unyielding, whereas in private settings the negotiators earnestly discuss potential options. By focusing on the issues and their differential priorities, negotiators can use different strategies on different issues.

Much of the research on strategies has focused on the more traditional concession/contending pattern. We know from experimental studies, for example, that time pressure can affect outcome of negotiations in that, when a single issue is being negotiated, lower demands, faster concessions, and a rapid agreement occur.

Cycle of Negotiations

Negotiations are often viewed as a cycle. At the start of negotiation a tough stand by one party is often followed by a moderate demand by the other party, and vice versa. This phenomenon is referred to as mismatching. This may simply relate to a distancing that disappears in the middle of the negotiation cycle when matching becomes the norm. At this point concession by one party will be followed by concession by the opposing party—interpreted by behavioral theorists as reinforcement for cooperation and movement toward the goal of agreement. Mismatching often returns at the end of the negotiation cycle. Although both parties have often moved toward compromise, they slow at the end and begin gauging how much they have given up in comparison to their opponent. Both sides also display the attitude that they may be at their limit of concession with a negotiator's "no man's land" standing between them. This last, often small gap is frequently difficult to close unless a time demand is placed on the parties. Concessions are, of course, tied to risk taking if an agreement is not achieved. In civil law negotiating, the expected judicial decision is important in determining how much risk either side is willing to take in achieving a settlement. Parties may break off negotiations if they anticipate a more favorable outcome at trial and when the costs of the trial are subtracted. Negotiation is risk-free—a trial is never risk-free, even if the party has a high level of confidence in the outcome. Nonetheless an evaluation of relative trial risk will usually assert itself in the negotiation cycle, particularly at the closing of negotiations when the party with less trial risk may be expected to take a firmer stand and use the differential to squeeze some last small concessions. The use of senior negotiators at the conclusion of negotiations also is effective in that, if authoritative firmness is needed, this is more effective and credible coming from high-status individuals, particularly if they have a history of carrying out their intentions. At the end of negotiations it is useful to provide external evidence that limits of concession have been reached and further demands cannot be met.

Being aware of the cycle of negotiations will often lead to overall strategies in approaching the talks. Often a pattern of setting high demands at the outset of negotiations allows a party to give regular concessions and move the discussions more rapidly. If the demands at the outset are too high, however, this may elicit anger from the other side and stall the process.

Less research has been conducted on problem solving as a negotiation tactic. Nonetheless it holds a great deal of promise. In this model both sides search for ways both to enhance their position and that of the other side as well. This promotes the win-win possibility. In laboratory experiments of problem solving, parties differentially prioritize multiple issues and each party *wins* on the issues it values most. *Logrolling* is the term often used to describe this method of problem solving. Win-win solutions also can be met by expanding the pie that is to be shared so that both parties receive a larger share than they originally anticipated, compensating the loser with something of value when a concession is necessary, cutting the loser's costs in the action, and actively creating new options that have not been previously brought to the bargaining table. In the famous Harvard Negotiation Project this last option was explored in detail with the goals, values, and interests of both parties analyzed and the goals of negotiation reconceptualized to fit them.

Personal Traits of Negotiators

The personal characteristics of negotiators have also received some scrutiny. Roger Fisher and William Ury (1981) describe effective negotiators as displaying the balance of firmness and flexibility. They must be firm on the fundamental interests but flexible on how to achieve the goals. Their participation in the Harvard Negotiation Project led them to an alternative to positional bargaining of concession and contention that they called principled negotiation or negotiation on the merits. They boiled their method down to four basic points:

1. Separate the people from the problem.
2. Focus on interests, not positions.
3. Generate a variety of possibilities before deciding what to do.
4. Insist that the result be based on some objective standard.

Fisher and Ury's premise is that participants in negotiation are problem solvers who can achieve a wise outcome efficiently and amicably. By not tying the problem to the people, individuals can go on to negotiate independent of trust. In exploring interests it is necessary to abandon a "bottom line." Decisions are delayed while a bank of options is built. The objective standard (e.g., market values, professional standards, precedent) allows results to be independent of will. Concessions are made to principle and reason, not pressure. Additional recommendations arising from Fisher and Ury's work on problem solving include brainstorming, forward looking, role reversal, and active listening to the other party. The latter involves repeating one's understanding of the other's issues to the opposing party. However, warmth to the other party, if excessive, signals weakness and tends to counteract the positive effects of active listening.

In negotiations you represent a constituent—an insurance company, an injured party, a parent, etc. Although it is natural to want to please the constituent, you also want to do some educating—educating the constituent on what the issues are and the development of realistic goals and time lines for settlement. Most constituents are eager to win rather than to resolve disputes. Reframing the situation will assist in achieving their understanding and cooperation, although this can be difficult at times. The benefit of a professional negotiator is that, in addition to skill and ability, the emotional element of disputes is neutralized to some extent.

Perceptions and Impressions

When you face the opposing legal counsel or agent in a negotiating situation, perceptions and impressions are often at work. Is the other lawyer someone you like and are attracted to? Do you perceive of the lawyer as fair and trustworthy? If asked, how would you describe the person in terms of intelligence, skill, ability, cooperativeness? What about the firm behind the lawyer—what are its collective traits and corporate culture in approaching the negotiating table? Our perceptions of these elements arise from our experience as well as the experiences shared by our colleagues. As important as these perceptions, however, are our self-perceptions. What are your perceptions of yourself as a lawyer? Laying aside false modesty or self-aggrandizement, realistically gauge the traits that would assist or hinder you in the negotiator's role. As well, what are your values and interests in the process and what are your risk preferences? How well are you matched with your opposing negotiator? Are you a good match or should you consider letting a colleague handle a particular negotiation?

Past successful negotiations between two parties lead to expectation of future successes. The negotiators' inner mental representation of the negotiating situation and their opponent guide their behavior and reactions to bargaining developments. We do not have a "personality profile" of the most successful negotiator—many of the successes appear tied to particular types of bargaining situations. Females succeed more in some, males in others. Machiavellian negotiators are more successful sometimes but are worse at others. A match between personality styles, opponent styles, and the complexities of individual negotiating situations are more plausible for success than simple analysis of personality traits. Repeatedly, however, a negotiator's cognitive ability has been cited as a potential advantage in the negotiating process. A higher cognitive ability leads to superior reasoning and problem solving in negotiations, both in exploring new ideas for negotiation and in being able to understand opponents' goals and perspectives of the conflict.

Creativity

It could be argued that creativity is the most valuable asset of a negotiator—the ability to create alternative solutions rather than to pound relentlessly against your opponents' wishes. Creativity, unlike sheer general intelligence, is a skill that can be learned and applied. Roger von Oech's (1983, 1986) work presents many exercises to open mental locks and identifies how to hunt for innovative solutions.

Good Will

Negotiation usually progresses best with the good will of two parties. However, this is not always the case. The other side may be more powerful and thus may assume an inflexible negotiating stance. The opponent may not participate in "responsible negotiation" but engage in personal attack. Fisher and Ury provide some excellent responses to dirty tricks by opposing negotiators. They also suggest negotiation *jujitsu*—do not push back when they push. Refuse to react by sidestepping their attack. Instead, use their strength by channeling it into exploring interests, inventing options for mutual gain, and searching for independent standards. Invite criticism and advice, recast attacks on you as attacks on the problem, ask questions, and use silence as a weapon. Play your game, not theirs.

Mediation

A further step in negotiation is bringing in a third party (the *neutral*), usually referred to as mediation. Although there is a current widespread implementation of mediation in legal practice, it is in reality an ancient approach to dispute resolution. It currently is seen in a wide variety of applications, including civil and criminal litigation and family and workplace disputes. As with other forms of negotiation, research and practice in mediation have input from many disciplines. Much of the early research on mediation derived from the study of international conflict, which grew to encompass labor-management disputes then to a wide application in legal circles.

Mediation has been shown to be an effective way of dispute resolution, and most participants have reported satisfaction with the process and outcome. It is most effective when conflict is of moderate or low rather than high intensity and when the parties are motivated to end the dispute. Some evidence suggests that it is also most effective when the parties have parity in power and the issues in dispute do not involve general principles but specific problems. Mediation appears most effective when the parties understand clearly that the next step is arbitration.

Mediators are most effective when the parties both have high trust in the individual and the mediation process. Mediators should be seen as neutral by both parties and conduct themselves overtly in an even-handed fashion. Fisher and Ury describe a typical mediation process that they term the "one-text procedure." Rather than having two parties construct their ideal resolution and modifying each to suit the other, the mediator alone builds a potential plan after surveying the issues and needs of the parties. He or she then asks for critiques from both parties on each successive draft of the plan and, when most of the issues have been settled, presents the plan as the best one that he or she can produce. The parties then are asked to respond in a yes or no fashion.

Mediation does not ask either party to abandon its position. Instead, the mediator helps the parties to understand the opposing position. This can happen in a caucus where the mediator meets separately with each party. The discovery and prioritizing of issues is the main task of mediation—along with presenting proposals of the mediator's construction, not of the parties directly.

Mediators can gain momentum and build confidence in the mediation process by arranging to get early agreement on simple and less-contentious issues. The mediator's effectiveness depends not only on trust but on warmth and friendliness with both parties, which helps to separate issues from persons. This is not to say that the mediator should not be forceful at times. Studies reveal that when hostility levels rise, the mediator is most effective when he or she is strong and controls the situation. A less intrusive style is best under lower-hostility conditions.

Mediation Cycle

Several researchers have described a mediation cycle that begins with setting the stage (reviewing ground rules and gathering information), then problem solving (posing issues and generating possibilities), and finally getting a workable agreement (pressing parties to accept a solution). Mediators in this model move from being less direct in the initial stages of the process to using pressure and compensation tactics in later stages. Judges who mediate are often seen to use strong-arm tactics in line with their high status and perceived authority.

As I posited earlier, negotiation is an essential skill for lawyers to develop and the new role as mediator is simply an extension of this ability, not a radical shift. Good negotiators will become good mediators. As the behavioral science of negotiator behavior continues to develop, mediators can benefit by continuous development with refinement of their skills and knowledge in this field.

APPENDIX **A**

Finding Expertise in Psychology

I presented this book as a review of the basic concepts and practices of psychologists as they may apply to forensic use. It was not my intent to suggest that this book might replace the need for you to retain a psychologist to advise or assist in the preparation of your case. Instead the information in the book should help you to employ and interact with a psychologist.

If you have never before retained a psychologist to assist you in a case, how do you go about finding one? The most reliable way is to use the same method you would use in seeking a qualified professional in any field—ask a trusted peer for recommendations. Beyond this there are a number of routes you can take to acquire names. First you should decide whether you require a professional or an academic expert or someone who can straddle both sides of the discipline. If you desire someone to comment on the scientific basis of an issue at trial, contacting the psychology department of the nearest college or university should yield results. At the very least it can provide you with leads if no one there has the specific expertise you seek. (A perusal of the telephone yellow pages will provide a listing of psychologists available in your vicinity, but it will not provide any information on their area of expertise or assurances of their abilities.)

Other sources of names are state, provincial, and national scientific, regulatory, and accreditation bodies. State and provincial bodies are responsible for regulation of the practice of psychology and maintain a directory of currently practicing psychologists. As well, the National Register of Health Services Providers in Psychology (and its Canadian equivalent) list psychologists who are licensed, certified, or registered at the independent-practice level; who hold a doctoral degree in psychology from a regionally accredited educational institution; and who have undergone at least two years of supervised experience in health services in psychology. A listing of specializations is provided by the listees, but this does not assure a level of competence in that specialty.

A number of independent professional boards have been established to provide a level of examination of credentials and competence in specialties of psychology. The oldest and most respected of these is the level of Diplomate, which is offered by the American Board of Professional Psychology. Among its specialties are forensic psychology and clinical neuropsychology. Although many very competent forensic psychologists (and clinical neuropsychologists) have not undergone these voluntary examinations, the attainment of this credential is an assurance of high levels of training and ability.

Additional databases developed commercially or by professional organizations list psychologists in forensic practice and narrow their specialty further.

American Psychological Association
   (founded in 1892)
750 First Street NE
Washington, DC 20002-4242
USA

Canadian Psychological Association
Vincent Road
Old Chelsea, Quebec, Canada
J0X 2N0

State and Provincial Boards
(current director and telephone number listed in the annual July issue of *American Psychologist*)

Alabama
Board of Examiners in Psychology
660 Adams Avenue
Suite 360
Montgomery, AL 36104

Alaska
Board of Psychologist and
   Psychological Associate Examiners
P.O. Box 110806
Juneau, AK 99811-0806

Alberta
College of Alberta Psychologists
Suite 2100
10123 - 99 St.
Edmonton, Alberta, Canada
T5J 3H1

Arizona
State Board of Psychologist
   Examiners
1400 West Washington, Room 230
Phoenix, AZ 85007

Arkansas
Board of Examiners in Psychology
101 East Capitol
Suite 415
Little Rock, AR 72201

British Columbia
College of Psychologists of British
   Columbia
1755 West Broadway, Suite 404
Vancouver, BC, Canada V6J 4S5

California
Board of Psychology
1422 Howe Avenue, Suite 22
Sacramento, CA 95825-3200

Colorado
Board of Psychologist Examiners
1560 Broadway, Suite 1340
Denver, CO 80202

Connecticut
Board of Examiners of Psychologists
150 Washington Street
Hartford, CT 06106

Delaware
Board of Examiners of Psychologists
Cannon Building, Suite 203
P.O. Box 1401
Dover, DE 19903

District of Columbia
Board of Psychology
614 H Street NW
Room 108
Washington, DC 20001

Florida
Board of Psychological Examiners
1940 North Monroe Street
Tallahassee, FL 32399-0788

Georgia
State Board of Examiners of
  Psychologists
166 Pryor Street SW
Atlanta, GA 30303

Guam
Board of Allied Health Examiners
P.O. Box 2816
Agana, Guam 96910

Hawaii
Board of Psychology
P.O. Box 3469
Honolulu, HI 96801

Idaho
Board of Psychologist Examiners
1109 Maine Street, Suite 220
Boise, ID 83702-5642

Illinois
Clinical Psychologist Licensing &
  Disciplinary Committee
320 West Washington Street, Third
  Floor
Springfield, IL 62786

Indiana
State Psychology Board
402 West Washington Street, Room
  041
Indianapolis, IN 46204

Iowa
Board of Psychology Examiners
Lucas State Office Building
32 East Twelfth Street, Fourth Floor
Des Moines, IA 50319-0075

Kansas
Behavioral Sciences Regulatory Board
712 South Kansas Avenue
Topeka, KS 66603-3817

Kentucky
State Board of Psychology
P.O. Box 456
Frankfort, KY 40602-0456

Louisiana
State Board of Examiners of
  Psychologists
11924 Justice Avenue, Suite A
Baton Rouge, LA 70816

Maine
Board of Examiners of Psychologists
Department of Professional and
 Financial Regulation
35 State House Station
Augusta, ME 04333

Manitoba
Psychological Association of
 Manitoba
59 Goulet Avenue
Suite 307
Winnipeg, MB Canada R2H 0R5

Maryland
Board of Examiners of Psychologists
4201 Patterson Avenue
Baltimore, MD 21215-2299

Massachusetts
Board of Registration of Psychologists
100 Cambridge Street, 15th Floor
Boston, MA 02202

Michigan
Board of Psychology
611 West Ottawa
Lansing, MI 48933

Minnesota
Board of Psychology
2700 University Avenue West, Room
 101
St. Paul, MN 55114-1095

Mississippi
Board of Psychological Examiners
812 North President Street
Jackson, MS 39202

Missouri
State Committee of Psychologists
3605 Missouri Boulevard
Jefferson City, MO 65109

Montana
Board of Psychologists
111 North Last Chance Gulch
P.O. Box 200513
Helena, MT 59620-0513

Nebraska
Board of Examiners of Psychologists
P.O. Box 95007
Lincoln, NE 68509-5007

Nevada
Board of Psychological Examiners
P.O. Box 2286
Reno, NV 89505-2286

New Brunswick
College of Psychologists of New
 Brunswick
P.O. Box 1194
Postal Station A
Fredericton, NB, Canada E3B 1B0

New Hampshire
Board of Examiners of Psychology
 and Mental Health Practice
105 Pleasant Street
Main Building
Concord, NH 03301

New Jersey
State Board of Psychological
 Examiners
P.O. Box 45017
Newark, NJ 07101

New Mexico
Board of Psychologist Examiners
P.O. Box 25101
725 St. Michael's Drive
Santa Fe, NM 87504

New York
Board for Psychology
New York State Education
 Department
Cultural Education Center
Room 3041
Albany, NY 12230

Newfoundland
P.O. Box 5666, Station C
St. John's, Newfoundland,
Canada A1C 5W8

North Carolina
Psychology Board
895 State Farm Road, Suite 102
Boone, NC 28607

North Dakota
State Board of Psychologist
 Examiners
1406 Second Street NW
Mandan, ND 58554

Nova Scotia
Board of Examiners in Psychology
5991 Spring Garden Road, Suite 1115
Halifax, NS, Canada B3H 1Y6

Ohio
State Board of Psychology
77 South High Street
Eighteenth Floor
Columbus, OH 43266-0321

Oklahoma
State Board of Examiners of
 Psychologists
1000 N.E. Tenth Street
Room 504
Oklahoma City, OK 73117-1299

Ontario
College of Psychologists of Ontario
1246 Yonge Street, Suite 201
Toronto, ON, Canada M4T 1W5

Oregon
Board of Psychologist Examiners
3218 Pringle Road SE
Salem, OR 97302-6309

Pennsylvania
State Board of Psychology
P.O. Box 2649
Harrisburg, PA 17105-2649

Quebec
Corporation Professionnelle des
 Psycholoques du Quebec
1100 Beaumont Avenue, #510
Mont-Royal, QU, Canada H3P 3H5

Rhode Island
Board of Psychology
104 Cannon Building
3 Capitol Hill
Providence, RI 02908

Saskatchewan
Psychological Association
1249 Eighth Street East
Saskatoon, SK, Canada S7H 0S5

South Carolina
Board of Examiners in Psychology
P.O. Box 11329
Columbia, SC 29211-1329

South Dakota
Board of Examiners of Psychologists
P.O. Box 654
Spearfish, SD 57783-0654

Tennessee
Board of Examiners in Psychology
283 Plus Park Boulevard
Nashville, TN 37247-1010

Texas
Board of Examiners of Psychologists
333 Guadalupe, Suite 2-450
Austin, TX 78701

Utah
Psychologist Licensing Board
P.O. Box 45805
Salt Lake City, UT 84145-0805

Vermont
Board of Psychological Examiners
Office of Professional Regulation
109 State Street
Montpelier, VT 05609-1106

Virginia
Board of Psychology
6606 West Broad Street, Fourth Floor
Richmond, VA 23230-1717

Washington
State Examining Board of Psychology
P.O. 47869
Olympia, WA 98504-7869

West Virginia
Board of Examiners of Psychologists
P.O. Box 910
Barrackville, WV 26559

Wisconsin
Psychology Examining Board
P.O. Box 8935
Madison, WI 53708-8935

Wyoming
Board of Psychology
2020 Carey Avenue, #201
Cheyenne, WY 82002

National Register of Health Service Providers in Psychology
1120 G Street NW
Washington, DC 20005
USA

Canadian Register of Health Service Providers in Psychology
37 Clarence Street
Suite #4
Ottawa, Ontario, Canada
K1N 5P4

American College of Forensic Psychology
Attorney's Directory of Forensic Psychologists
Box 5870
Balboa Island, CA 92662
USA

American Board of Clinical Neuropsychology
A Specialty of the American Board of Professional Psychology
2100 E. Broadway, Suite 313
Columbia, MO 65201-6082
USA

American Board of Forensic Psychology
A Specialty of the American Board of Professional Psychology
2100 E. Broadway, Suite 313
Columbia, MO 65201-6082
USA

*American Board of Professional
  Neuropsychology*
Wilmington Health Associates, PA
1202 Medical Center Drive
Wilmington, NC 28401
USA

American Board of Forensic Examiners
1658 South Cobblestone Court
Springfield, MO 65809
USA

National Forensic Center
Forensic Services Directory
17 Temple Terrace
Lawrenceville, NJ 08648
USA

APPENDIX B

Ethical Principles of Psychologists and Code of Conduct

Copyright ©1992 by the American Psychological Association. Reprinted with permission.

Ethical Principles of Psychologists and Code of Conduct

CONTENTS

INTRODUCTION

PREAMBLE

GENERAL PRINCIPLES
Principle A: Competence
Principle B: Integrity
Principle C: Professional and Scientific Responsibility
Principle D: Respect for People's Rights and Dignity
Principle E: Concern for Others' Welfare
Principle F: Social Responsibility

ETHICAL STANDARDS

1. General Standards
1.01 Applicability of the Ethics Code
1.02 Relationship of Ethics and Law
1.03 Professional and Scientific Relationship
1.04 Boundaries of Competence
1.05 Maintaining Expertise
1.06 Basis for Scientific and Professional Judgments
1.07 Describing the Nature and Results of Psychological Services
1.08 Human Differences
1.09 Respecting Others
1.10 Nondiscrimination
1.11 Sexual Harassment
1.12 Other Harassment
1.13 Personal Problems and Conflicts
1.14 Avoiding Harm
1.15 Misuse of Psychologists' Influence
1.16 Misuse of Psychologists' Work
1.17 Multiple Relationships
1.18 Barter (With Patients or Clients)
1.19 Exploitative Relationships
1.20 Consultations and Referrals
1.21 Third-Party Requests for Services
1.22 Delegation to and Supervision of Subordinates
1.23 Documentation of Professional and Scientific Work
1.24 Records and Data
1.25 Fees and Financial Arrangements
1.26 Accuracy in Reports to Payors and Funding Sources
1.27 Referrals and Fees

2. Evaluation, Assessment, or Intervention
2.01 Evaluation, Diagnosis, and Interventions in Professional Context
2.02 Competence and Appropriate Use of Assessments and Interventions
2.03 Test Construction
2.04 Use of Assessment in General and With Special Populations
2.05 Interpreting Assessment Results
2.06 Unqualified Persons
2.07 Obsolete Tests and Outdated Test Results
2.08 Test Scoring and Interpretation Services
2.09 Explaining Assessment Results
2.10 Maintaining Test Security

3. Advertising and Other Public Statements
3.01 Definition of Public Statements
3.02 Statements by Others
3.03 Avoidance of False or Deceptive Statements
3.04 Media Presentations
3.05 Testimonials
3.06 In-Person Solicitation

4. Therapy
4.01 Structuring the Relationship
4.02 Informed Consent to Therapy
4.03 Couple and Family Relationships
4.04 Providing Mental Health Services to Those Served by Others
4.05 Sexual Intimacies With Current Patients or Clients
4.06 Therapy With Former Sexual Partners
4.07 Sexual Intimacies With Former Therapy Patients
4.08 Interruption of Services
4.09 Terminating the Professional Relationship

5. Privacy and Confidentiality
5.01 Discussing the Limits of Confidentiality
5.02 Maintaining Confidentiality
5.03 Minimizing Intrusions on Privacy
5.04 Maintenance of Records
5.05 Disclosures
5.06 Consultations
5.07 Confidential Information in Databases
5.08 Use of Confidential Information for Didactic or Other Purposes
5.09 Preserving Records and Data
5.10 Ownership of Records and Data
5.11 Withholding Records for Nonpayment

6. Teaching, Training Supervision, Research, and Publishing
6.01 Design of Education and Training Programs
6.02 Descriptions of Education and Training Programs
6.03 Accuracy and Objectivity in Teaching
6.04 Limitation on Teaching
6.05 Assessing Student and Supervisee Performance
6.06 Planning Research
6.07 Responsibility
6.08 Compliance With Law and Standards
6.09 Institutional Approval
6.10 Research Responsibilities
6.11 Informed Consent to Research
6.12 Dispensing With Informed Consent
6.13 Informed Consent in Research Filming or Recording
6.14 Offering Inducements for Research Participants
6.15 Deception in Research
6.16 Sharing and Utilizing Data
6.17 Minimizing Invasiveness
6.18 Providing Participants With Information About the Study
6.19 Honoring Commitments
6.20 Care and Use of Animals in Research
6.21 Reporting of Results
6.22 Plagiarism
6.23 Publication Credit
6.24 Duplicate Publication of Data
6.25 Sharing Data
6.26 Professional Reviewers

7. Forensic Activities
7.01 Professionalism
7.02 Forensic Assessments
7.03 Clarification of Role
7.04 Truthfulness and Candor
7.05 Prior Relationships
7.06 Compliance With Law and Rules

8. Resolving Ethical Issues
8.01 Familiarity With Ethics Code
8.02 Confronting Ethical Issues
8.03 Conflicts Between Ethics and Organizational Demands
8.04 Informal Resolution of Ethical Violations
8.05 Reporting Ethical Violations
8.06 Cooperating With Ethics Committees
8.07 Improper Complaints

INTRODUCTION

The American Psychological Association's (APA's) Ethical Principles of Psychologists and Code of Conduct (hereinafter referred to as the Ethics Code) consists of an Introduction, a Preamble, six General Principles (A–F), and specific Ethical Standards. The Introduction discusses the intent, organization, procedural considerations, and scope of application of the Ethics Code. The Preamble and General Principles are *aspirational* goals to guide psychologists toward the highest ideals of psychology. Although the Preamble and General Principles are not themselves enforceable rules, they should be considered by psychologists in arriving at an ethical course of action and may be considered by ethics bodies in interpreting the Ethical Standards. The Ethical Standards set forth *enforceable* rules for conduct as psychologists. Most of the Ethical Standards are written broadly, in order to apply to psychologists in varied roles, although the application of an Ethical Standard may vary depending on the context. The Ethical Standards are not exhaustive. The fact that a given conduct is not specifically addressed by the Ethics Code does not mean that it is necessarily either ethical or unethical.

Membership in the APA commits members to adhere to the APA Ethics Code and to the rules and procedures used to implement it. Psychologists and students, whether or not they are APA members, should be aware that the Ethics Code may be applied to them by state psychology boards, courts, or other public bodies.

This Ethics Code applies only to psychologists' work-related activities, that is, activities that are part of the psychologists' scientific and professional functions or that are psychological in nature. It includes the clinical or counseling practice of psychology, research, teaching, supervision of trainees, development of assessment instruments, conducting assessments, educational counseling, organizational consulting, social intervention, administration, and other activities as well. These work-related activities can be distinguished from the purely private conduct of a psychologist, which ordinarily is not within the purview of the Ethics Code.

The Ethics Code is intended to provide standards of professional conduct that can be applied by the APA and by other bodies that choose to adopt them. Whether or not a psychologist has violated the Ethics Code does not by itself determine whether he or she is legally liable in a court action, whether a contract is enforceable, or whether other legal consequences occur. These results are based on legal rather than ethical rules. However, compliance with or violation of the Ethics Code may be admissible as evidence in some legal proceedings, depending on the circumstances.

In the process of making decisions regarding their professional behavior, psychologists must consider this Ethics Code, in addition to applicable laws and psychology board regulations. If the Ethics Code establishes a higher standard of conduct than is required by law, psychologists must meet the higher ethical standard. If the Ethics Code standard appears to conflict with the requirements of law, then psychologists make known their commitment to the Ethics Code and take steps to resolve the conflict in a responsible manner. If neither law nor the Ethics Code resolves an issue, psychologists should consider other professional materials[1] and the dictates of their own conscience, as well as seek consultation with others within the field when this is practical.

The procedures for filing, investigating, and resolving complaints of unethical conduct are described in the current Rules and Procedures of the APA Ethics Committee. The actions that APA may take for violations of the Ethics Code include actions such as reprimand, censure, termination of

---

This version of the APA Ethics Code was adopted by the American Psychological Association's Council of Representatives during its meeting, August 13 and 16, 1992, and is effective beginning December 1, 1992. Inquiries concerning the substance or interpretation of the APA Ethics Code should be addressed to the Director, Office of Ethics, American Psychological Association, 750 First Street, NE, Washington, DC 20002-4242.

This Code will be used to adjudicate complaints brought concerning alleged conduct occurring on or after the effective date. Complaints regarding conduct occurring prior to the effective date will be adjudicated on the basis of the version of the Code that was in effect at the time the conduct occurred, except that no provisions repealed in June 1989, will be enforced even if an earlier version contains the provision. The Ethics Code will undergo continuing review and study for future revisions; comments on the Code may be sent to the above address.

The APA has previously published its Ethical Standards as follows:

American Psychological Association. (1953). *Ethical standards of psychologists*. Washington, DC: Author.
American Psychological Association. (1958). Standards of ethical behavior for psychologists. *American Psychologist, 13*, 268–271.
American Psychological Association. (1963). Ethical standards of psychologists. *American Psychologist, 18*, 56–60.
American Psychological Association. (1968). Ethical standards of psychologists. *American Psychologist, 23*, 357–361.
American Psychological Association. (1977, March). Ethical standards of psychologists. *APA Monitor*, pp. 22–23.
American Psychological Association. (1979). *Ethical standards of psychologists*. Washington, DC: Author.
American Psychological Association. (1981). Ethical principles of psychologists. *American Psychologist, 36*, 633–638.
American Psychological Association. (1990). Ethical principles of psychologists (Amended June 2, 1989). *American Psychologist, 45*, 390–395.

Request copies of the APA's Ethical Principles of Psychologists and Code of Conduct from the APA Order Department, 750 First Street, NE, Washington, DC 20002-4242, or phone (202) 336-5510.

---

[1]Professional materials that are most helpful in this regard are guidelines and standards that have been adopted or endorsed by professional psychological organizations. Such guidelines and standards, whether adopted by the American Psychological Association (APA) or its Divisions, are not enforceable as such by this Ethics Code, but are of educative value to psychologists, courts, and professional bodies. Such materials include, but are not limited to, the APA's *General Guidelines for Providers of Psychological Services* (1987), *Specialty Guidelines for the Delivery of Services by Clinical Psychologists, Counseling Psychologists, Industrial/ Organizational Psychologists, and School Psychologists* (1981), *Guidelines for Computer Based Tests and Interpretations* (1987), *Standards for Educational and Psychological Testing* (1985), *Ethical Principles in the Conduct of Research With Human Participants* (1982), *Guidelines for Ethical Conduct in the Care and Use of Animals* (1986), *Guidelines for Providers of Psychological Services to Ethnic, Linguistic, and Culturally Diverse Populations* (1990), and *Publication Manual of the American Psychological Association* (3rd ed., 1983). Materials not adopted by APA as a whole include the APA Division 41 (Forensic Psychology)/American Psychology–Law Society's *Specialty Guidelines for Forensic Psychologists* (1991).

APA membership, and referral of the matter to other bodies. Complainants who seek remedies such as monetary damages in alleging ethical violations by a psychologist must resort to private negotiation, administrative bodies, or the courts. Actions that violate the Ethics Code may lead to the imposition of sanctions on a psychologist by bodies other than APA, including state psychological associations, other professional groups, psychology boards, other state or federal agencies, and payors for health services. In addition to actions for violation of the Ethics Code, the APA Bylaws provide that APA may take action against a member after his or her conviction of a felony, expulsion or suspension from an affiliated state psychological association, or suspension or loss of licensure.

PREAMBLE

Psychologists work to develop a valid and reliable body of scientific knowledge based on research. They may apply that knowledge to human behavior in a variety of contexts. In doing so, they perform many roles, such as researcher, educator, diagnostician, therapist, supervisor, consultant, administrator, social interventionist, and expert witness. Their goal is to broaden knowledge of behavior and, where appropriate, to apply it pragmatically to improve the condition of both the individual and society. Psychologists respect the central importance of freedom of inquiry and expression in research, teaching, and publication. They also strive to help the public in developing informed judgments and choices concerning human behavior. This Ethics Code provides a common set of values upon which psychologists build their professional and scientific work.

This Code is intended to provide both the general principles and the decision rules to cover most situations encountered by psychologists. It has as its primary goal the welfare and protection of the individuals and groups with whom psychologists work. It is the individual responsibility of each psychologist to aspire to the highest possible standards of conduct. Psychologists respect and protect human and civil rights, and do not knowingly participate in or condone unfair discriminatory practices.

The development of a dynamic set of ethical standards for a psychologist's work-related conduct requires a personal commitment to a lifelong effort to act ethically; to encourage ethical behavior by students, supervisees, employees, and colleagues, as appropriate; and to consult with others, as needed, concerning ethical problems. Each psychologist supplements, but does not violate, the Ethics Code's values and rules on the basis of guidance drawn from personal values, culture, and experience.

GENERAL PRINCIPLES

Principle A: Competence

Psychologists strive to maintain high standards of competence in their work. They recognize the boundaries of their particular competencies and the limitations of their expertise. They provide only those services and use only those techniques for which they are qualified by education, training, or experience. Psychologists are cognizant of the fact that the competencies required in serving, teaching, and/or studying groups of people vary with the distinctive characteristics of those groups. In those areas in which recognized professional standards do not yet exist, psychologists exercise careful judgment and take appropriate precautions to protect the welfare of those with whom they work. They maintain knowledge of relevant scientific and professional information related to the services they render, and they recognize the need for ongoing education. Psychologists make appropriate use of scientific, professional, technical, and administrative resources.

Principle B: Integrity

Psychologists seek to promote integrity in the science, teaching, and practice of psychology. In these activities psychologists are honest, fair, and respectful of others. In describing or reporting their qualifications, services, products, fees, research, or teaching, they do not make statements that are false, misleading, or deceptive. Psychologists strive to be aware of their own belief systems, values, needs, and limitations and the effect of these on their work. To the extent feasible, they attempt to clarify for relevant parties the roles they are performing and to function appropriately in accordance with those roles. Psychologists avoid improper and potentially harmful dual relationships.

Principle C: Professional and Scientific Responsibility

Psychologists uphold professional standards of conduct, clarify their professional roles and obligations, accept appropriate responsibility for their behavior, and adapt their methods to the needs of different populations. Psychologists consult with, refer to, or cooperate with other professionals and institutions to the extent needed to serve the best interests of their patients, clients, or other recipients of their services. Psychologists' moral standards and conduct are personal matters to the same degree as is true for any other person, except as psychologists' conduct may compromise their professional responsibilities or reduce the public's trust in psychology and psychologists. Psychologists are concerned about the ethical compliance of their colleagues' scientific and professional conduct. When appropriate, they consult with colleagues in order to prevent or avoid unethical conduct.

Principle D: Respect for People's Rights and Dignity

Psychologists accord appropriate respect to the fundamental rights, dignity, and worth of all people. They respect the rights of individuals to privacy, confidentiality, self-determination, and autonomy, mindful that legal and other obligations may lead to inconsistency and conflict with the exercise of these rights. Psychologists are aware of cultural, individual, and role differences, including those due to age, gender, race, ethnicity, national origin, religion, sexual orientation, disability, language, and socioeconomic status.

Psychologists try to eliminate the effect on their work of biases based on those factors, and they do not knowingly participate in or condone unfair discriminatory practices.

Principle E: Concern for Others' Welfare

Psychologists seek to contribute to the welfare of those with whom they interact professionally. In their professional actions, psychologists weigh the welfare and rights of their patients or clients, students, supervisees, human research participants, and other affected persons, and the welfare of animal subjects of research. When conflicts occur among psychologists' obligations or concerns, they attempt to resolve these conflicts and to perform their roles in a responsible fashion that avoids or minimizes harm. Psychologists are sensitive to real and ascribed differences in power between themselves and others, and they do not exploit or mislead other people during or after professional relationships.

Principle F: Social Responsibility

Psychologists are aware of their professional and scientific responsibilities to the community and the society in which they work and live. They apply and make public their knowledge of psychology in order to contribute to human welfare. Psychologists are concerned about and work to mitigate the causes of human suffering. When undertaking research, they strive to advance human welfare and the science of psychology. Psychologists try to avoid misuse of their work. Psychologists comply with the law and encourage the development of law and social policy that serve the interests of their patients and clients and the public. They are encouraged to contribute a portion of their professional time for little or no personal advantage.

ETHICAL STANDARDS

1. General Standards

These General Standards are potentially applicable to the professional and scientific activities of all psychologists.

1.01 Applicability of the Ethics Code

The activity of a psychologist subject to the Ethics Code may be reviewed under these Ethical Standards only if the activity is part of his or her work-related functions or the activity is psychological in nature. Personal activities having no connection to or effect on psychological roles are not subject to the Ethics Code.

1.02 Relationship of Ethics and Law

If psychologists' ethical responsibilities conflict with law, psychologists make known their commitment to the Ethics Code and take steps to resolve the conflict in a responsible manner.

1.03 Professional and Scientific Relationship

Psychologists provide diagnostic, therapeutic, teaching, research, supervisory, consultative, or other psychological services only in the context of a defined professional or scientific relationship or role. (See also Standards 2.01, Evaluation, Diagnosis, and Interventions in Professional Context, and 7.02, Forensic Assessments.)

1.04 Boundaries of Competence

(a) Psychologists provide services, teach, and conduct research only within the boundaries of their competence, based on their education, training, supervised experience, or appropriate professional experience.

(b) Psychologists provide services, teach, or conduct research in new areas or involving new techniques only after first undertaking appropriate study, training, supervision, and/or consultation from persons who are competent in those areas or techniques.

(c) In those emerging areas in which generally recognized standards for preparatory training do not yet exist, psychologists nevertheless take reasonable steps to ensure the competence of their work and to protect patients, clients, students, research participants, and others from harm.

1.05 Maintaining Expertise

Psychologists who engage in assessment, therapy, teaching, research, organizational consulting, or other professional activities maintain a reasonable level of awareness of current scientific and professional information in their fields of activity, and undertake ongoing efforts to maintain competence in the skills they use.

1.06 Basis for Scientific and Professional Judgments

Psychologists rely on scientifically and professionally derived knowledge when making scientific or professional judgments or when engaging in scholarly or professional endeavors.

1.07 Describing the Nature and Results of Psychological Services

(a) When psychologists provide assessment, evaluation, treatment, counseling, supervision, teaching, consultation, research, or other psychological services to an individual, a group, or an organization, they provide, using language that is reasonably understandable to the recipient of those services, appropriate information beforehand about the nature of such services and appropriate information later about results and conclusions. (See also Standard 2.09, Explaining Assessment Results.)

(b) If psychologists will be precluded by law or by organizational roles from providing such information to particular individuals or groups, they so inform those individuals or groups at the outset of the service.

1.08 Human Differences

Where differences of age, gender, race, ethnicity, national origin, religion, sexual orientation, disability, language, or socioeconomic status significantly affect psychologists' work concerning particular individuals or groups, psychologists obtain the training, experience, consultation, or supervision necessary to ensure the competence of their services, or they make appropriate referrals.

1.09 Respecting Others

In their work-related activities, psychologists respect the rights of others to hold values, attitudes, and opinions that differ from their own.

1.10 Nondiscrimination

In their work-related activities, psychologists do not engage in unfair discrimination based on age, gender, race, ethnicity, national origin, religion, sexual orientation, disability, socioeconomic status, or any basis proscribed by law.

1.11 Sexual Harassment

(a) Psychologists do not engage in sexual harassment. Sexual harassment is sexual solicitation, physical advances, or verbal or nonverbal conduct that is sexual in nature, that occurs in connection with the psychologist's activities or roles as a psychologist, and that either: (1) is unwelcome, is offensive, or creates a hostile workplace environment, and the psychologist knows or is told this; or (2) is sufficiently severe or intense to be abusive to a reasonable person in the context. Sexual harassment can consist of a single intense or severe act or of multiple persistent or pervasive acts.

(b) Psychologists accord sexual-harassment complainants and respondents dignity and respect. Psychologists do not participate in denying a person academic admittance or advancement, employment, tenure, or promotion, based solely upon their having made, or their being the subject of, sexual-harassment charges. This does not preclude taking action based upon the outcome of such proceedings or consideration of other appropriate information.

1.12 Other Harassment

Psychologists do not knowingly engage in behavior that is harassing or demeaning to persons with whom they interact in their work based on factors such as those persons' age, gender, race, ethnicity, national origin, religion, sexual orientation, disability, language, or socioeconomic status.

1.13 Personal Problems and Conflicts

(a) Psychologists recognize that their personal problems and conflicts may interfere with their effectiveness. Accordingly, they refrain from undertaking an activity when they know or should know that their personal problems are likely to lead to harm to a patient, client, colleague, student, research participant, or other person to whom they may owe a professional or scientific obligation.

(b) In addition, psychologists have an obligation to be alert to signs of, and to obtain assistance for, their personal problems at an early stage, in order to prevent significantly impaired performance.

(c) When psychologists become aware of personal problems that may interfere with their performing work-related duties adequately, they take appropriate measures, such as obtaining professional consultation or assistance, and determine whether they should limit, suspend, or terminate their work-related duties.

1.14 Avoiding Harm

Psychologists take reasonable steps to avoid harming their patients or clients, research participants, students, and others with whom they work, and to minimize harm where it is foreseeable and unavoidable.

1.15 Misuse of Psychologists' Influence

Because psychologists' scientific and professional judgments and actions may affect the lives of others, they are alert to and guard against personal, financial, social, organizational, or political factors that might lead to misuse of their influence.

1.16 Misuse of Psychologists' Work

(a) Psychologists do not participate in activities in which it appears likely that their skills or data will be misused by others, unless corrective mechanisms are available. (See also Standard 7.04, Truthfulness and Candor.)

(b) If psychologists learn of misuse or misrepresentation of their work, they take reasonable steps to correct or minimize the misuse or misrepresentation.

1.17 Multiple Relationships

(a) In many communities and situations, it may not be feasible or reasonable for psychologists to avoid social or other nonprofessional contacts with persons such as patients, clients, students, supervisees, or research participants. Psychologists must always be sensitive to the potential harmful effects of other contacts on their work and on those persons with whom they deal. A psychologist refrains from entering into or promising another personal, scientific, professional, financial, or other relationship with such persons if it appears likely that such a relationship reasonably might impair the psychologist's objectivity or otherwise interfere with the psychologist's effectively performing his or her functions as a psychologist, or might harm or exploit the other party.

(b) Likewise, whenever feasible, a psychologist refrains from taking on professional or scientific obligations when preexisting relationships would create a risk of such harm.

(c) If a psychologist finds that, due to unforeseen factors, a potentially harmful multiple relationship has arisen, the psychologist attempts to resolve it with due regard for the best interests of the affected person and maximal compliance with the Ethics Code.

1.18 Barter (With Patients or Clients)

Psychologists ordinarily refrain from accepting goods, services, or other nonmonetary remuneration from patients or clients in return for psychological services because such arrangements create inherent potential for conflicts, exploitation, and distortion of the professional relationship. A psychologist may participate in bartering only if (1) it is not clinically contraindicated, and (2) the relationship is not exploitative. (See also Standards 1.17, Multiple Relationships, and 1.25, Fees and Financial Arrangements.)

1.19 Exploitative Relationships

(a) Psychologists do not exploit persons over whom they have supervisory, evaluative, or other authority such as students, supervisees, employees, research participants, and clients or patients. (See also Standards 4.05–4.07 regarding sexual involvement with clients or patients.)

(b) Psychologists do not engage in sexual relationships with students or supervisees in training over whom the psychologist has evaluative or direct authority, because such relationships are so likely to impair judgment or be exploitative.

1.20 Consultations and Referrals

(a) Psychologists arrange for appropriate consultations and referrals based principally on the best interests of their patients or clients, with appropriate consent, and subject to other relevant considerations, including applicable law and contractual obligations. (See also Standards 5.01, Discussing the Limits of Confidentiality, and 5.06, Consultations.)

(b) When indicated and professionally appropriate, psychologists cooperate with other professionals in order to serve their patients or clients effectively and appropriately.

(c) Psychologists' referral practices are consistent with law.

1.21 Third-Party Requests for Services

(a) When a psychologist agrees to provide services to a person or entity at the request of a third party, the psychologist clarifies to the extent feasible, at the outset of the service, the nature of the relationship with each party. This clarification includes the role of the psychologist (such as therapist, organizational consultant, diagnostician, or expert witness), the probable uses of the services provided or the information obtained, and the fact that there may be limits to confidentiality.

(b) If there is a foreseeable risk of the psychologist's being called upon to perform conflicting roles because of the involvement of a third party, the psychologist clarifies the nature and direction of his or her responsibilities, keeps all parties appropriately informed as matters develop, and resolves the situation in accordance with this Ethics Code.

1.22 Delegation to and Supervision of Subordinates

(a) Psychologists delegate to their employees, supervisees, and research assistants only those responsibilities that such persons can reasonably be expected to perform competently, on the basis of their education, training, or experience, either independently or with the level of supervision being provided.

(b) Psychologists provide proper training and supervision to their employees or supervisees and take reasonable steps to see that such persons perform services responsibly, competently, and ethically.

(c) If institutional policies, procedures, or practices prevent fulfillment of this obligation, psychologists attempt to modify their role or to correct the situation to the extent feasible.

1.23 Documentation of Professional and Scientific Work

(a) Psychologists appropriately document their professional and scientific work in order to facilitate provision of services later by them or by other professionals, to ensure accountability, and to meet other requirements of institutions or the law.

(b) When psychologists have reason to believe that records of their professional services will be used in legal proceedings involving recipients of or participants in their work, they have a responsibility to create and maintain documentation in the kind of detail and quality that would be consistent with reasonable scrutiny in an adjudicative forum. (See also Standard 7.01, Professionalism, under Forensic Activities.)

1.24 Records and Data

Psychologists create, maintain, disseminate, store, retain, and dispose of records and data relating to their research, practice, and other work in accordance with law and in a manner that permits compliance with the requirements of this Ethics Code. (See also Standard 5.04, Maintenance of Records.)

1.25 Fees and Financial Arrangements

(a) As early as is feasible in a professional or scientific relationship, the psychologist and the patient, client, or other appropriate recipient of psychological services reach an agreement specifying the compensation and the billing arrangements.

(b) Psychologists do not exploit recipients of services or payors with respect to fees.

(c) Psychologists' fee practices are consistent with law.

(d) Psychologists do not misrepresent their fees.

(e) If limitations to services can be anticipated because of limitations in financing, this is discussed with the patient, client, or other appropriate recipient of services as early as is feasible. (See also Standard 4.08, Interruption of Services.)

(f) If the patient, client, or other recipient of services does not pay for services as agreed, and if the psychologist wishes to use collection agencies or legal measures to collect the fees, the psychologist first informs the person that such measures will be taken and provides that person an opportunity to make prompt payment. (See also Standard 5.11, Withholding Records for Nonpayment.)

1.26 Accuracy in Reports to Payors and Funding Sources

In their reports to payors for services or sources of research funding, psychologists accurately state the nature of the research or service provided, the fees or charges, and where applicable, the identity of the provider, the findings, and the diagnosis. (See also Standard 5.05, Disclosures.)

1.27 Referrals and Fees

When a psychologist pays, receives payment from, or divides fees with another professional other than in an employer–employee relationship, the payment to each is based on the services (clinical, consultative, administrative, or other) provided and is not based on the referral itself.

2. Evaluation, Assessment, or Intervention

2.01 Evaluation, Diagnosis, and Interventions in Professional Context

(a) Psychologists perform evaluations, diagnostic services, or interventions only within the context of a defined professional relationship. (See also Standard 1.03, Professional and Scientific Relationship.)

(b) Psychologists' assessments, recommendations, reports, and psychological diagnostic or evaluative statements are based on information and techniques (including personal interviews of the individual when appropriate) sufficient to provide appropriate substantiation for their findings. (See also Standard 7.02, Forensic Assessments.)

2.02 Competence and Appropriate Use of Assessments and Interventions

(a) Psychologists who develop, administer, score, interpret, or use psychological assessment techniques, interviews, tests, or instruments do so in a manner and for purposes that are appropriate in light of the research on or evidence of the usefulness and proper application of the techniques.

(b) Psychologists refrain from misuse of assessment techniques, interventions, results, and interpretations and take reasonable steps to prevent others from misusing the information these techniques provide. This includes refraining from releasing raw test results or raw data to persons, other than to patients or clients as appropriate, who are not qualified to use such information. (See also Standards 1.02, Relationship of Ethics and Law, and 1.04, Boundaries of Competence.)

2.03 Test Construction

Psychologists who develop and conduct research with tests and other assessment techniques use scientific procedures and current professional knowledge for test design, standardization, validation, reduction or elimination of bias, and recommendations for use.

2.04 Use of Assessment in General and With Special Populations

(a) Psychologists who perform interventions or administer, score, interpret, or use assessment techniques are familiar with the reliability, validation, and related standardization or outcome studies of, and proper applications and uses of, the techniques they use.

(b) Psychologists recognize limits to the certainty with which diagnoses, judgments, or predictions can be made about individuals.

(c) Psychologists attempt to identify situations in which particular interventions or assessment techniques or norms may not be applicable or may require adjustment in administration or interpretation because of factors such as individuals' gender, age, race, ethnicity, national origin, religion, sexual orientation, disability, language, or socioeconomic status.

2.05 Interpreting Assessment Results

When interpreting assessment results, including automated interpretations, psychologists take into account the various test factors and characteristics of the person being assessed that might affect psychologists' judgments or reduce the accuracy of their interpretations. They indicate any significant reservations they have about the accuracy or limitations of their interpretations.

2.06 Unqualified Persons

Psychologists do not promote the use of psychological assessment techniques by unqualified persons. (See also Standard 1.22, Delegation to and Supervision of Subordinates.)

2.07 Obsolete Tests and Outdated Test Results

(a) Psychologists do not base their assessment or intervention decisions or recommendations on data or test results that are outdated for the current purpose.

(b) Similarly, psychologists do not base such decisions or recommendations on tests and measures that are obsolete and not useful for the current purpose.

2.08 Test Scoring and Interpretation Services

(a) Psychologists who offer assessment or scoring procedures to other professionals accurately describe the purpose, norms, validity, reliability, and applications of the procedures and any special qualifications applicable to their use.

(b) Psychologists select scoring and interpretation services (including automated services) on the basis of evidence of the validity of the program and procedures as well as on other appropriate considerations.

(c) Psychologists retain appropriate responsibility for the appropriate application, interpretation, and use of assessment instruments, whether they score and interpret such tests themselves or use automated or other services.

2.09 Explaining Assessment Results

Unless the nature of the relationship is clearly explained to the person being assessed in advance and precludes provision of an explanation of results (such as in some organizational consulting, preemployment or security screenings, and forensic evaluations), psychologists ensure that an explanation of the results is provided using language that is reasonably understandable to the person assessed or to another legally authorized person on behalf of the client. Regardless of whether the scoring and interpretation are done by the psychologist, by assistants, or by automated or other outside services, psychologists take reasonable steps to ensure that appropriate explanations of results are given.

2.10 Maintaining Test Security

Psychologists make reasonable efforts to maintain the integrity and security of tests and other assessment techniques consistent with law, contractual obligations, and in a manner that permits compliance with the requirements of this Ethics Code. (See also Standard 1.02, Relationship of Ethics and Law.)

3. Advertising and Other Public Statements

3.01 Definition of Public Statements

Psychologists comply with this Ethics Code in public statements relating to their professional services, products, or publications or to the field of psychology. Public statements include but are not limited to paid or unpaid advertising, brochures, printed matter, directory listings, personal resumes or curricula vitae, interviews or comments for use in media, statements in legal proceedings, lectures and public oral presentations, and published materials.

3.02 Statements by Others

(a) Psychologists who engage others to create or place public statements that promote their professional practice, products, or activities retain professional responsibility for such statements.

(b) In addition, psychologists make reasonable efforts to prevent others whom they do not control (such as employers, publishers, sponsors, organizational clients, and representatives of the print or broadcast media) from making deceptive statements concerning psychologists' practice or professional or scientific activities.

(c) If psychologists learn of deceptive statements about their work made by others, psychologists make reasonable efforts to correct such statements.

(d) Psychologists do not compensate employees of press, radio, television, or other communication media in return for publicity in a news item.

(e) A paid advertisement relating to the psychologist's activities must be identified as such, unless it is already apparent from the context.

3.03 Avoidance of False or Deceptive Statements

(a) Psychologists do not make public statements that are false, deceptive, misleading, or fraudulent, either because of what they state, convey, or suggest or because of what they omit, concerning their research, practice, or other work activities or those of persons or organizations with which they are affiliated. As examples (and not in limitation) of this standard, psychologists do not make false or deceptive statements concerning (1) their training, experience, or competence; (2) their academic degrees; (3) their credentials; (4) their institutional or association affiliations; (5) their services; (6) the scientific or clinical basis for, or results or degree of success of, their services; (7) their fees; or (8) their publications or research findings. (See also Standards 6.15, Deception in Research, and 6.18, Providing Participants With Information About the Study.)

(b) Psychologists claim as credentials for their psychological work, only degrees that (1) were earned from a regionally accredited educational institution or (2) were the basis for psychology licensure by the state in which they practice.

3.04 Media Presentations

When psychologists provide advice or comment by means of public lectures, demonstrations, radio or television programs, prerecorded tapes, printed articles, mailed material, or other media, they take reasonable precautions to ensure that (1) the statements are based on appropriate psychological literature and practice, (2) the statements are otherwise consistent with this Ethics Code, and (3) the recipients of the information are not encouraged to infer that a relationship has been established with them personally.

3.05 Testimonials

Psychologists do not solicit testimonials from current psychotherapy clients or patients or other persons who because of their particular circumstances are vulnerable to undue influence.

3.06 In-Person Solicitation

Psychologists do not engage, directly or through agents, in uninvited in-person solicitation of business from actual or potential psychotherapy patients or clients or other persons who because of their particular circumstances are vulnerable to undue influence. However, this does not preclude attempting to implement appropriate collateral contacts with significant others for the purpose of benefiting an already engaged therapy patient.

4. Therapy

4.01 Structuring the Relationship

(a) Psychologists discuss with clients or patients as early as is feasible in the therapeutic relationship appropriate issues, such as the nature and anticipated course of therapy, fees, and confidentiality. (See also Standards 1.25, Fees and Financial Arrangements, and 5.01, Discussing the Limits of Confidentiality.)

(b) When the psychologist's work with clients or patients will be supervised, the above discussion includes that fact, and the name of the supervisor, when the supervisor has legal responsibility for the case.

(c) When the therapist is a student intern, the client or patient is informed of that fact.

(d) Psychologists make reasonable efforts to answer patients' questions and to avoid apparent misunderstandings about therapy. Whenever possible, psychologists provide oral and/or written information, using language that is reasonably understandable to the patient or client.

4.02 Informed Consent to Therapy

(a) Psychologists obtain appropriate informed consent to therapy or related procedures, using language that is reasonably understandable to participants. The content of informed consent will vary depending on many circumstances; however, informed consent generally implies that the person (1) has the capacity to consent, (2) has been informed of significant information concerning the procedure, (3) has freely and without undue influence expressed consent, and (4) consent has been appropriately documented.

(b) When persons are legally incapable of giving informed consent, psychologists obtain informed permission from a legally authorized person, if such substitute consent is permitted by law.

(c) In addition, psychologists (1) inform those persons who are legally incapable of giving informed consent about the proposed interventions in a manner commensurate with the persons' psychological capacities, (2) seek their assent to those interventions, and (3) consider such persons' preferences and best interests.

4.03 Couple and Family Relationships

(a) When a psychologist agrees to provide services to several persons who have a relationship (such as husband and wife or parents and children), the psychologist attempts to clarify at the outset (1) which of the individuals are patients or clients and (2) the relationship the psychologist will have with each person. This clarification includes the role of the psychologist and the probable uses of the services provided or the information obtained. (See also Standard 5.01, Discussing the Limits of Confidentiality.)

(b) As soon as it becomes apparent that the psychologist may be called on to perform potentially conflicting roles (such as marital counselor to husband and wife, and then witness for one party in a divorce proceeding), the psychologist attempts to clarify and adjust, or withdraw from, roles appropriately. (See also Standard 7.03, Clarification of Role, under Forensic Activities.)

4.04 Providing Mental Health Services to Those Served by Others

In deciding whether to offer or provide services to those already receiving mental health services elsewhere, psychologists carefully consider the treatment issues and the potential patient's or client's welfare. The psychologist discusses these issues with the patient or client, or another legally authorized person on behalf of the client, in order to minimize the risk of confusion and conflict, consults with the other service providers when appropriate, and proceeds with caution and sensitivity to the therapeutic issues.

4.05 Sexual Intimacies With Current Patients or Clients

Psychologists do not engage in sexual intimacies with current patients or clients.

4.06 Therapy With Former Sexual Partners

Psychologists do not accept as therapy patients or clients persons with whom they have engaged in sexual intimacies.

4.07 Sexual Intimacies With Former Therapy Patients

(a) Psychologists do not engage in sexual intimacies with a former therapy patient or client for at least two years after cessation or termination of professional services.

(b) Because sexual intimacies with a former therapy patient or client are so frequently harmful to the patient or client, and because such intimacies undermine public confidence in the psychology profession and thereby deter the public's use of needed services, psychologists do not engage in sexual intimacies with former therapy patients and clients even after a two-year interval except in the most unusual circumstances. The psychologist who engages in such activity after the two years following cessation or termination of treatment bears the burden of demonstrating that there has been no exploitation, in light of all relevant factors, including (1) the amount of time that has passed since therapy terminated, (2) the nature and duration of the therapy, (3) the circumstances of termination, (4) the patient's or client's personal history, (5) the patient's or client's current mental status, (6) the likelihood of adverse impact on the patient or client and others, and (7) any statements or actions made by the therapist during the course of therapy suggesting or inviting the possibility of a posttermination sexual or romantic relationship with the patient or client. (See also Standard 1.17, Multiple Relationships.)

4.08 Interruption of Services

(a) Psychologists make reasonable efforts to plan for facilitating care in the event that psychological services are interrupted by factors such as the psychologist's illness, death, unavailability, or relocation or by the client's relocation or financial limitations. (See also Standard 5.09, Preserving Records and Data.)

(b) When entering into employment or contractual relationships, psychologists provide for orderly and appropriate resolution of responsibility for patient or client care in the event that the employment or contractual relationship ends, with paramount consideration given to the welfare of the patient or client.

4.09 Terminating the Professional Relationship

(a) Psychologists do not abandon patients or clients. (See also Standard 1.25e, under Fees and Financial Arrangements.)

(b) Psychologists terminate a professional relationship when it becomes reasonably clear that the patient or client no longer needs the service, is not benefiting, or is being harmed by continued service.

(c) Prior to termination for whatever reason, except where precluded by the patient's or client's conduct, the psychologist discusses the patient's or client's views and needs, provides appropriate pretermination counseling, suggests alternative service providers as appropriate, and takes other reasonable steps to facilitate transfer of responsibility to another provider if the patient or client needs one immediately.

5. Privacy and Confidentiality

These Standards are potentially applicable to the professional and scientific activities of all psychologists.

5.01 Discussing the Limits of Confidentiality

(a) Psychologists discuss with persons and organizations with whom they establish a scientific or professional relationship (including, to the extent feasible, minors and their legal representatives) (1) the relevant limitations on confidentiality, including limitations where applicable in group, marital, and family therapy or in organizational consulting, and (2) the foreseeable uses of the information generated through their services.

(b) Unless it is not feasible or is contraindicated, the discussion of confidentiality occurs at the outset of the relationship and thereafter as new circumstances may warrant.

(c) Permission for electronic recording of interviews is secured from clients and patients.

5.02 Maintaining Confidentiality

Psychologists have a primary obligation and take reasonable precautions to respect the confidentiality rights of those with whom they work or consult, recognizing that confidentiality may be established by law, institutional rules, or professional or scientific relationships. (See also Standard 6.26, Professional Reviewers.)

5.03 Minimizing Intrusions on Privacy

(a) In order to minimize intrusions on privacy, psychologists include in written and oral reports, consultations, and the like, only information germane to the purpose for which the communication is made.

(b) Psychologists discuss confidential information obtained in clinical or consulting relationships, or evaluative data concerning patients, individual or organizational clients, students, research participants, supervisees, and employees, only for appropriate scientific or professional purposes and only with persons clearly concerned with such matters.

5.04 Maintenance of Records

Psychologists maintain appropriate confidentiality in creating, storing, accessing, transferring, and disposing of records under their control, whether these are written, automated, or in any other medium. Psychologists maintain and dispose of records in accordance with law and in a manner that permits compliance with the requirements of this Ethics Code.

5.05 Disclosures

(a) Psychologists disclose confidential information without the consent of the individual only as mandated by law, or where permitted by law for a valid purpose, such as (1) to provide needed professional services to the patient or the individual or organizational client, (2) to obtain appropriate professional consultations, (3) to protect the patient or client or others from harm, or (4) to obtain payment for services, in which instance disclosure is limited to the minimum that is necessary to achieve the purpose.

(b) Psychologists also may disclose confidential information with the appropriate consent of the patient or the individual or organizational client (or of another legally authorized person on behalf of the patient or client), unless prohibited by law.

5.06 Consultations

When consulting with colleagues, (1) psychologists do not share confidential information that reasonably could lead to the identification of a patient, client, research participant, or other person or organization with whom they have a confidential relationship unless they have obtained the prior consent of the person or organization or the disclosure cannot be avoided, and (2) they share information only to the extent necessary to achieve the purposes of the consultation. (See also Standard 5.02, Maintaining Confidentiality.)

5.07 Confidential Information in Databases

(a) If confidential information concerning recipients of psychological services is to be entered into databases or systems of records available to persons whose access has not been consented to by the recipient, then psychologists use coding or other techniques to avoid the inclusion of personal identifiers.

(b) If a research protocol approved by an institutional review board or similar body requires the inclusion of personal identifiers, such identifiers are deleted before the information is made accessible to persons other than those of whom the subject was advised.

(c) If such deletion is not feasible, then before psychologists transfer such data to others or review such data collected by others, they take reasonable steps to determine that appropriate consent of personally identifiable individuals has been obtained.

5.08 Use of Confidential Information for Didactic or Other Purposes

(a) Psychologists do not disclose in their writings, lectures, or other public media, confidential, personally identifiable information concerning their patients, individual or organizational clients, students, research participants, or other recipients of their services that they obtained during the course of their work, unless the person or organization has consented in writing or unless there is other ethical or legal authorization for doing so.

(b) Ordinarily, in such scientific and professional presentations, psychologists disguise confidential information concerning such persons or organizations so that they are not individually identifiable to others and so that discussions do not cause harm to subjects who might identify themselves.

5.09 Preserving Records and Data

A psychologist makes plans in advance so that confidentiality of records and data is protected in the event of the psychologist's death, incapacity, or withdrawal from the position or practice.

5.10 Ownership of Records and Data

Recognizing that ownership of records and data is governed by legal principles, psychologists take reasonable and lawful steps so that records and data remain available to the extent needed to serve the best interests of patients, individual or organizational clients, research participants, or appropriate others.

5.11 Withholding Records for Nonpayment

Psychologists may not withhold records under their control that are requested and imminently needed for a patient's or client's treatment solely because payment has not been received, except as otherwise provided by law.

6. Teaching, Training Supervision, Research, and Publishing

6.01 Design of Education and Training Programs

Psychologists who are responsible for education and training programs seek to ensure that the programs are competently designed, provide the proper experiences, and meet the requirements for licensure, certification, or other goals for which claims are made by the program.

6.02 Descriptions of Education and Training Programs

(a) Psychologists responsible for education and training programs seek to ensure that there is a current and accurate description of the program content, training goals and objectives, and requirements that must be met for satisfactory completion of the program. This information must be made readily available to all interested parties.

(b) Psychologists seek to ensure that statements concerning their course outlines are accurate and not misleading, particularly regarding the subject matter to be covered, bases for evaluating progress, and the nature of course experiences. (See also Standard 3.03, Avoidance of False or Deceptive Statements.)

(c) To the degree to which they exercise control, psychologists responsible for announcements, catalogs, brochures, or advertisements describing workshops, seminars, or other non-degree-granting educational programs ensure that they accurately describe the audience for which the program is intended, the educational objectives, the presenters, and the fees involved.

6.03 Accuracy and Objectivity in Teaching

(a) When engaged in teaching or training, psychologists present psychological information accurately and with a reasonable degree of objectivity.

(b) When engaged in teaching or training, psychologists recognize the power they hold over students or supervisees and therefore make reasonable efforts to avoid engaging in conduct that is personally demeaning to students or supervisees. (See also Standards 1.09, Respecting Others, and 1.12, Other Harassment.)

6.04 Limitation on Teaching

Psychologists do not teach the use of techniques or procedures that require specialized training, licensure, or expertise, including but not limited to hypnosis, biofeedback, and projective techniques, to individuals who lack the prerequisite training, legal scope of practice, or expertise.

6.05 Assessing Student and Supervisee Performance

(a) In academic and supervisory relationships, psychologists establish an appropriate process for providing feedback to students and supervisees.

(b) Psychologists evaluate students and supervisees on the basis of their actual performance on relevant and established program requirements.

6.06 Planning Research

(a) Psychologists design, conduct, and report research in accordance with recognized standards of scientific competence and ethical research.

(b) Psychologists plan their research so as to minimize the possibility that results will be misleading.

(c) In planning research, psychologists consider its ethical acceptability under the Ethics Code. If an ethical issue is unclear, psychologists seek to resolve the issue through consultation with institutional review boards, animal care and use committees, peer consultations, or other proper mechanisms.

(d) Psychologists take reasonable steps to implement appropriate protections for the rights and welfare of human participants, other persons affected by the research, and the welfare of animal subjects.

6.07 Responsibility

(a) Psychologists conduct research competently and with due concern for the dignity and welfare of the participants.

(b) Psychologists are responsible for the ethical conduct of research conducted by them or by others under their supervision or control.

(c) Researchers and assistants are permitted to perform only those tasks for which they are appropriately trained and prepared.

(d) As part of the process of development and implementation of research projects, psychologists consult those with expertise concerning any special population under investigation or most likely to be affected.

6.08 Compliance With Law and Standards

Psychologists plan and conduct research in a manner consistent with federal and state law and regulations, as well as professional standards governing the conduct of research, and particularly those standards governing research with human participants and animal subjects.

6.09 Institutional Approval

Psychologists obtain from host institutions or organizations appropriate approval prior to conducting research, and they provide accurate information about their research proposals. They conduct the research in accordance with the approved research protocol.

6.10 Research Responsibilities

Prior to conducting research (except research involving only anonymous surveys, naturalistic observations, or similar research), psychologists enter into an agreement with participants that clarifies the nature of the research and the responsibilities of each party.

6.11 Informed Consent to Research

(a) Psychologists use language that is reasonably understandable to research participants in obtaining their appropriate informed consent (except as provided in Standard 6.12, Dispensing With Informed Consent). Such informed consent is appropriately documented.

(b) Using language that is reasonably understandable to participants, psychologists inform participants of the nature of the research; they inform participants that they are free to participate or to decline to participate or to withdraw from the research; they explain the foreseeable consequences of declining or withdrawing; they inform participants of significant factors that may be expected to influence their willingness to participate (such as risks, discomfort, adverse effects, or limitations on confidentiality, except as provided in Standard 6.15, Deception in Research); and they explain other aspects about which the prospective participants inquire.

(c) When psychologists conduct research with individuals such as students or subordinates, psychologists take special care to protect the prospective participants from adverse consequences of declining or withdrawing from participation.

(d) When research participation is a course requirement or opportunity for extra credit, the prospective participant is given the choice of equitable alternative activities.

(e) For persons who are legally incapable of giving informed consent, psychologists nevertheless (1) provide an appropriate explanation, (2) obtain the participant's assent, and (3) obtain appropriate permission from a legally authorized person, if such substitute consent is permitted by law.

6.12 Dispensing With Informed Consent

Before determining that planned research (such as research involving only anonymous questionnaires, naturalistic observations, or certain kinds of archival research) does not require the informed consent of research participants, psychologists consider applicable regulations and institutional review board requirements, and they consult with colleagues as appropriate.

6.13 Informed Consent in Research Filming or Recording

Psychologists obtain informed consent from research participants prior to filming or recording them in any form, unless the research involves simply naturalistic observations in public places and it is not anticipated that the recording will be used in a manner that could cause personal identification or harm.

6.14 Offering Inducements for Research Participants

(a) In offering professional services as an inducement to obtain research participants, psychologists make clear the nature of the services, as well as the risks, obligations, and limitations. (See also Standard 1.18, Barter [With Patients or Clients].)

(b) Psychologists do not offer excessive or inappropriate financial or other inducements to obtain research participants, particularly when it might tend to coerce participation.

6.15 Deception in Research

(a) Psychologists do not conduct a study involving deception unless they have determined that the use of deceptive techniques is justified by the study's prospective scientific, educational, or applied value and that equally effective alternative procedures that do not use deception are not feasible.

(b) Psychologists never deceive research participants about significant aspects that would affect their willingness to participate, such as physical risks, discomfort, or unpleasant emotional experiences.

(c) Any other deception that is an integral feature of the design and conduct of an experiment must be explained to participants as early as is feasible, preferably at the conclusion of their participation, but no later than at the conclusion of the research. (See also Standard 6.18, Providing Participants With Information About the Study.)

6.16 Sharing and Utilizing Data

Psychologists inform research participants of their anticipated sharing or further use of personally identifiable research data and of the possibility of unanticipated future uses.

6.17 Minimizing Invasiveness

In conducting research, psychologists interfere with the participants or milieu from which data are collected only in a manner that is warranted by an appropriate research design and that is consistent with psychologists' roles as scientific investigators.

6.18 Providing Participants With Information About the Study

(a) Psychologists provide a prompt opportunity for participants to obtain appropriate information about the nature, results, and conclusions of the research, and psychologists attempt to correct any misconceptions that participants may have.

(b) If scientific or humane values justify delaying or withholding this information, psychologists take reasonable measures to reduce the risk of harm.

6.19 Honoring Commitments

Psychologists take reasonable measures to honor all commitments they have made to research participants.

6.20 Care and Use of Animals in Research

(a) Psychologists who conduct research involving animals treat them humanely.

(b) Psychologists acquire, care for, use, and dispose of animals in compliance with current federal, state, and local laws and regulations, and with professional standards.

(c) Psychologists trained in research methods and experienced in the care of laboratory animals supervise all procedures involving animals and are responsible for ensuring appropriate consideration of their comfort, health, and humane treatment.

(d) Psychologists ensure that all individuals using animals under their supervision have received instruction in research methods and in the care, maintenance, and handling of the species being used, to the extent appropriate to their role.

(e) Responsibilities and activities of individuals assisting in a research project are consistent with their respective competencies.

(f) Psychologists make reasonable efforts to minimize the discomfort, infection, illness, and pain of animal subjects.

(g) A procedure subjecting animals to pain, stress, or privation is used only when an alternative procedure is unavailable and the goal is justified by its prospective scientific, educational, or applied value.

(h) Surgical procedures are performed under appropriate anesthesia; techniques to avoid infection and minimize pain are followed during and after surgery.

(i) When it is appropriate that the animal's life be terminated, it is done rapidly, with an effort to minimize pain, and in accordance with accepted procedures.

6.21 Reporting of Results

(a) Psychologists do not fabricate data or falsify results in their publications.

(b) If psychologists discover significant errors in their published data, they take reasonable steps to correct such errors in a correction, retraction, erratum, or other appropriate publication means.

6.22 Plagiarism

Psychologists do not present substantial portions or elements of another's work or data as their own, even if the other work or data source is cited occasionally.

6.23 Publication Credit

(a) Psychologists take responsibility and credit, including authorship credit, only for work they have actually performed or to which they have contributed.

(b) Principal authorship and other publication credits accurately reflect the relative scientific or professional contributions of the individuals involved, regardless of their relative status. Mere possession of an institutional position, such as Department Chair, does not justify authorship credit. Minor contributions to the research or to the writing for publications are appropriately acknowledged, such as in footnotes or in an introductory statement.

(c) A student is usually listed as principal author on any multiple-authored article that is substantially based on the student's dissertation or thesis.

6.24 Duplicate Publication of Data

Psychologists do not publish, as original data, data that have been previously published. This does not preclude republishing data when they are accompanied by proper acknowledgment.

6.25 Sharing Data

After research results are published, psychologists do not withhold the data on which their conclusions are based from other competent professionals who seek to verify the substantive claims through reanalysis and who intend to use such data only for that purpose, provided that the confidentiality of the participants can be protected and unless legal rights concerning proprietary data preclude their release.

6.26 Professional Reviewers

Psychologists who review material submitted for publication, grant, or other research proposal review respect the confidentiality of and the proprietary rights in such information of those who submitted it.

7. Forensic Activities

7.01 Professionalism

Psychologists who perform forensic functions, such as assessments, interviews, consultations, reports, or expert testimony, must comply with all other provisions of this Ethics Code to the extent that they apply to such activities. In addition, psychologists base their forensic work on appropriate knowledge of and competence in the areas underlying such work, including specialized knowledge concerning special populations. (See also Standards 1.06, Basis for Scientific and Professional Judgments; 1.08, Human Differences; 1.15, Misuse of Psychologists' Influence; and 1.23, Documentation of Professional and Scientific Work.)

7.02 Forensic Assessments

(a) Psychologists' forensic assessments, recommendations, and reports are based on information and techniques (including personal interviews of the individual, when appropriate) sufficient to provide appropriate substantiation for their findings. (See also Standards 1.03, Professional and Scientific Relationship; 1.23, Documentation of Professional and Scientific Work; 2.01, Evaluation, Diagnosis, and Interventions in Professional Context; and 2.05, Interpreting Assessment Results.)

(b) Except as noted in (c), below, psychologists provide written or oral forensic reports or testimony of the psychological characteristics of an individual only after they have conducted an examination of the individual adequate to support their statements or conclusions.

(c) When, despite reasonable efforts, such an examination is not feasible, psychologists clarify the impact of their limited information on the reliability and validity of their reports and testimony, and they appropriately limit the nature and extent of their conclusions or recommendations.

7.03 Clarification of Role

In most circumstances, psychologists avoid performing multiple and potentially conflicting roles in forensic matters. When psychologists may be called on to serve in more than one role in a legal proceeding—for example, as consultant or expert for one party or for the court and as a fact witness—they clarify role expectations and the extent of confidentiality in advance to the extent feasible, and thereafter as changes occur, in order to avoid compromising their professional judgment and objectivity and in order to avoid misleading others regarding their role.

7.04 Truthfulness and Candor

(a) In forensic testimony and reports, psychologists testify truthfully, honestly, and candidly and, consistent with applicable legal procedures, describe fairly the bases for their testimony and conclusions.

(b) Whenever necessary to avoid misleading, psychologists acknowledge the limits of their data or conclusions.

7.05 Prior Relationships

A prior professional relationship with a party does not preclude psychologists from testifying as fact witnesses or from testifying to their services to the extent permitted by applicable law. Psychologists appropriately take into account ways in which the prior relationship might affect their professional objectivity or opinions and disclose the potential conflict to the relevant parties.

7.06 Compliance With Law and Rules

In performing forensic roles, psychologists are reasonably familiar with the rules governing their roles. Psychologists are aware of the occasionally competing demands placed upon them by these principles and the requirements of the court system, and attempt to resolve these conflicts by making known their commitment to this Ethics Code and taking steps to resolve the conflict in a responsible manner. (See also Standard 1.02, Relationship of Ethics and Law.)

8. Resolving Ethical Issues

8.01 Familiarity With Ethics Code

Psychologists have an obligation to be familiar with this Ethics Code, other applicable ethics codes, and their application to psychologists' work. Lack of awareness or misunderstanding of an ethical standard is not itself a defense to a charge of unethical conduct.

8.02 Confronting Ethical Issues

When a psychologist is uncertain whether a particular situation or course of action would violate this Ethics Code, the psychologist ordinarily consults with other psychologists knowledgeable about ethical issues, with state or national psychology ethics committees, or with other appropriate authorities in order to choose a proper response.

8.03 Conflicts Between Ethics and Organizational Demands

If the demands of an organization with which psychologists are affiliated conflict with this Ethics Code, psychologists clarify the nature of the conflict, make known their commitment to the Ethics Code, and to the extent feasible, seek to resolve the conflict in a way that permits the fullest adherence to the Ethics Code.

8.04 Informal Resolution of Ethical Violations

When psychologists believe that there may have been an ethical violation by another psychologist, they attempt to resolve the issue by bringing it to the attention of that individual if an informal resolution appears appropriate and the intervention does not violate any confidentiality rights that may be involved.

8.05 Reporting Ethical Violations

If an apparent ethical violation is not appropriate for informal resolution under Standard 8.04 or is not resolved properly in that fashion, psychologists take further action appropriate to the situation, unless such action conflicts with confidentiality rights in ways that cannot be resolved. Such action might include referral to state or national committees on professional ethics or to state licensing boards.

8.06 Cooperating With Ethics Committees

Psychologists cooperate in ethics investigations, proceedings, and resulting requirements of the APA or any affiliated state psychological association to which they belong. In doing so, they make reasonable efforts to resolve any issues as to confidentiality. Failure to cooperate is itself an ethics violation.

8.07 Improper Complaints

Psychologists do not file or encourage the filing of ethics complaints that are frivolous and are intended to harm the respondent rather than to protect the public.

APPENDIX C

Guidelines for Child Custody Evaluations in Divorce Proceedings

Copyright ©1994 by the American Psychological Association. Reprinted with permission.

Guidelines

Guidelines for Child Custody Evaluations in Divorce Proceedings

Introduction

Decisions regarding child custody and other parenting arrangements occur within several different legal contexts, including parental divorce, guardianship, neglect or abuse proceedings, and termination of parental rights. The following guidelines were developed for psychologists conducting child custody evaluations, specifically within the context of parental divorce. These guidelines build upon the American Psychological Association's *Ethical Principles of Psychologists and Code of Conduct* (APA, 1992) and are aspirational in intent. *As guidelines, they are not intended to be either mandatory or exhaustive. The goal of the guidelines is to promote proficiency in using psychological expertise in conducting child custody evaluations.*

Parental divorce requires a restructuring of parental rights and responsibilities in relation to children. If the parents can agree to a restructuring arrangement, which they do in the overwhelming proportion (90%) of divorce custody cases (Melton, Petrila, Poythress, & Slobogin, 1987), there is no dispute for the court to decide. However, if the parents are unable to reach such an agreement, the court must help to determine the relative allocation of decision making authority and physical contact each parent will have with the child. The courts typically apply a "best interest of the child" standard in determining this restructuring of rights and responsibilities.

Psychologists provide an important service to children and the courts by providing competent, objective, impartial information in assessing the best interests of the child; by demonstrating a clear sense of direction and purpose in conducting a child custody evaluation; by performing their roles ethically; and by clarifying to all involved the nature and scope of the evaluation. The Ethics Committee of the American Psychological Association has noted that psychologists' involvement in custody disputes has at times raised questions in regard to the misuse of psychologists' influence, sometimes resulting in complaints against psychologists being brought to the attention of the APA Ethics Committee (APA Ethics Committee, 1985; Hall & Hare-Mustin, 1983; Keith-Spiegel & Koocher, 1985; Mills, 1984) and raising questions in the legal and forensic literature (Grisso, 1986; Melton et al., 1987; Mnookin, 1975; Ochroch, 1982; Okpaku, 1976; Weithorn, 1987).

Particular competencies and knowledge are required for child custody evaluations to provide adequate and appropriate psychological services to the court. Child custody evaluation in the context of parental divorce can be an extremely demanding task. For competing parents the stakes are high as they participate in a process fraught with tension and anxiety. The stress on the psychologist/evaluator can become great. Tension surrounding child custody evaluation can become further heightened when there are accusations of child abuse, neglect, and/or family violence.

Psychology is in a position to make significant contributions to child custody decisions. Psychological data and expertise, gained through a child custody evaluation, can provide an additional source of information and an additional perspective not otherwise readily available to the court on what appears to be in a child's best interest, and thus can increase the fairness of the determination the court must make.

Guidelines for Child Custody Evaluations In Divorce Proceedings

I. Orienting Guidelines: Purpose of a Child Custody Evaluation

1. The primary purpose of the evaluation is to assess the best psychological interests of the child. The primary consideration in a child custody evaluation is to assess the individual and family factors that affect the best psychological interests of the child. More specific questions may be raised by the court.

2. The child's interests and well-being are paramount. In a child custody evaluation, the child's interests and well-being are paramount. Parents competing for custody, as well as others, may have legitimate concerns, but the child's best interests must prevail.

These guidelines were drafted by the Committee on Professional Practice and Standards (COPPS), a committee of the Board of Professional Affairs (BPA), with input from the Committee on Children, Youth, and Families (CYF). They were adopted by the Council of Representatives of the American Psychological Association in February 1994.

COPPS members in 1991–1993 were Richard Cohen, Alex Carballo Dieguez, Kathleen Dockett, Sam Friedman, Colette Ingraham, John Northman, John Robinson, Deborah Tharinger, Susana Urbina, Phil Witt, and James Wulach; BPA liaisons in 1991–1993 were Richard Cohen, Joseph Kobos, and Rodney Lowman; CYF members were Don Routh and Carolyn Swift.

Correspondence concerning this article should be addressed to the Practice Directorate, American Psychological Association, 750 First Street, NE, Washington, DC 20002-4242.

3. The focus of the evaluation is on parenting capacity, the psychological and developmental needs of the child, and the resulting fit. In considering psychological factors affecting the best interests of the child, the psychologist focuses on the parenting capacity of the prospective custodians in conjunction with the psychological and developmental needs of each involved child. This involves (a) an assessment of the adults' capacities for parenting, including whatever knowledge, attributes, skills, and abilities, or lack thereof, are present; (b) an assessment of the psychological functioning and developmental needs of each child and of the wishes of each child where appropriate; and (c) an assessment of the functional ability of each parent to meet these needs, including an evaluation of the interaction between each adult and child.

The values of the parents relevant to parenting, ability to plan for the child's future needs, capacity to provide a stable and loving home, and any potential for inappropriate behavior or misconduct that might negatively influence the child also are considered. Psychopathology may be relevant to such an assessment, insofar as it has impact on the child or the ability to parent, but it is not the primary focus.

II. General Guidelines: Preparing for a Child Custody Evaluation

4. The role of the psychologist is that of a professional expert who strives to maintain an objective, impartial stance. The role of the psychologist is as a professional expert. The psychologist does not act as a judge, who makes the ultimate decision applying the law to all relevant evidence. Neither does the psychologist act as an advocating attorney, who strives to present his or her client's best possible case. The psychologist, in a balanced, impartial manner, informs and advises the court and the prospective custodians of the child of the relevant psychological factors pertaining to the custody issue. The psychologist should be impartial regardless of whether he or she is retained by the court or by a party to the proceedings. If either the psychologist or the client cannot accept this neutral role, the psychologist should consider withdrawing from the case. If not permitted to withdraw, in such circumstances, the psychologist acknowledges past roles and other factors that could affect impartiality.

5. The psychologist gains specialized competence.

A. A psychologist contemplating performing child custody evaluations is aware that special competencies and knowledge are required for the undertaking of such evaluations. Competence in performing psychological assessments of children, adults, and families is necessary but not sufficient. Education, training, experience, and/or supervision in the areas of child and family development, child and family psychopathology, and the impact of divorce on children help to prepare the psychologist to participate competently in child custody evaluations. The psychologist also strives to become familiar with applicable legal standards and procedures, including laws governing divorce and custody adjudications in his or her state or jurisdiction.

B. The psychologist uses current knowledge of scientific and professional developments, consistent with accepted clinical and scientific standards, in selecting data collection methods and procedures. The *Standards for Educational and Psychological Testing* (APA, 1985) are adhered to in the use of psychological tests and other assessment tools.

C. In the course of conducting child custody evaluations, allegations of child abuse, neglect, family violence, or other issues may occur that are not necessarily within the scope of a particular evaluator's expertise. If this is so, the psychologist seeks additional consultation, supervision, and/or specialized knowledge, training, or experience in child abuse, neglect, and family violence to address these complex issues. The psychologist is familiar with the laws of his or her state addressing child abuse, neglect, and family violence and acts accordingly.

6. The psychologist is aware of personal and societal biases and engages in nondiscriminatory practice. The psychologist engaging in child custody evaluations is aware of how biases regarding age, gender, race, ethnicity, national origin, religion, sexual orientation, disability, language, culture, and socioeconomic status may interfere with an objective evaluation and recommendations. The psychologist recognizes and strives to overcome any such biases or withdraws from the evaluation.

7. The psychologist avoids multiple relationships. Psychologists generally avoid conducting a child custody evaluation in a case in which the psychologist served in a therapeutic role for the child or his or her immediate family or has had other involvement that may compromise the psychologist's objectivity. This should not, however, preclude the psychologist from testifying in the case as a fact witness concerning treatment of the child. In addition, during the course of a child custody evaluation, a psychologist does not accept any of the involved participants in the evaluation as a therapy client. Therapeutic contact with the child or involved participants following a child custody evaluation is undertaken with caution.

A psychologist asked to testify regarding a therapy client who is involved in a child custody case is aware of the limitations and possible biases inherent in such a role and the possible impact on the ongoing therapeutic relationship. Although the court may require the psychologist to testify as a fact witness regarding factual information he or she became aware of in a professional relationship with a client, that psychologist should generally decline the role of an expert witness who gives a professional opinion regarding custody and visitation issues (see Ethical Standard 7.03) unless so ordered by the court.

III. Procedural Guidelines: Conducting a Child Custody Evaluation

8. The scope of the evaluation is determined by the evaluator, based on the nature of the referral question. The scope of the custody-related evaluation is determined by the nature of the question or issue raised by the referring person or the court, or is inherent in the situation. Although comprehensive child custody evaluations generally require an evaluation of all parents or guardians and children, as well as observations of interactions between them, the scope of the assessment in a particular case may be limited to evaluating the parental capacity of one parent without attempting to compare the parents or to make recommendations. Likewise, the scope may be limited to evaluating the child. Or a psychologist may be asked to critique the assumptions and methodology of the assessment of another mental health professional. A psychologist also might serve as an expert witness in the area of child development, providing expertise to the court without relating it specifically to the parties involved in a case.

9. The psychologist obtains informed consent from all adult participants and, as appropriate, informs child participants. In undertaking child custody evaluations, the psychologist ensures that each adult participant is aware of (a) the purpose, nature, and method of the evaluation; (b) who has requested the psychologist's services; and (c) who will be paying the fees. The psychologist informs adult participants about the nature of the assessment instruments and techniques and informs those participants about the possible disposition of the data collected. The psychologist provides this information, as appropriate, to children, to the extent that they are able to understand.

10. The psychologist informs participants about the limits of confidentiality and the disclosure of information. A psychologist conducting a child custody evaluation ensures that the participants, including children to the extent feasible, are aware of the limits of confidentiality characterizing the professional relationship with the psychologist. The psychologist informs participants that in consenting to the evaluation, they are consenting to disclosure of the evaluation's findings in the context of the forthcoming litigation and in any other proceedings deemed necessary by the courts. A psychologist obtains a waiver of confidentiality from all adult participants or from their authorized legal representatives.

11. The psychologist uses multiple methods of data gathering. The psychologist strives to use the most appropriate methods available for addressing the questions raised in a specific child custody evaluation and generally uses multiple methods of data gathering, including, but not limited to, clinical interviews, observation, and/or psychological assessments. Important facts and opinions are documented from at least two sources whenever their reliability is questionable. The psychologist, for example, may review potentially relevant reports (e.g., from schools, health care providers, child care providers, agencies, and institutions). Psychologists may also interview extended family, friends, and other individuals on occasions when the information is likely to be useful. If information is gathered from third parties that is significant and may be used as a basis for conclusions, psychologists corroborate it by at least one other source wherever possible and appropriate and document this in the report.

12. The psychologist neither overinterprets nor inappropriately interprets clinical or assessment data. The psychologist refrains from drawing conclusions not adequately supported by the data. The psychologist interprets any data from interviews or tests, as well as any questions of data reliability and validity, cautiously and conservatively, seeking convergent validity. The psychologist strives to acknowledge to the court any limitations in methods or data used.

13. The psychologist does not give any opinion regarding the psychological functioning of any individual who has not been personally evaluated. This guideline, however, does not preclude the psychologist from reporting what an evaluated individual (such as the parent or child) has stated or from addressing theoretical issues or hypothetical questions, so long as the limited basis of the information is noted.

14. Recommendations, if any, are based on what is in the best psychological interests of the child. Although the profession has not reached consensus about whether psychologists ought to make recommendations about the final custody determination to the courts, psychologists are obligated to be aware of the arguments on both sides of this issue and to be able to explain the logic of their position concerning their own practice.

If the psychologist does choose to make custody recommendations, these recommendations should be derived from sound psychological data and must be based on the best interests of the child in the particular case. Recommendations are based on articulated assumptions, data, interpretations, and inferences based upon established professional and scientific standards. Psychologists guard against relying on their own biases or unsupported beliefs in rendering opinions in particular cases.

15. The psychologist clarifies financial arrangements. Financial arrangements are clarified and agreed upon prior to commencing a child custody evaluation. When billing for a child custody evaluation, the psychologist does not misrepresent his or her services for reimbursement purposes.

16. The psychologist maintains written records. All records obtained in the process of conducting a child custody evaluation are properly maintained and filed in accord with the APA *Record Keeping Guidelines* (APA, 1993) and relevant statutory guidelines.

All raw data and interview information are recorded with an eye toward their possible review by other psychologists or the court, where legally permitted. Upon request, appropriate reports are made available to the court.

REFERENCES

American Psychological Association. (1985). *Standards for educational and psychological testing.* Washington, DC: Author.

American Psychological Association. (1992). Ethical principles of psychologists and code of conduct. *American Psychologist, 47,* 1597–1611.

American Psychological Association. (1993). *Record keeping guidelines.* Washington, DC: Author.

American Psychological Association, Ethics Committee. (1985). *Annual report of the American Psychological Association Ethics Committee.* Washington, DC: Author.

Grisso, T. (1986). *Evaluating competencies: Forensic assessments and instruments.* New York: Plenum.

Hall, J. E., & Hare-Mustin, R. T. (1983). Sanctions and the diversity of ethical complaints against psychologists. *American Psychologist, 38,* 714–729.

Keith-Spiegel, P., & Koocher, G. P. (1985). *Ethics in psychology.* New York: Random House.

Melton, G. B., Petrila, J., Poythress, N. G., & Slobogin, C. (1987). *Psychological evaluations for the courts: A handbook for mental health professionals and lawyers.* New York: Guilford Press.

Mills, D. H. (1984). Ethics education and adjudication within psychology. *American Psychologist, 39,* 669–675.

Mnookin, R. H. (1975). Child-custody adjudication: Judicial functions in the face of indeterminacy. *Law and Contemporary Problems, 39,* 226–293.

Ochroch, R. (1982, August). *Ethical pitfalls in child custody evaluations.* Paper presented at the 90th Annual Convention of the American Psychological Association, Washington, DC.

Okpaku, S. (1976). Psychology: Impediment or aid in child custody cases? *Rutgers Law Review, 29,* 1117–1153.

Weithorn, L. A. (Ed.). (1987). *Psychology and child custody determinations: Knowledge, roles, and expertise.* Lincoln: University of Nebraska Press.

OTHER RESOURCES

State Guidelines

Georgia Psychological Association. (1990). *Recommendations for psychologists' involvement in child custody cases.* Atlanta, GA: Author.

Metropolitan Denver Interdisciplinary Committee on Child Custody. (1989). *Guidelines for child custody evaluations.* Denver, CO: Author.

Nebraska Psychological Association. (1986). *Guidelines for child custody evaluations.* Lincoln, NE: Author.

New Jersey State Board of Psychological Examiners. (1993). *Specialty guidelines for psychologists in custody/visitation evaluations.* Newark, NJ: Author.

North Carolina Psychological Association. (1993). *Child custody guidelines.* Unpublished manuscript.

Oklahoma Psychological Association. (1988). *Ethical guidelines for child custody evaluations.* Oklahoma City, OK: Author.

Forensic Guidelines

Committee on Ethical Guidelines for Forensic Psychologists. (1991). Specialty guidelines for forensic psychologists. *Law and Human Behavior, 6,* 655–665.

Pertinent Literature

Ackerman, M. J., & Kane, A. W. (1993). *Psychological experts in divorce, personal injury and other civil actions.* New York: Wiley.

American Psychological Association, Board of Ethnic Minority Affairs. (1991). *Guidelines for providers of psychological services to ethnic, linguistic, and culturally diverse populations.* Washington, DC: American Psychological Association.

American Psychological Association, Committee on Women in Psychology and Committee on Lesbian and Gay Concerns. (1988). *Lesbian parents and their children: A resource paper for psychologists.* Washington, DC: American Psychological Association.

Beaber, R. J. (1982, Fall). Custody quagmire: Some psycholegal dilemmas. *Journal of Psychiatry & Law,* 309–326.

Bennett, B. E., Bryant, B. K., VandenBos, G. R., & Greenwood, A. (1990). *Professional liability and risk management.* Washington, DC: American Psychological Association.

Bolocofsky, D. N. (1989). Use and abuse of mental health experts in child custody determinations. *Behavioral Sciences and the Law, 7*(2), 197–213.

Bozett, F. (1987). *Gay and lesbian parents.* New York: Praeger.

Bray, J.H. (1993). What's the best interest of the child?: Children's adjustment issues in divorce. *The Independent Practitioner. 13,* 42–45.

Bricklin, B. (1992). Data-based tests in custody evaluations. *American Journal of Family Therapy, 20,* 254–265.

Cantor, D. W., & Drake, E. A. (1982). *Divorced parents and their children: A guide for mental health professionals.* New York: Springer.

Chesler, P. (1991). *Mothers on trial: The battle for children and custody.* New York: Harcourt Brace Jovanovich.

Deed, M. L. (1991). Court-ordered child custody evaluations: Helping or victimizing vulnerable families. *Psychotherapy, 28,* 76–84.

Falk, P. J. (1989). Lesbian mothers: Psychosocial assumptions in family law. *American Psychologist, 44,* 941–947.

Gardner, R. A. (1989). *Family evaluation in child custody mediation, arbitration, and litigation.* Cresskill, NJ: Creative Therapeutics.

Gardner, R. A. (1992). *The parental alienation syndrome: A guide for mental health and legal professionals.* Cresskill, NJ: Creative Therapeutics.

Gardner, R. A. (1992). *True and false accusations of child abuse.* Cresskill, NJ: Creative Therapeutics.

Goldstein, J., Freud, A., & Solnit, A. J. (1980). *Before the best interests of the child.* New York: Free Press.

Goldstein, J., Freud, A., & Solnit, A. J. (1980). *Beyond the best interests of the child.* New York: Free Press.

Goldstein, J., Freud, A., Solnit, A. J., & Goldstein, S. (1986). *In the best interests of the child.* New York: Free Press.

Grisso, T. (1990). Evolving guidelines for divorce/custody evaluations. *Family and Conciliation Courts Review, 28*(1), 35–41.

Halon, R. L. (1990). The comprehensive child custody evaluation. *American Journal of Forensic Psychology, 8*(3), 19–46.

Hetherington, E. M. (1990). Coping with family transitions: Winners, losers, and survivors. *Child Development, 60,* 1–14.

Hetherington, E. M., Stanley-Hagen, M., & Anderson, E. R. (1988). Marital transitions: A child's perspective. *American Psychologist, 44,* 303–312.

Johnston, J., Kline, M., & Tschann, J. (1989). Ongoing postdivorce conflict: Effects on children of joint custody and frequent access. *Journal of Orthopsychiatry, 59,* 576–592.

Koocher, G. P., & Keith-Spiegel, P. C. (1990). *Children, ethics, and the law: Professional issues and cases.* Lincoln: University of Nebraska Press.

Kreindler, S. (1986). The role of mental health professions in custody and access disputes. In R. S. Parry, E. A. Broder, E. A. G. Schmitt, E. B. Saunders, & E. Hood (Eds.), *Custody disputes: Evaluation and intervention.* New York: Free Press.

Martindale, D. A., Martindale, J. L., & Broderick, J. E. (1991). Providing expert testimony in child custody litigation. In P. A. Keller & S. R. Heyman (Eds.), *Innovations in clinical practice: A source book* (Vol. 10, pp. 481–497). Sarasota, FL: Professional Resource Exchange.

Patterson, C. J. (in press). Children of lesbian and gay parents. *Child Development.*

Pennsylvania Psychological Association, Clinical Division Task Force on Child Custody Evaluation. (1991). *Roles for psychologists in child custody disputes.* Unpublished manuscript.

Saunders, T. R. (1991). An overview of some psycholegal issues in child physical and sexual abuse. *Psychotherapy in Private Practice, 9*(2), 61–78.

Schutz, B. M., Dixon, E. B., Lindenberger, J. C., & Ruther, N. J. (1989). *Solomon's sword: A practical guide to conducting child custody evaluations.* San Francisco: Jossey-Bass.

Stahly, G. B. (1989, August 9). *Testimony on child abuse policy to APA Board.* Paper presented at the meeting of the American Psychological Association Board of Directors, New Orleans, LA.

Thoennes, N., & Tjaden, P. G. (1991). The extent, nature, and validity of sexual abuse allegations in custody/visitation disputes. *Child Abuse & Neglect, 14,* 151–163.

Wallerstein, J. S., & Blakeslee, S. (1989). *Second chances: Men, women, and children a decade after divorce.* New York: Ticknor & Fields.

Wallerstein, J. S., & Kelly, J. B. (1980). *Surviving the breakup.* New York: Basic Books.

Weissman, H. N. (1991). Child custody evaluations: Fair and unfair professional practices. *Behavioral Sciences and the Law, 9,* 469–476.

Weithorn, L. A., & Grisso, T. (1987). Psychological evaluations in divorce custody: Problems, principles, and procedures. In L. A. Weithorn (Ed.), *Psychology and child custody determinations* (pp. 157–158). Lincoln: University of Nebraska Press.

White, S. (1990). The contamination of children's interviews. *Child Youth and Family Services Quarterly, 13*(3), 6, 17–18.

Wyer, M. M., Gaylord, S. J., & Grove, E. T. The legal context of child custody evaluations. In L. A. Weithorn (Ed.), *Psychology and child custody determinations* (pp. 3–23). Lincoln: University of Nebraska Press.

APPENDIX D

Glossary

The vocabulary of psychology continues to evolve and expand. As well, some of the terms we use, while borrowing from the common vocabulary, have specific meaning. This brief list defines some common terms that you may see in a psychological report or hear in testimony.

achievement tests. Designed to assess level of information learned.

addiction. Physical dependence upon a substance, with features such as tolerance and withdrawal symptoms. The term *dependence* has largely replaced this term in formal diagnosis and it includes cognitive and behavioral indicators in addition to physical symptoms.

affect. Often used interchangeably with emotion, but refers more to the observable aspects of this internal feeling. *Mood* usually refers to sustained emotional presentation whereas *affect* is more variable. Affect may be referred to as *blunted*—no intensity; *flat*—no signs of emotional expression; *labile*—highly variable with abrupt shifts in direction of emotion; *restricted*—reduction of intensity but not as severe as blunted.

amnesia. Memory loss. It can be retrograde (amnesia for events before trauma) or anteriorgrade (amnesia for events after trauma). It can be due to drugs, neurological injury, or psychological trauma (dissociative amnesia).

aphasia. Inability to express oneself effectively through speech (expressive or motor aphasia) or loss of verbal comprehension (receptive or sensory aphasia).

aptitude. An individual's capacity and ability for particular types of work.

ataxia. Muscular incoordination, particularly when attempting voluntary movement.

attention. Directing one's consciousness upon only one task or stimulus (internal or external).

baseline. Measurement of behavior before treatment is initiated.

behavioral medicine. An interdisciplinary field that integrates behavioral and medical knowledge to understand, control, and prevent disease.

biofeedback. A method for electronically recording and amplifying physiological responses (e.g., heart rate), and providing feedback to the person with the goal of regulating or controlling the response.

catatonia. Motoric immobility, extreme negativism, and mutism that is often accompanied by stereotypic movements and speech.

confabulation. Production of fictitious memories to fill in the gaps (seen often in alcoholics).

confirmation bias. The tendency to seek out information that confirms one's preconceived ideas.

control group. A group of subjects matched to the experimental group but not exposed to the active treatment under investigation.

cognition. The group of mental activities associated with thinking, knowing, and remembering.

conversion. A physical symptom that arises from psychological sources (e.g., anxiety) and is not intentionally produced.

defense mechanism. A means, in psychoanalytic theory, for the ego to reduce anxiety by unconsciously distorting reality.

delusion. False belief that is firmly sustained despite incontrovertible and obvious proof that the belief is not true.

dementia. Irrecoverable, deteriorated mental state with loss of cognitive abilities (including memory), which may result from a variety of causes (e.g., alcohol, disease).

depersonalization. Feelings of unreality or strangeness with regard to the immediate environment or one's person.

derealization. Feeling of detachment from immediate surroundings.

disorientation. Inability of a person to tell the time of day, date, season, where they are or who they are.

dissociation. A split in consciousness that allows thoughts and actions to occur simultaneously without mutual awareness.

dysarthria. Difficult and defective production of speech.

flashback. A sudden recurrence of a memory or perceptual feeling from the past that is experienced as if the person were reliving the episode.

flight of ideas. Accelerated flow of speech with abrupt topic changes.

functional disorder. A disorder not explained by structural organic causes.

grandiosity. Inflated estimate of one's worth or other specific characteristic.

hallucination. A sensory perception without external stimulation (e.g., hearing voices when no sound is presented).

ideas of reference. The reading of meaning into unconnected events.

idiopathic. Of unknown cause.

incidence. The number of new cases of a disorder occurring during a specified time.

illusion. A misinterpretation of a sensory experience.

learning. A relatively permanent change in a person's behavior or knowledge due to experience.

mean. The arithmetic average that is obtained by adding the individual scores and dividing by the number of scores.

mood. A sustained emotion that affects one's general view of the world.

nature-nurture controversy. The issue over the relative contributions of learning and genetics in the development of behavior.

panic attack. Discrete period of sudden intense feeling of terror or apprehension.

paranoid ideation. Suspiciousness or the belief one is being followed, persecuted, or treated unfairly.

pathognomic. A symptom or symptoms that are specifically diagnostic of a condition or disorder.

percentile rank. The percentage of scores in a distribution that an individual score exceeds.

personality. A sum of persistent characteristic manners and behaviors.

phobia. Persistent, irrational fear of situations or objects, often with active avoidance.

pressured speech. Excess verbalizations that are delivered quickly; also, when the speaker is difficult to interrupt.

prevalence. Total percentage of individuals suffering a disorder.

projective. Tests made up of ambiguous stimuli that the subject is asked to interpret with the responses theorized to reflect inner feelings and conflicts.

prodromal. Initial stage of a disorder before full appearance of symptoms.

profile. A method of visually displaying scores on a test that makes comparisons to the mean from a standardized group.

psychomotor retardation. Generalized slowing of physical and emotional reactions.

psychopathology. The study of abnormal behavior or mental disorders.

psychotic. Disorder in which a person loses contact with reality, often accompanied by perceptual distortions and delusions.

psychotropic. Drugs that have a special action on behavior.

reliability. The degree to which tests yield consistent results.

sequelae. Conditions following and resulting from a disease or condition.

somatic. Pertaining to the body.

standard deviation. The measure of the variability of scores in a distribution indicating the average differences in the scores and their mean.

standard score. A test score calculated to reflect the distance from the mean in terms of standard deviations.

standardization. A defined norm that has been developed by measuring a standardization group to which individuals will be compared.

stressor. Internal or external events that promote stress.

symptom. A sign or occurrence that may indicate pathological change.

syndrome. A group of symptoms that collectively characterize a particular disorder or disease process.

transference. A psychoanalytic theory that the patient transfers some emotion linked with another relationship to the therapist.

validity. The degree to which a test measures that which it is designed to measure.

variable. Any measurable dimension that fluctuates over time.

Bibliography

1. Psychology and Law: Strange Bedfellows

Bartol, C. R., & Bartol, A. M. History of forensic psychology. 1987. In I. B. Weiner and A. K. Hess, eds. *Handbook of forensic psychology*. New York: John Wiley & Sons.

Kagehiro, D. K., and Laufer, W. S., eds. 1992. *Handbook of psychology and the law*. New York: Springer.

Kimble, G. A. 1984. Psychology's two cultures. *American Psychologist*, 39:833-839.

Melton, G. B. 1987. Bringing psychology to the legal system: Opportunities, obstacles and efficacy. *American Psychologist*, 42:488-495.

Münsterberg, H. 1908. *On the witness stand: Essays on psychology and crime*. New York: The McClure Co.

Nietzel, M. T. and Dillehay, R. C. 1986. *Psychological consultation in the courtroom*. New York: Pergamon Press.

Ogloff, J. R. P., ed. 1992. *Law and psychology: The broadening of the discipline*. Durham, N.C.: Carolina Academic Press.

Rogers, R. 1986. *Conducting insanity evaluations*. New York: Van Nostrand Reinhold Co.

Slovenko, R. 1987. Civil competency. In I. B. Weiner and A. K. Hess, eds. *Handbook of forensic psychology*. New York: John Wiley & Sons.

2. Models of Behavior

Frank, G. 1967. *The Boston Strangler*. New York: New American Library.

Hearnshaw, L. S. 1987. *The shaping of modern psychology*. New York: Routledge.

Leahey, T. H. 1992. *A history of psychology: Main currents in psychological thought*. 3rd ed. New Jersey: Prentice Hall.

Leyton, E. 1986. *Hunting humans: The rise of the modern multiple murderer*. Toronto: McClelland & Stewart.

Lowry, R. 1971. *The evolution of psychological theory (1650 to the present)*. Chicago: Aldine Publishing Co.

3. Psychological Research and Assessment Methods

Anastasi, A. 1988. *Psychological testing*. 6th ed. New York: Macmillan.

Buros, O. K. 1985. *The ninth mental measurement year book*. Vols. I and II. Highland Park, N.J.: Grypham Press.

Cronbach, L. J. 1990. *Essentials of psychological testing*. New York: Harper & Row.

Haney, C. 1980. Psychology and legal change: On the limits of factual jurisprudence. *Law and Human Behavior*, 4:147-200.

Isaac, S., with Michael, W. B. 1971. *Handbook in research and evaluation*. San Diego, Calif.: Edits Publishers.

Kuhn, T. S. 1970. *The structure of scientific revolutions*. Chicago, Ill.: University of Chicago Press.

4. Personality Tests

American Psychological Association. 1996. Statement on the disclosure of test data. *American Psychologist*, 51:644-648.

Ben-Porath, Y. S., Graham, J. R., Hall, G. C. N., Hirschman, R. D., and Zaragoza, M. S. 1995. *Forensic applications of the MMPI-2*. Thousand Oaks, Calif.: Sage Publications.

Graham, J. R. 1993. *MMPI-2: Assessing personality and psychopathology*. 2nd ed. New York: Oxford University Press.

Kaplan, R. M., and Saccuzzo, D. P. 1993. *Psychological testing: principles, applications and issues*. 3rd ed. Belmont, Calif.: Brook/Cole.

McCann, J. T. and Dyer, F. J. 1996. *Forensic assessment with the Millon Inventories*. New York: The Guilford Press.

Pope, K. S., Butcher, J. N., and Seelen, J. 1993. *The MMPI, MMPI-2 and MMPI-A in court: A practical guide for expert witnesses and attorneys*. Washington, D.C.: American Psychological Association.

Tranel, D. 1994. The release of psychological data to nonexperts: Ethical and legal considerations. *Professional Psychology: Research and Practice*, 25:33-38.

5. Cognitive and Neuropsychological Assessment

Doerr, H. O., and Carlin, A. S., eds. 1991. *Forensic neuropsychology: Legal and scientific bases*. New York: The Guilford Press.

Faust, D., Ziskin, J., and Hiers, J. B. 1991. *Brain damage claims: Coping with neuropsychological evidence* (2 volumes). Los Angeles: Law and Psychology Press.

Lezak, M. D. 1995. *Neuropsychological assessment*. 3rd ed. New York: Oxford University Press.

Spreen, O., and Strauss, E. 1991. *A compendium of neuropsychological tests*. New York: Oxford University Press.

6. Other Tests

Kendall-Tackett, K. A., Williams, L. M., and Finkelhor, D. 1993. Impact of sexual abuse on children: A review and synthesis of recent empirical studies. *Psychological Bulletin*, 113:164-180.

Koocher, G. P., Goodman, G. S., White, C. S., Friedrich, W. N., Sivan, A. B., and Reynolds, C. R. 1995. Psychological science and the use of anatomically detailed dolls in child sexual-abuse assessments. *Psychological Bulletin*, 118:199-222.

Loftus, E. F. 1993. The reality of repressed memories. *American Psychologist*, 48:518-537.

Lowman, R. L. 1991. *The clinical practice of career assessment: Interests, abilities and personality*. Washington, D.C.: American Psychological Association.

Orne, M. T. 1979. The use and misuse of hypnosis in court. *International Journal of Clinical and Experimental Hypnosis*, 27:311-341.

Rogers, R., ed. 1988. *Clinical assessment of malingering and deception*. New York: The Guilford Press.

Turk, D. C., and Melzack, R., eds. 1992. *Handbook of pain assessment*. New York: The Guilford Press.

Undeutsch, U. 1989. The development of statement reality analysis. In J. C. Yuille, ed. *Credibility assessment*. Dordreccht, The Netherlands.

Wakefield, H., and Underwager, R. 1991. Sexual abuse allegations in divorce and child custody disputes. *Behavioral Sciences and the Law*, 9:451-468.

Wakefield, H., and Underwager, R. 1992. Recovered memories of alleged sexual abuse: Lawsuits against parents. *Behavioral Sciences and the Law*, 10:483-507.

Webster, C. D., and Eaves, D. (with Douglas, D. and Wintrup, A.). 1995. *The HCR-20 scheme: The assessment of dangerousness and risk*. Burnaby, Simon Fraser University and Forensic Psychiatric Services Commission of British Columbia.

Yuille, J. C., Hunter, R., Joffe, R., and Zaparniuk, J. 1993. Interviewing children in sexual abuse cases. In G. Goodman and B. Bottoms, eds. *Understanding and improving children's testimony: Clinical, developmental and legal implications*. New York: The Guilford Press.

7. Diagnosis: Understanding the *Diagnostic and Statistical Manual of Mental Disorders* (DSM–IV)

American Psychiatric Association. 1994. *Diagnostic and statistical manual of mental disorders*. 4th ed. Washington, D.C.: American Psychiatric Association.

Kaplan, H. I., and Sadock, B. J. 1995. *Comprehensive textbook of psychiatry*. 6th ed. Baltimore: Williams & Wilkins.

Paykel, E. S., ed. 1992. *Handbook of affective disorders*. New York: The Guilford Press.

8. Treatment

Bergin, A. E., and Garfield, S. L., eds. 1994. *Handbook of psychotherapy and behavior change*. 4th ed. New York: Wiley.

Bezchlibnyk-Butler, K., and Jeffries, J. J., eds. 1996. *Clinical handbook of psychotropic drugs*. 6th ed. Seattle, Wash.: Hogrefe & Huber Publishers.

Comer, R. J. 1995. *Abnormal psychology*. 2nd ed. New York: W. H. Freeman and Co.

Consumer Reports. November 1995. Mental health: Does therapy help?

Kane, J. M., and Lieberman, J. A., eds. 1992. *Adverse effects of psychotropic drugs*. New York: The Guilford Press.

Mash, E. J., and Barkley, R., eds. 1989. *Treatment of childhood disorders*. New York: The Guilford Press.

Schatzberg, A. F., and Nemeroff, C. B., eds. 1995. *The American Psychiatric Press textbook of psychopharmacology*. Washington, D.C.: American Psychiatric Press.

9. Psychological Testimony

American Psychology–Law Society and Division 41 of the American Psychological Association. 1991. Specialty guidelines for forensic psychologists. *Law and Human Behavior*, 15:655-665.

Bank, S. C., and Poythress, N. G. 1982. The elements of persuasion in expert testimony. *The Journal of Psychiatry and the Law* (Summer):173-204.

Brodsky, S. L. 1991. *Testifying in court: Guidelines and maxims for the expert witness*. Washington, D.C.: American Psychological Association.

Evans, D. R. 1987. The psychologist as an expert witness in civil and criminal litigation. *Canadian Psychology*, 28:274-279.

Fersch, E. A. 1980. Ethical issues for psychologists in court settings. In J. Monahan, ed. *Who is the client? The ethics of psychological intervention in the criminal justice system*. Washington, D.C.: American Psychological Association.

Gibbs, M. S., Sigal, J., Adams, B., and Grossman, B. 1989. Cross-examination of the expert witness: Do hostile tactics affect impressions of a simulated jury? *Behavioral Sciences and the Law*, 7:275-281.

Rogers, R., Bagby, R. M., and Perera, C. 1993. Can Ziskin withstand his own criticisms? Problems with his model of cross-examination. *Behavioral Sciences and the Law*, 11:223-233.

Rogers, R., and Mitchell, C. N. 1991. *Mental health experts and the criminal courts*. Scarborough, Ontario: Carswell.

Ziskin, J., and Faust, D. 1995. *Coping with psychiatric and psychological testimony*. 5th ed. Marina del Rey, Calif.: Law and Psychology Press.

10. Psychological Consultation on Legal Issues

Ceci, S. J. 1994. Cognitive and social factors in children's testimony. In Sales, B. D., and VandenBos, G. R., eds. *Psychology in Litigation and Legislation*, Washington, D.C.: American Psychological Association.

Ceci, S. J., and Bruck, M. 1995. *Jeopardy in the courtroom: A scientific analysis of children's testimony*. Washington, D.C.: American Psychological Association.

Darden, C. (with J. Walter). 1996. *In contempt*. New York: HarperCollins.

Follingstad, D. R. 1985. Systematic jury selection: the quest for a scientific approach. In C. P. Ewing, ed. *Psychology, psychiatry and the law: A clinical and forensic handbook*. Sarasota, Fla.: Professional Resource Exchange.

Frederick, J. T. 1995. *Mastering voir dire and jury selection: Gaining an edge in questioning and selecting a jury*. Chicago: American Bar Association, 1995.

Garry, M., and Loftus, E. F. 1994. Pseudomemories without hypnosis. *International Journal of Clinical and Experimental Hypnosis*, 17:363-378.

Kassin, S. M., and Wrightsman, L. S., eds. 1985. *The psychology of evidence and trial procedure*. Beverly Hills, Calif.: Sage Publications.

Kraus, E., and Bonora, B. 1987. *Jurywork: Systematic techniques*. New York: Clark Boardman Co.

Nietzel, M. T., and Dillehay, R. C. 1986. *Psychological consultation in the courtroom*. New York: Pergamon Press.

Penrod, S. D., and Cutler, B. M. 1987. Assessing the competence of juries. In Weiner, I. B., and Hess, A. K., eds. *Handbook of forensic psychology*. New York: John Wiley & Sons.

Wrightsman, L. S., Nietzel, M. T., and Fortune, W. H. 1994. *Psychology and the legal system*. 3rd ed. Pacific Grove, Calif.: Brooks/Cole Publishing Co.

11. Negotiation and Mediation

Carnevale, P. J., and Pruitt, D. G. 1992. Negotiation and mediation. *Annual Review of Psychology*, 43:531-582.

Fisher, R., and Ury, W. 1981. *Getting to yes: Negotiating agreement without giving in*. New York: Penguin.

Folberg, J., and Taylor, A. 1984. *Mediation: A comprehensive guide to resolving conflicts without litigation*. San Francisco: Jossey-Bass.

Thompson, L. 1990. Negotiation behavior and outcomes: Empirical evidence and theoretical issues. *Psychological Bulletin*, 108:515-532.

Tzu, S. 1988. *The art of war*. (Translated by Thomas Cleary) Boston, Mass.: Shambhala Publications.

Von Oech, R. 1983. *A whack on the side of the head: How to unlock your mind for innovation*. New York: Warner Books.

Von Oech, R. 1986. *A kick in the seat of the pants: Using your explorer, artist, judge and warrior to be more creative*. New York: Harper & Row Publishers.

Wall, J. A., Jr., and Rude, D. E. 1985 Judicial mediation: techniques, strategies and situational effects. *Journal of Social Issues*, 41:47-63.

Wall, J. A., Jr., and Rude, D. E. 1987. Judge's mediation of settlement negotiations. *Journal of Applied Psychology*, 72:234-239.